MAKE
YOUR
MONEY
GROW

KIPLINGER'S

MAKE YOUR MONEY GROW

By Theodore J. Miller
Editor, *Changing Times* Magazine

KIPLINGER BOOKS, Washington, D.C.

Published by
The Kiplinger Washington Editors, Inc.
1729 H Street, NW
Washington, DC 20006

Library of Congress Cataloging-in-Publication Data

Kiplinger's make your money grow.

   Rev. ed. of: Make your money grow. 1981.
   Includes index.
   1. Finance, Personal.   I. Miller, Theodore
II. Make your money grow.
HG179.M255 1988   332.024   88-131
ISBN 0-938721-05-4

ISBN 0-938721-03-8 (pbk.)

First printing. Printed in the United States of America.

ACKNOWLEDGEMENTS

A book with the breadth and scope of *Make Your Money Grow* is by necessity the work of many people. Staff members of *Changing Times* magazine generated most of the original material on which each of the book's three editions has been based. For readers who find help here, the following people–current or former editors, writers or research reporters for the magazine, deserve the credit: Adrienne Blum, Janet Bodnar, Priscilla Brandon, Fred Frailey, William Giese, Joan Goldwasser, Nancy Henderson, Ed Henry, Bertha Kainen, Jeffrey Kosnett, Kevin McCormally, Andrea Meditch, Sherri Miller, Daniel Moreau, Jerome Oelbaum, Morton Paulson, Paul Plawin, Marshall Rens, Suzan Richmond, Ronaleen Roha, Charles Schaeffer, Manuel Schiffres, Mark Solheim, Lindy Spellman and Wendy Van Cott.

A number of people should be singled out for their contributions. Priscilla Brandon handled most of the revisions for Part Two of the current edition, and Suzan Richmond did the same for Part Three. The editor is also indebted to Dayl Sanders for her assistance in getting the project launched. David Harrison, Director of Books for the Kiplinger Washington Editors, did an exemplary job of guiding the volume through the various stages of its rebirth. Lise Metzger did the copyediting and proofreading, assisted early on by Jennifer Lorenzo. The cover and book were designed by Nicolas Fasciano. The index was prepared by Kim McClung. Gail Fisher coded the copy for typesetting. Don Fragale, with the assistance of Milie Thompson, made certain we achieved the highest quality of printing and production.

Finally, the editor is thankful to his wife, Carolyn Clark Miller, and his son, Jason, for their encouragement and patience.

CONTENTS

Introduction by **KNIGHT A. KIPLINGER**
Editor in Chief, *Changing Times*

PART ONE

MAKING THE MOST OF WHAT YOU HAVE

PART TWO

THE ROOF OVER YOUR HEAD

PART FOUR

INVESTMENTS FOR TODAY AND TOMORROW

INTRODUCTION

Y ou can't live well by accident. If there ever was a time when you could achieve financial success through fitful effort combined with a little good luck, that time is long since past.

To cope with the many choices and many challenges, you've got to have a plan. It doesn't have to be a fancy financial blueprint drawn up by a professional consultant, although you may want to seek professional counsel as part of the process. At the very least, you can start by taking stock of where you are now and where you want to end up. Then you'll be ready to chart your course between today and the future.

The only certainty of modern life is uncertainty—or put another way, the certainty of change. Back at the beginning of the 1980s, some people thought they would be living forever in a climate of double-digit inflation and interest rates in the mid teens. Capital had fled from traditional financial investments into the anti-inflation havens of hard assets—gold, real estate, fine arts. But every economic excess breeds a corrective reaction, and the economic recovery of the mid '80s—strong growth, falling interest rates and lower inflation—caught many people by surprise. A few years later, the long, steep rise in the stock market mesmerized some investors into thinking it would continue forever, without the occasional pauses and corrections which have always characterized the stock market.

As you prepare for tomorrow, don't ever believe that the circumstances of the moment, however rosy or grim they may seem, are going to last forever. Odds are, when the general public begins to assume the permanence of any given situation—a rising stock market, for example—the swing of the pendulum is imminent, or has already begun.

This new edition of *Make Your Money Grow* is designed to help you get a grip on your personal finances, set realistic goals, and design your own plans for achieving those goals. It is a complete personal-finance manual, with sections on all the major areas of money management, such as budgeting, savings and investment, buying a home, tax planning, all kinds of insurance, getting ready for retirement, and the rudiments of estate planning. There are, of course, entire books written on each of these subjects, and you might need to consult some of them for more detail. But I think you'll be pleasantly surprised that most of what you really need to know is included here.

This book epitomizes an approach to personal money management that has evolved over many years in the pages of *Changing Times,* the Kiplinger magazine. It is straightforward, clearly presented, and free of tricks and gimmicks.

When *Changing Times* was founded in 1947 as the first magazine of personal-finance guidance, it undertook to educate the young families of postwar America on the basics of sound money management. It urged investment in growth stocks rather than low-yield savings accounts. It deciphered the mysteries of life insurance. It explained how mutual funds can make portfolio management and diversification affordable to the small investor. It offered proven techniques for reducing the bite of income taxes.

We at *Changing Times* have long cautioned our readers against the temptations of get-rich-quick schemes. Considering how few families achieve true financial security in their lifetimes, we think getting rich slowly is challenging enough.

Even sophisticated investors who wouldn't fall for a blatant scam are sometimes victims of their own impatience, expecting every investment they make to beat the market in any given time frame. Not content to wait out periods of slower appreciation, they often sell quality assets too low.

Some investment manuals lead you to believe that the peaks and valleys of the stock market can be timed with some precision, enabling you to trade in and out of the market for maximum gain. We disagree. Most studies show that "dollar cost averaging"—the evenly spaced investing of small sums on a regular timetable, in markets high and low and in between—will beat the market "timers" in the long run.

The next decade will be a time of extraordinary ferment in the American and world economies. Despite signs of rising protectionism around the world, we at the Kiplinger organization believe that the opposite trend—expanding world trade and a closer knitting of national economies—will accelerate. Barriers to the free flow of goods, capital and even labor will gradually crumble in the face of persuasive evidence that open markets benefit all nations. American management and labor will be subject to constant pressures of streamlining, cost reduction and technological innovation.

Fortunately, there are ample signs America is up to the challenge. American elementary and secondary education, which had slipped in the last couple of decades, is turning around. American higher education—long the best in the world—continues to be a magnet for the best and brightest youths from all over the world, drawn to our colleges and graduate schools by the excellence of the American research establishment.

In virtually all of the major technologies—supercomputing, microelectronics, biotechnology, robotics, energy generation and storage, fiber-optic communications—American research is the equal of or superior to that of every other nation. A shortcoming of America in recent years—slowness in translating American technology into marketable products—is being corrected by closer cooperation between universities and corporations.

Just as American manufacturing productivity has boomed during the mid 1980s, service-sector productivity—sluggish in recent years—will have its turn to shine in the 1990s. Part of the improvement will come from increasing competition in international services; much will come from demographic factors—the boost from an aging, more experienced labor force.

The American savings rate has been depressed in recent years by the inflation-driven rise in household assets (which apparently has made many people think they don't have to save much money to increase their net worth) and by the large population bulge of young families, who traditionally don't save much while buying their first homes, cars and furniture. But as the Baby Boomers mature into high-earning middle-agers, it's reasonable to expect the national savings rate will rise.

Some forecasters are predicting a decline of American living standards in the decade ahead; we see a continued rise in real personal incomes. Over the past 15 years, most groups of Americans have experienced an improvement in their financial lot. The improvement has been very uneven, with retirees and employed women experiencing the greatest improvement in living standards, while several age segments of younger workers have barely held their own, adjusted for inflation.

Managing your personal finances in these times of turmoil will be one of the greatest challenges you will face. You'll have to change gears occasionally, as the rate of inflation rises and falls, taking interest rates with them. The proliferation of investment choices will continue unabated, although most Americans will find their needs are met by a narrow mix of stalwart assets like real estate, stocks and fixed-income instruments.

We at *Changing Times* hope this book will give you a framework of information and common sense that will serve you well in the many financial climates you'll encounter in the years to come.

KNIGHT A. KIPLINGER

Part One

MAKING THE MOST
OF WHAT YOU HAVE

HOW TO TAKE CHARGE OF YOUR MONEY

Money. When you consider the importance most of us place on it, or at least on the sense of security money can provide, it is surprising how many people have only a vague idea of how much they possess. The purpose of this book is to show you how to use the money you have to build a more secure future, and it begins by helping you do some personal financial stocktaking. Determining your current net worth is the first step in developing plans for making it grow.

This isn't a complex or difficult job. In fact, it consists of just two basic steps: First you add up the value of everything you own, then you subtract from it the total of all your debts. The form on pages 21 and 22 will help you do that. But before you turn to it, it will be useful to take the preliminary step of calculating your cash flow, which will give you a good look at what's happening to the money that passes through your hands every day. It will pay off in valuable information about the state of your financial affairs and help you get them under control.

If you haven't been keeping close track of the dollars, filling in the cash-flow form (page 18) should bring you up to date.

You can't remember every little detail, of course, but you

YOUR CASH FLOW

INCOME	TOTAL FOR YEAR	MONTHLY AVERAGE
Take-home Pay		
Dividends, Capital Gains, Interest		
Bonuses		
Other		
Total Income		

EXPENDITURES

Mortgage or Rent		
Taxes not withheld		
Food		
Utilities and Fuel		
Insurance Premiums		
Household Maintenance		
Auto (gas, oil, maintenance, repairs)		
Other Transportation		
Loans		
Medical Bills not covered by insurance		
Clothing Purchases and Care		
Savings and Investments		
Charity		
Recreation and Entertainment		
Miscellaneous		
Total Expenditures		

SUMMARY

Total Income		
Minus Total Expenditures		
surplus (+) or deficit (−)		

should be able to locate exact figures for some expenses—mortgage or rent, for example, and insurance premiums—and you can estimate others by thinking of them in weekly or monthly terms and multiplying to get the year's total. Go over your checkbook, paid bills, credit card slips, receipts from stores, cleaners, garages, restaurants. The more actual expenditures you can pinpoint, the more you'll know about your spending habits when you're through.

No matter how this exercise comes out, you're confronted with the evidence of your spending and forced to make some judgments about it. The results will show one of three things.

Income and expenditures are roughly in balance. Making it from one year to the next without getting into a hole may be something of a feat these days, but before you start patting yourself on the back, check your totals again. How much did you put into savings, compared with what you spent on recreation, gifts or clothing? Out-of-whack entries in those or other categories of discretionary spending could mean trouble is brewing. There's more to sensible spending than balancing the books. You have to balance your priorities, too.

You took in more than you spent. This isn't necessarily a good sign, either. Since your cash-flow statement includes savings and investments, you shouldn't have any money left over. Any apparent surplus is probably created by a failure to remember and record all your spending.

You spent more than you took in. This is the clearest signal of imminent danger. When current expenditures outrun income, the money has to come from somewhere. You've either been dipping into savings, borrowing money or buying on credit. You can get away with it for a while, and there may be times when it's smart to borrow to buy something that will appreciate rapidly and cost more later. But as a regular practice, it's bad money management that can cost you dearly in the long run.

Examine your cash-flow statement carefully, looking for places where your money might be dribbling away. As you proceed with this chapter, you should begin to spot some ways to plug the leaks.

HOW MUCH ARE YOU WORTH?

Now you have a picture of how you're handling the money that comes your way. But performing a cash-flow analysis for a single year doesn't give you much information about the cumulative impact on your financial worth of all the cash that's been flowing through your hands for all of your adult life. Compiling a net-worth statement will show you this, and a form for doing so is on pages 21 and 22. Here's how to use it.

Assets. In compiling this part of the statement, begin with cash: what you've got on hand, what's in your checking account, and what you may have squirreled away elsewhere. Next come funds in savings accounts and certificates of deposit. If you own U.S. savings bonds, check with an institution that sells them to get the current (not face) value. Premium payments on a whole life insurance policy contribute to your assets by increasing the policy's cash value, the amount you'd get if you cashed it in. Your agent or a table in the policy can tell you the current cash value. Ditto for finding the surrender value of any annuities you own.

Settling on figures to enter as the current value of your pension and profit-sharing plans is probably the toughest part. A program that will provide you with retirement income is surely an important asset, but it's difficult (although by no means impossible) to put a present-day dollar value on income you're supposed to receive in the future. For purposes of this statement, include in your net worth only the amount you could withdraw in cash if you quit your job. Your personnel office should be able to provide that figure. If you have an individual retirement account or Keogh plan, list its current balance, but remember that you'll be charged a penalty if you withdraw funds prematurely (see Chapter 24).

Your home is likely to be your biggest asset, so it's especially important that the value you assign to it be accurate. Don't list what it cost you or take a wild guess at its present value.

Find out what similar homes in your area have sold for recently (a list of such sale prices should be available in the local land-records office) or ask a real estate agent for an estimate of current market value. Try to get reliable estimates of the value

YOUR NET WORTH

ASSETS

Cash in Checking Accounts	
Cash in Savings Accounts	
Savings Certificates	
U.S. Savings Bonds (current value)	
Cash Value of Life Insurance	
Market Value of House or Apartment	
Market Value of other Real Estate	
Surrender Value of Annuities	
Equity in Pension and Profit-Sharing Plans	
Market Value of IRA or Keogh Plan	
Market Value of Securities	
Stocks	
Bonds	
Mutual Fund Shares	
Other	
Current Value of Durable Possessions	
Automobiles	
Household Furnishings	
Household Appliances and Equipment	
Furs and Jewelry	
Precious Metals	
Collectibles	
Recreation and Hobby Equipment	
Loans Receivable	
Interest in a Business	
Other Assets	
Total Assets	

LIABILITIES

Current Bills Outstanding	
Installment Debts	

continued

Auto Loan _____	
Taxes Due _____	
Balance Due on Mortgages _____	
Other Liabilities _____	
Total Liabilities _____	

SUMMARY

Assets _____	
Minus Liabilities _____	
Net Worth _____	

of any other real estate or business interests you own, too.

The current market value of securities—stocks, bonds, mutual funds—is easy enough to find in the financial pages of a newspaper. If your securities aren't listed, ask a stockbroker.

You can get a good idea of what your car is worth by consulting a car-price guide, such as the Kelly Blue Book or the guide published by the National Automobile Dealers Association. Banks that make auto loans usually have copies of those guides, as do many public libraries. For help in putting a value on a boat, motorcycle or other vehicle, contact a dealer or check the prices of comparable models in the classified ads.

You'll probably have to rely on ballpark figures when valuing household furnishings, appliances and other personal belongings. It's best to be conservative in your estimates. One conservative approach is to "guesstimate" that what's inside your home is worth about 10% of the value of the home itself. Or make your own item-by-item estimate and then slash it by 50%. Use estimated resale value (not purchase price) of antiques, furs, jewelry, and stamp or coin collections.

Liabilities. If you're like most Americans, there's a string of debits tied to your list of assets. Filling out this portion of the form may be painful, but it shouldn't be difficult. Most liabilities are obvious, and whoever you owe probably reminds you of the debt on a regular basis.

Start with current bills—what you owe the doctor and

plumber, for example, plus this month's utility bill, college tuition payment, credit card charges. Next list all charge accounts and installment debts, with the balance due in each case. There's a separate category on the form for your car loan and another one for taxes coming due. Your home mortgage is probably your largest single liability, and an amortization schedule should indicate exactly how much you still owe on it. Do you have any other loans outstanding or stock bought on margin? Whatever you owe is a liability that diminishes your net worth.

Now it's time to fill in the bottom line. If you sold all your assets and paid all your debts, what would be left over? That's your net worth.

The bottom line.   With all the figures at hand, it's easy to compute your asset-to-debt ratio and compare your position with that of the average American. Just divide the total of your assets by the sum of your liabilities. If you have $100,000 in assets, for example, and your liabilities total $20,000, then your asset-to-debt ratio is 5 to 1. In the late 1980s, according to the *Changing Times* Personal Prosperity Index, the average asset-to-debt ratio for U.S. households was about 6.3 to 1, meaning that for every $1 of debt, households had $6.30 in assets.

But the importance of figuring your net worth goes beyond satisfying any curiosity about how you stack up against the mythical average American. Pulling all the figures together can be a first step toward starting or revising a budget that can show you ways to beef up your assets and trim your liabilities. To do that, you need to set some goals.

HOW TO SET FINANCIAL GOALS

You probably don't expect to attain great wealth in your lifetime. Simple financial security would do, if only you knew what it meant. It's a slippery notion, all right, but it does have a few characteristics you can grab onto. It means:

Having a steady source of income. This means your job, or your business if you're self-employed, or income from investments. Future income is the bedrock on which financial security is built.

Anticipating long- and short-term needs. Cars break down,

household appliances wear out, roofs spring leaks. Kids grow to college age, and someday you'll want to retire. These are expenses you have to provide for with savings and investments. *Being protected against financial catastrophes.* In a word, insurance. You need it in sufficient amounts to cover your life, health, family and possessions. Without insurance, the best-laid financial plans can be wiped out in an instant.

Getting further ahead each year. If you stand pat, inflation will loot your financial reserves just as surely as if you were throwing the money away. You have to be alert for opportunities to make your money grow.

The most important step toward financial security is to translate it into your own terms. What, exactly, are your personal financial goals? If you have trouble sorting them out, try classifying them as either "wants" or "needs." Go a step further and add long-term or short-term to the description. Now you have some labels you can use for figuring out your priorities.

Say you're going to need a new car soon. Gathering the money for a down payment without dipping into savings would be short-term need, priority number one. Same for your youngster's braces, perhaps, or a new winter coat.

Long-term needs, such as contributions to a retirement fund, can get priority number two. Yearning for a vacation in Bermuda this spring? That's a short-term want, priority number three. The outboard motorboat you'd like to own before too many years go by is a long-term want, so it gets a four.

You could shift priorities around, of course, and use lots more numbers. Actual goals and their priorities will vary with your circumstances. The important thing is to give serious thought to your goals and try to anticipate the expenses coming up, whether they're close at hand or several years away.

The best way to achieve your goals is to assign target dates to each of them. If you think October would be the best time to buy a car, for instance, and you want at least $2,000 on hand for a down payment, solidify that objective by putting it in writing. That gives you a basis for action: You have to find some way of allocating expenditures that will allow you to accumulate $2,000 by October. The progress you make toward this and other specific goals becomes the gauge of your progress toward the ultimate goal, which is financial security.

The trouble is, the cash often runs out before the priorities do. That's where budgeting comes in. It's your best bet for distributing limited resources intelligently among competing priorities.

WHAT A BUDGET CAN DO

You'll find a suggested budget format on pages 27 and 28. There's space there for a month's expenditures. Use that format as a model to make your own budget sheets, or make copies of what's there to give you space for more months. Think of it as a planning device, a means of setting and reaching goals. You project future expenditures now, record them when they're made, and see whether your projections were any good. If not, you adjust your planning or your spending, whichever is out of line.

Some of your projections will be easy. You probably know what your mortgage or rent payments will be in the months ahead. Same for the premiums coming due on insurance policies you currently have in force. So why budget for them? Because by recording these and other fixed expenditures as monthly outgo, you can see at a glance how much of your income is committed to current or future expenses. That should stop you from spending it on something else.

Under variable expenditures go the items over which you have some degree of control. This is the place to test your cost-cutting skills. Watch for patterns that may signal trouble. If the miscellaneous line keeps growing bigger, your record-keeping may be careless.

Use the record of last year's spending that you compiled on pages 21 and 22 as the basis for the coming year's budget projections. Work only a couple of months ahead at first, until you get the hang of it. Then you can budget further ahead. After a while you'll want to apply the same principles to long-term goal-setting by forecasting the growth of your net worth and all the little pieces that compose it. Then you can keep track of the progress you're making by comparing each year's projected growth with the actual results.

MAKING THE BUDGET WORK

The beauty of a budget is that it alerts you to trouble while you still have time to do something about it. You're forced to find out why expenditures are climbing and take action. If the electric bill is higher because the rates were raised, you'll have to revise your monthly forecasts for that budget item and figure out whether other items need to be cut to pay for it.

Sometimes, though, your budget can flash danger signs that are more difficult to pinpoint. If you start picking up distress signals, run your budget through these checks:

Have you been inattentive? Perhaps you got in this fix because you didn't watch what was going on. Examine budget categories where spending overshot allocations. Pay particular attention to items that involve charge account buying and credit card spending. The finance charges generated by revolving credit alone may be enough to force you out of bounds.

Are you behind the times? You may be in trouble not because you've been doing unnecessary spending, but because your necessary spending now costs more. This is everyone's inflation experience, whether or not they budget. In fact, those who budget sometimes have more trouble coping with inflation than other people, because budgets usually tie spending objectives to preexisting price levels. You should revise your budget from time to time to keep it in touch with reality.

Do you need more flexibility? Consider the couple who thought they were doing fine without a budget of any kind, until their checks suddenly began bouncing all over town. With their two-salary income, they told each other, there was simply no excuse for such embarrassment. So they vowed to budget and for the first time ever sat down to list their normal expenses and match them against their normal income.

To their delight, they found not only that there was enough money to go around but also that it would be perfectly realistic to fund a savings program, which they had talked about but never started. They promptly drew up a budget that included a

SUGGESTED BUDGET FORMAT

INCOME

MONTH: _____

	Projected	Actual	(+) or (−)
Take-home Pay _____			
Other _____			
Total			

FIXED EXPENDITURES

	Projected	Actual	(+) or (−)
Mortgage or Rent _____			
Taxes not withheld from Pay _____			
Installment and Credit Card Payments _____			
Insurance Premiums Life			
Auto			
Home			
Health and other			
Savings/Investments Vacation Fund			
Emergency Fund			
Investment Fund			
Other			
Subtotal			

VARIABLE EXPENDITURES

	Projected	Actual	(+) or (−)
Food and Beverages _____			
Fuel and Utilities Gas or Oil			
Electricity			
Telephone			
Water and Sewer			
Household Operation and Maintenance _____			
Automobile Gas and Oil			
Repairs			
Public Transportation _____			
Clothing Mom			
Dad			
Kids			

continued

Pocket Money	Mom			
	Dad			
	Kids			
Personal Care (haircuts, cosmetics, etc.)				
Recreation, Entertainment				
Medical and Dental				
Charity				
Special Expenses (tuition, alimony, etc.)				
Miscellaneous				
Subtotal				
Plus Fixed Expenditures				
Total				

heroic chunk of savings each month, and they happily set forth on their road to affluence.

It didn't work. In their enthusiasm they had been both too ambitious and too rigid. They had tried to shovel too much into savings. They budgeted every penny of the remainder but neglected to allow for the little unforeseen expenses that are too petty to budget for but add up nevertheless.

Moral: Don't torture yourself. Don't aim for spartan goals. Allow yourself leeway. It is better to budget a bit too much in a few headings (certainly including "miscellaneous" or "contingencies") than to end each month robbing Peter to pay Paul. After all, the purpose of a budget is not to make impossible dreams come true but to make attainable goals come more easily.

Are you doing somebody else's thing? The Bureau of Labor Statistics once invented a hypothetical urban family of four, and it periodically computed itemized budgets for this family, just to see how much it would cost them to live. This was a useful exercise and often revealing. But if by wild chance yours happened to be an urban family of four with precisely the same income, it is unlikely you could have lived by the BLS budget.

Next to a will, a budget is probably the most intimate financial document you can create. It embodies decisions you make about how you will allocate your resources. And many intangibles help shape those decisions—your goals, aspirations, values, hopes, anxieties, life-style, commitments and, to an important degree, even the expectations of people whose expectations you regard as worthy of honoring.

Thus, you may be John Doe Average and pull off-the-rack pants over one-size-fits-all socks every morning of the year, but you can't live by somebody else's budget. Yours has to be tailored to your measure, by you.

Most people approach this task by listing first the expenditures about which they feel they have no choice whatever. If anything is left over, only then do they consider expenditures they might make from free choice. Budgeting doesn't have to proceed this grimly, however. A few people begin at the other end. First they put down their desired goals, such as "enough money to buy a 30-foot boat by 1992." Then they budget to attain those goals of choice before distributing the remainder among items most people would rank as first-order necessities—shelter, food, clothing and the like.

It takes a strong-minded person to budget wishes first, needs later. But it can work, which only goes to show how highly personal the whole budgeting process can be.

MAKE YOUR MONEY GROW 2

MANAGING THE DAY-TO-DAY FLOW

WAYS TO SQUEEZE THE MOST OUT OF EVERY DOLLAR

The money that flows through your hands on a regular basis, if managed properly, can work to increase your income. The difference between lackadaisical and smart money management can be hundreds of dollars a year. That could be cash in your pocket or cash down the drain.

A few years ago, earning money on your cash flow was chiefly a matter of timing. You carefully timed the transfer of your funds from a savings account (where it earned interest) to a checking account (where it didn't) just in time to write the checks to pay your bills. These days that's unnecessary. Thanks to the deregulation of financial institutions and the marketing ingenuity of the people who run them, you now have a choice of accounts in which your cash automatically earns interest and check-writing money is available when you need it. (Because of the difference in yields on some checking and money-market accounts, however, it may still be advantageous to shuttle money between the two when large amounts are involved.)

There are so many of these kinds of accounts that they have understandably become a source of some confusion. This chapter will help you sort through their various features to locate the one that serves you best. The first step is to review your current money-handling practices to make sure you're adhering to five common-sense principles of smart money management.

1. Don't accumulate idle cash. Do you often delay depositing checks? Do you neglect to cash traveler's checks after a trip? Do you keep large amounts of cash around? All those practices deprive you of the opportunity to increase your interest income.

2. Don't prepay bills. Paying bills before they are due won't improve your credit standing; it's the persistently late payers who worry the banks and other creditors. Prepaying only reduces the time your money can be earning interest for you.

3. Don't overwithhold taxes. Many people deliberately have too much taken out of their salaries to avoid a large tax bill in April or to accumulate a refund. Those excess withholdings could be put where they earn interest to help pay taxes.

4. Maximize your savings. Never before have ordinary people had such abundant opportunities for maximizing the return on their savings—certificates of deposit with a wide range of maturities and rates, money-market mutual funds, checking accounts that pay rates once available only on long-term deposits. Now you can use many of the cash-management techniques developed by large corporations, even though you deal in far smaller sums.

To succeed, however, you must begin with an accurate, up-to-date record of the funds you have. Use the form on page 34 to list all your savings funds, the institutions where they are held, the names in which the accounts are registered, the rate the money is earning and when the money can be withdrawn.

Standard passbook-account money can be considered immediately available. So, too, can money-market funds, NOW accounts, money-market deposit accounts and U.S. savings bonds, although you won't receive the full interest on the bonds if they are cashed in before their initial maturity. For certificates of deposit, enter the maturity dates. Certificates can be redeemed beforehand, but normally you must pay an interest penalty. The registered owner's name is important, because his or her signature is required for withdrawal.

What these accounts have in common is that they constitute savings, not investments. What's the difference? Availability and risk. With the exception of certificates of deposit, the funds are usually available immediately without penalty. With the exception of money-market funds, they are as safe as money can be—either in insured accounts or, in the case of savings bonds, backed by the U.S. Treasury. Even money-market funds, the vast majority of which are neither guaranteed nor insured, are quite safe because of the nature and term of the investments they make (see Chapter 17). And certificates of deposit, although they must be held to their maturity dates to pay the maximum yield, can be made to behave like shorter-term instruments by following the next money-management principle.

5. *Stagger your maturities.* One usually reliable principle of saving holds that the longer the term, the higher the rate. A 30-year bond, for example, should offer a higher rate than a ten-year bond. A five-year certificate of deposit normally provides a better return than a one-year certificate, and a one-year certificate usually pays more than a savings account. Periods of rapid inflation can knock these relationships cockeyed, and short-term rates may actually rise higher than long-term rates. As inflation subsides, the traditional relationship between long- and short-term rates is restored, but the uncertainties of the financial marketplace make it unwise to commit much of your money for too long.

With certificates, you can reduce the risks of long-term commitment by staggering the maturities, so that some certificates are always coming due in the near future. Then, if you don't need the cash, you can rotate the maturing certificates back into long or short maturities, depending on rates available.

If you want further protection against getting locked into a low rate or being caught short for ready money, arrange to have the interest from some of the certificates paid out on a quarterly or semiannual basis. That gives you a constant stream of cash for use or reinvestment. You will lose part of the extra return

SAVINGS RECORD

ACCOUNT, INSTITUTION	REGISTERED OWNER	AMOUNT	WHEN AVAILABLE
Standard Savings Accounts			
Total			
Certificates of Deposit			
Total			
U.S. Savings Bonds			
Total			
Other (e.g., Money-Market Funds, NOW Accounts)			
Total			
Grand Total			

you'd get from leaving interest in the account for compounding, but it's a relatively small cost to pay for retaining your liquidity. Also, in an emergency you can pledge a certificate as collateral for a loan. Some institutions will let you specify maturity dates for certificates, so you can time maturities to coincide with your need for the principal—for a tuition payment, for example.

The aim of all these money-management principles is to keep your money working. What's available for savings and investments probably represents a small fraction of your weekly or monthly income; most of what you bring home must soon be paid out as rent, mortgage, utilities and other living expenses. Nevertheless, the short periods that money is in your possession represent interest-earning opportunities, and there are several ways to take advantage of them.

MONEY-MARKET FUNDS

These can be excellent cash-management tools, especially when you want to park savings someplace while you ponder longer-term investments. Because of the volatile nature of interest rates in recent years, many people have come to consider money-market funds as a permanent part of their savings plans.

The funds invest in very short-term debt instruments, such as corporate commercial paper (IOUs from a company, in effect) and Treasury bills. Although $1,000 is a common minimum initial investment, some funds are available for less, and virtually all impose lower requirements for subsequent investments. Shares are generally redeemable at any time by mail or telephone, and you can arrange to have the funds wired or mailed directly to your bank.

With most of the funds, you can write checks on your account, although the high minimum for checks—usually $250 or $500—makes money-market funds unsuitable for everyday bill-paying. These funds are discussed in detail in Chapter 17.

INTEREST-EARNING CHECKING ACCOUNTS

Sometimes called NOW (Negotiable Order of Withdrawal) accounts, these are convenient ways to keep your money working and quickly available at the same time. But interest-earning checking accounts often have enough strings attached to keep small depositors from sharing in the potential benefits. In fact, the profusion of service charges, minimum balances, fees for checks, and other fine print can create what seems to be an impenetrable jungle.

Remember this: The key to choosing the right NOW account lies in the minimum-balance requirement. If you don't maintain it, you'll probably have to pay a service charge, and what you pay could actually exceed what you earn in interest. Suppose, for example, you kept an average balance of about $900 in a NOW account on which you got 5¼% interest but which had a $1,000 minimum-balance requirement. You'd earn about $3.95 a month, but you'd also pay a service charge because your balance was under the minimum. If that charge were, say $5, you'd lose about a dollar a month.

Savings and loan associations often require a smaller minimum balance than banks and charge smaller service fees. Credit unions may offer even better terms on their NOW accounts, which they call share draft accounts. But you could still end up losing out on interest because of the way some institutions compute it. Here are the key questions to consider when you're trying to decide whether a NOW account will pay off for you or when you're comparing one account to another.

How is the minimum balance determined? Some institutions tote up your balance at the end of each day; if it falls below the minimum for even one day in a monthly cycle, you're charged the full service fee. An average minimum-balance requirement gives you more leeway. Your account can drop to zero for days at a time, but as long as you deposit enough to bring the average up to the minimum, you won't have to pay a service charge.

Although the minimum balance required at one bank may sound like a better deal than the higher average balance required at another, it may not be. Industry studies show that the average balance in a typical checking account usually runs about twice the minimum balance. At that rate, a $500 average balance requirement could be considered comparable to a minimum balance requirement of about $250.

How are charges assessed? If your balance dips below the

minimum, you may be charged for every check written during the month or only for those written while your balance was too low. Sometimes check fees aren't charged at all, no matter how little you have in your account, unless you write more than a specified number of checks, usually around 15 to 20.

In addition to monthly service and check fees, you may run into another kind of NOW account charge—loss of interest for all or part of the period when your account dips below a certain amount.

Of course, you can avoid all service charges simply by keeping the required minimum balance. But even this tactic could cost you money: If you had to increase your NOW account balance by shifting money from a higher-paying account, you'd lose interest on the transferred funds.

There's still a good chance you'd come out ahead, though, especially if your alternative is a passbook account. But if your money is earning considerably more, you could be better off leaving it where it is.

How is interest calculated? NOW accounts generally pay interest daily, but there are some exceptions. At credit unions, for instance, dividends paid on share draft accounts may be based on the lowest balance during a dividend period, which is often a month or a quarter. This quirk can dull the interest edge some credit unions have over bank and savings and loan NOW accounts. But since credit unions often don't set minimum-balance requirements or service charges, share draft accounts can still be a good deal, especially if fees would eat into your earnings at a bank or savings and loan.

You'll get the best deal if interest is figured from day of deposit to day of withdrawal or on your average daily balance. In either case you get credit for all the money you have in your account, and compounding sweetens the deal even more.

If you're accustomed to keeping a very low balance, you might be better off with a traditional checking account that pays no interest. Regular checking-account fees are generally set below the fees for NOW accounts, so even though you're not earning any interest, you could be better off with the traditional account.

MONEY-MARKET DEPOSIT ACCOUNTS

The main attraction of MMDAs is that they usually pay higher rates than NOW accounts on high balances. The main drawback is that transfers from the account—that is, checks or other movements of the money—are often limited. MMDAs are meant for savings, not for funds to which you need ready and repeated access. Institutions often charge fees if your account falls below their minimum-balance requirement.

ASSET MANAGEMENT ACCOUNTS

This type of account, which is offered by several brokerage firms and a growing number of banks, can be a good vehicle for managing your cash if you have a lot of it and feel you can use the other services such accounts deliver.

Merrill Lynch, which introduced the idea with its Cash Management Account more than a decade ago, requires a minimum initial balance of $20,000 in stocks, bonds, cash, mutual fund shares, or a combination of the four. CMA customers get a line of credit, unlimited check-writing privileges on their money-market funds and several other services. The fee is $65 a year. Other accounts require smaller minimum balances and may provide slightly different services.

As money-management tools, asset management accounts are valuable because of the detailed consolidated records you get from their monthly statements and the easy access they provide to several alternative investment instruments. These accounts are described in more detail in Chapter 4.

KEEPING TRACK OF IT ALL

As we go through the daily routine of earning and spending money, we generate a blizzard of paperwork—some created by ourselves, some by those we deal with. Some of that paper can be thrown away; some you should keep. In fact, good record-keeping is an essential part of sound money management. The following is a guide to the kinds of records to keep, and why.

Tax records. Canceled checks, receipts and myriad other documents may be required for federal and state income tax purposes, both to calculate how much you owe and to justify deductions, exemptions, and other tax items. You should be prepared to present concrete evidence to the government in case of an audit. However, you can lighten your files by eliminating superfluous items and discarding records after they have served their purpose. For instance, you can dispose of weekly or monthly salary statements once you have checked them against the annual W-2 wage form.

Often, a canceled check that relates directly to an entry on your return is sufficient without supplementary documents. The canceled check for a medical expense doesn't have to be supported by the original bill unless the nature of the expense is ambiguous. A check to a physician leaves little doubt as to the service involved, but you would want to back up a check to a drugstore with a detailed receipt, because the check could cover either deductible drugs or nondeductible cosmetics.

Sometimes you can and should create a record to protect yourself. If a charity fails to give you a receipt for donated goods, draw up a list with the used-market value of each item, the name of the organization, and the date of the contribution.

Precise records are particularly important for business travel- and entertainment-expense deductions. If you expect to claim business expenses, write to your Internal Revenue Service district office for a copy of Publication 463, *Travel, Entertainment and Gift Expenses,* which explains the regulations and record-keeping requirements.

How long should you keep tax records? The law allows the IRS three years to challenge a return under ordinary circumstances, and six years when you have understated income by more than 25%. In cases of fraud, there is no limit.

You may be able to obtain substitutes for lost tax records from the person who made the payment to you or to whom you made the payment. The IRS generally stores returns for six years and can furnish copies for $4.25 per return regardless of length of the return. Write to the IRS center to which the return was originally sent. Include your check, social security number and notarized signature.

For detailed suggestions on tax record-keeping, see Chapter 21.

Stock and bond certificates. These should be kept in your safe-deposit box or, if you prefer, in the brokerage firm's vault. Mutual funds retain custody of shares unless the owner requests the certificates.

If you lose a certificate, immediately notify the issuing company or its transfer agent (your broker can find the name for you). You will probably be sent a set of replacement forms, including an application for an indemnity bond. The bond insures the company against loss if the missing shares are cashed illegally. You can expect to be charged a fee for the bond based on the value of the shares. Once the bond is obtained, the company can issue a new certificate.

Stock purchase and sale confirmations. The broker's purchase statement showing the number of shares, the price, commission and taxes, if any, should be filed with the certificates. You will need that information eventually to figure your gain or loss for tax purposes when you sell the shares. The broker's sales statement goes with your current year's tax material.

Investment dividends. It's helpful to log dividend payments each year in a separate record to guard against company errors or lost checks. You can discard your tally after matching it against the annual dividend summary the company sends you (and the IRS). However, you should maintain an ongoing record of capital-distribution dividends, because they have to be figured into the gain or loss reported for taxes when the shares are sold.

Savings passbooks and certificates. They're not as difficult or costly to replace as stock certificates, but their loss could cause some inconvenience. Bank procedures for handling lost passbooks and certificates vary. You may be given new ones with no fuss or bother. In some cases, though, withdrawals from the account might be temporarily restricted.

Homeownership and rental records. When you buy or sell a house, keep all the records you receive. They are not all necessarily essential from a legal standpoint, but they may have other important uses. The deed, for example, doesn't fully protect your ownership of the property until it is recorded at the county or municipal land office. However, it may give a precise description of the property. Similarly, the survey map provided is a convenient reference for locating boundaries when you put up a fence, a toolshed or other structures.

The payment records of the transaction will probably be needed for tax purposes either that year or at some future time. Your share of the regular real estate tax is deductible the same year you pay it. Special land-transfer taxes are ordinarily not deductible, but they can be added to the cost of the house in calculating the capital gain when you sell it.

Any permanent improvements you make to property— central air-conditioning, a porch, a patio, a garage—can also be added to the cost of the property when you sell. The canceled checks to contractors or the receipted bills should be put away for long-term safekeeping.

Maintenance costs for painting, papering and the like do not qualify as permanent improvements, but they can be deducted from the sales proceeds of a property as a fixing-up expense if the work is done within 90 days before the sale. If there's any possibility that you might sell in the near future, hang on to those records.

When you rent a house or apartment, your legal and financial relationship with the landlord rests on the lease. You may need it to verify particular provisions from time to time. Keep it handy.

Warranties, service agreements. Try to assemble in one place all your warranties, appliance instruction booklets and agreements covering such services as lawn care and termite inspection, and periodically remove the out-of-date ones. If you buy an appliance without a printed guarantee, retain the canceled check or paid bill in case you have to make a claim against the retailer or manufacturer. They could be obligated to correct defects, even without an explicit warranty, under the legal principle that any product should adequately perform its designated function.

Automobile records. Keep your automobile title certificate in a safe-deposit box. You can probably obtain a replacement from the state motor vehicle department, but that could be difficult, particularly if the dealer who sold the car has gone out of business and you haven't kept the original bill of sale.

Keeping receipts or a running log of work you have done on the car can help you maintain it properly and presumably lengthen its life. Such records are a must for a new car in order to keep the warranty in force.

Passports. Don't throw out an expired passport. You can use it to satisfy some of the application requirements for a new one. If you lose your passport while traveling abroad, notify the nearest American consular office immediately. If you're at home, report the loss to the Passport Office, Department of State, 1425 K St., N.W., Washington, D.C. 20524.

Insurance policies. Life insurance policies are best kept in a safe place, quickly and easily accessible to your heirs. A safe-deposit box might not always be the best location because there may be a delay before your heirs can get permission to open the box. Ask your bank how long it usually takes to gain access. The company can replace lost policies.

Auto, house and other property policies should be readily accessible at home so you can verify the provisions when making claims.

Birth, death, marriage records. These are vital for many legal and financial purposes, so protect them in your safe-deposit box. If you've lost any, apply for a replacement now, before it's needed, because you could run into a long wait.

For the names and addresses of the state agencies to get in touch with for copies, write to the Superintendent of Documents, U.S. Government Printing Office, Washington, D.C. 20402. Ask for *Where to Write for Vital Records,* GPO 017-022-01008–9. The cost is $1.50, and you must include a check or money order with your request.

Many people leave the original copy of their will in the custody of their attorney and keep one duplicate in their own safe-deposit box and another at home. If you don't have a regular lawyer, put the original in your safe-deposit box.

Pension and profit-sharing records. Before retirement your prospective pension benefits are likely to change with your salary and length of service, so you need to keep only the last annual statement issued by your employer or union. If you leave the company before retirement, with rights to a pension that starts at some future date, make absolutely sure to preserve a record of how much you will receive and when payments will begin. In some plans the employee is given the annuity policy that will provide the pension payments. In others your rights may be recorded only in the plan's files, and it is up to you to apply for that pension when you're eligible.

Loan contracts. Even though you may be keeping the canceled checks for the payments on a loan, the contract spelling out the credit terms might be required to settle differences with the lender and for tax purposes. Similarly, when you make a loan to someone, the note constitutes the best evidence of the terms.

Unfortunately, the one loan document borrowers rarely receive before the debt is paid off is their home mortgage and the attached note covering the payments. You should be able to obtain a copy of the note and the mortgage from the lending institution or a copy of the mortgage and deed from the land office where it was recorded.

Military service records. The two key documents for most veterans are the discharge certificate and the service record. If you qualify for disability benefits, retain the original letter from the Veterans Administration specifying the amount you're entitled to. You might need it if you should have to enter a VA hospital.

Put the discharge, service record and disability letter in a safe-deposit box, and make copies for home reference if you like. To replace lost VA records, contact the nearest VA office.

Appraisal records. If your home is damaged or destroyed by fire, the claims process will go much more smoothly if your safe-deposit box contains detailed, up-to-date information on your personal possessions, especially collectibles such as antique furniture, paintings, silver and anything else on the fine-arts rider of your insurance policy. (The same is true after a theft from your home.) Make a complete descriptive inventory of your possessions and get periodic professional appraisals of the more valuable items. Include good-quality photographs of each item as well as photos of whole rooms of your home showing things in their usual location. Videotapes can also be useful for this purpose.

USING CREDIT WISELY

HOW TO TELL IF YOU OWE TOO MUCH

Just as your income and expenses differ from those of other people, so does your debt limit. A few years ago, a good argument could be made for the tactic of borrowing to the hilt, taking advantage of tax deductions on the interest, then paying back the loans in so-called cheaper dollars. Several years of relatively tame inflation, coupled with the phasing out of tax deductions for consumer interest, have put an end to that kind of thinking.

But how much debt is too much? A long-standing rule of thumb holds that monthly payments on debts (not including the home mortgage, which is considered more of an investment) should not exceed 20% of take-home pay. The closer you get to that 20% ceiling, the greater your risk of over-indebtedness. And as mortgage payments consume a greater and greater proportion of income, that 20% may even be a little high. But there are so many variables involved that a general guideline isn't much help. Debt is a personal thing, and the answer to the question of how much you can afford is personal, too.

You probably have a pretty good idea of whether you're heading for trouble. Too much debt gives off these warning signals: You find it more and more difficult each month to make ends meet. You rely heavily on overtime pay and income from moonlighting. You pay only the minimum due on your charge-account bills and sometimes juggle payments, stalling one creditor to pay another. You struggle to save even small amounts and don't have enough set aside to get you through such upsets as a pay cut or the need to replace a major appliance.

Even if you're getting along fine, you should take a hard look at your debt situation occasionally in light of your own limits.

Begin by filling out the form on pages 48 and 49. Use your checkbook for help with the section on expenses. Where you have to estimate, be realistic, not hopeful. (If you filled out the cash-flow form on page 18, this form will be easy.)

Add the total of current monthly expenses to the amount that equals one-twelfth of your annual expenses. Subtract that sum from your monthly income and you'll have the maximum amount you can commit to monthly payments. The total of your payments on current debts tells you how much you've already committed. What's left over, if anything, is theoretically available for other purposes, including incurring new debt. But first determine how prudent that would be.

In sizing up your debt, you should pay attention not only to how much you have to pay off each month but also to how many months into the future you'll be stuck with those payments. If you quit using credit today, for example, how long would it take to pay your installment debts? Six months? A year? Longer?

Using the form shows you the maximum amount you can afford to pay on debts each month. How close you want to come to that limit is a personal decision based on a number of considerations. How much future flexibility have you forfeited to your debts? How secure is your household income? Can you count on raises every year? Are you locked into your present job because your monthly payments won't let you take the pay cut that might go along with a change in careers? How far down the road have payments on today's debts pushed the starting date for your retirement investment program?

There's no hard and fast rule on how much outstanding debt

is prudent or makes sense. What's important is to set a debt limit that considers what you can afford today and, just as important, what it means to your future.

THE SMART WAY TO MANAGE YOUR CREDIT

You won't get the full benefit of your credit capacity unless you manage it like the asset it is. That means shopping for the best terms and making credit work for you, not against you. Even a cheap loan is no bargain if you don't have the money to keep up the payments.

There are different kinds of credit, sources of credit and prices for credit. It pays you, literally, to know the differences.

Here are some credit truisms worth bearing in mind: Finance companies generally charge higher interest rates than banks, which generally charge higher rates than credit unions. Secured loans cost less than unsecured loans, but some kinds of collateral provide better security than others. For example, you'll get a lower rate on a new-car loan than on a used-car loan. The longer the term of a loan, the lower the monthly payments, but the more you'll end up paying in interest.

When you're shopping for the best deal, the basis of comparison to use is the annual percentage rate (APR), which is the relative cost of credit on a yearly basis. The federal Truth in Lending Act requires that lenders use the APR when referring to interest rates, so you can be sure you're comparing apples with apples. However, lenders also use other methods of computing interest—notably add-on and discount rates—that make the interest sound lower but can actually be double the equivalent APR. For example, a 12% add-on rate on a 12-month loan is equivalent to an annual percantage rate of 21.46%, and a 12% discount rate for the same term is equivalent to an APR of 24.28%.

The basic difference between add-on and discount rates and the APR is that in the first two cases the interest is expressed as a percentage of the original amount, whereas the APR is figured on the unpaid balance, which shrinks as you pay off the loan. This difference can result in significant variations in the amount of interest you pay. On a $1,000 loan at 12% add-on for

48

12 months you'd pay $120 in interest; on the same loan at 12% discount you'd end up paying $136.36. But at 12% APR the total cost to you would be only $66.19.

If the interest rate you're quoted sounds suspiciously low, or if the lender quotes you only a monthly dollar payment, make sure to get the APR. The mathematical calculations involved are complicated, but all lenders have tables that do the work, and financial calculators are set up to do it. If you're unsure of a rate you're quoted, check it with another lender or with a standard library reference, such as *The Cost of Personal Borrowing in the United States*.

SIZING UP YOUR DEBTS

See page 46 for directions on how to use these numbers in setting a personal debt limit.

MONTHLY INCOME

Your Take-home Pay	
Spouse's Take-home Pay	
Other Regular Income	
Total	

MONTHLY EXPENSES

Rent or Mortgage	
Food	
Utilities (oil, gas, water, sewage, telephone, electricity)	
Savings and Investment	
Insurance	
Charitable Contributions	
Transportation and Auto Expenses	
Entertainment	
All Other	
Total	

continued

ANNUAL EXPENSES

Taxes (not deducted from pay or included in mortgage payment) _____	
Insurance (not paid monthly) _____	
Medical and Dental Bills _____	
School Costs _____	
Major Purchases and Repairs _____	
Vacation _____	
Clothing _____	
All Other _____	
Total	

*Divide the total by 12 to find the
amount that should be set aside
each month to cover these expenses:* $ _____

PAYMENTS ON CURRENT DEBTS

Personal Loans (lender and purpose)	MONTHLY PAYMENT	BALANCE	MONTHS LEFT
_____			
_____			
_____			
Charge Accounts and Other Installment Payments			
_____			
_____			
_____			
Total			

MAKING THE BEST USE OF CREDIT CARDS

Used wisely, credit cards can be the closest you'll ever come to free money. The smartest way to use bank cards, such as Visa and MasterCard, and other cards that charge interest on the unpaid balance, is to pay your bill in full each month. These cards sometimes allow a grace period of 25 to 30 days from the date you're billed before you're assessed interest. If you pay the bill in full before it runs out, you get, in effect, a free loan. And if you make your purchases right after your billing date, you can stretch the term of this free-money period to nearly two months.

Such grace periods aren't universally available, however. Many banks have shifted to a system under which new purchases start accumulating interest on the date of the purchase if you carry over a balance from the previous month. This system is also popular among department stores that issue their own credit cards. Nevertheless, you can still keep the cost of your multipurpose cards—Visa and MasterCard—under control if you keep an eye on the charges you're paying. They include:

Annual fees. The charges range from $10 to $20; $15 is a common amount and $17 is about average.

Transaction fees. Transaction fees take dead aim at those people at the top of bank hit lists: the so-called free riders who use credit cards as a convenience but pay off their balances before incurring any interest charges. One approach is to levy a small fee each time the card is used. Some card issuers take a different tack, charging customers only if they pay their bills in full each month. Cardholders who extend their payments and run up interest charges aren't charged the fee.

High interest rates. Interest rates are set by the bank or savings and loan that issues your credit card, not by the card company. Issuers have to keep under the interest limits set by the state in which their headquarters are chartered. But that's rarely much comfort because the limits are often 18% to 20% or more.

Other fees and charges. These include minimum monthly payment requirements, transaction fees and interest on cash advances, charges for paying late, and charges for exceeding your credit limit.

FINDING THE BEST BANK CARD DEAL

Actually, the great variety of credit card charges can work to your advantage. If you aren't satisfied with the terms your bank is offering, you may be able to find a less expensive plan somewhere else. The way you use your credit card will determine which pricing deal works out best for you.

Do you pay your bill in full every month? If so, a 24% APR won't affect you, but being charged interest from the date of purchase will.

Do you use your card frequently? If you do, paying a flat annual fee may be a better deal than paying each time you use the card.

Do you carry over balances from month to month? Then look for the lowest interest rate and fee combination.

Do you rely on your card mostly as a form of identification? In that case, a transaction fee could end up costing you very little.

Here's how much an account would cost annually under three pricing schemes, assuming an unpaid balance of $200 a month.

	BANK A	**BANK B**	**BANK C**
Percentage Rate	18%	21%	24%
Interest Charges	$36	$42	$48
Fee	$12	12 cents per transaction, or $8.64 a year based on six transactions per month	none
Total Annual Cost	$48	$50.64	$48

There are at least a couple of organizations that can help you choose and use bank-issued credit cards. Bankcard Holders of America (BHA) is a nonprofit consumer group that provides advice and information about credit rights and follows developments in the field. An annual membership fee of $18 gets you a newsletter published six times a year, access to a toll-free hot line for advice about disputes with card issuers, and a list of banks that offer low-interest, no-fee credit cards. BHA also publishes a number of helpful pamphlets on credit rights and billing. The address is 460 Spring Park Place, Suite 1000, Herndon, Va. 22070.

For $10, The Consumer Credit Card Rating Service (P.O. Box 5219, Ocean Park Station, Santa Monica, Cal. 90405) will send you a kit that lists hundreds of card issuers, their rates, grace periods and other information you can use to match your credit habits with the best deal available.

TRAVEL AND ENTERTAINMENT CARDS

If you have two bank cards and you're being charged a $15 annual fee for each of them, you can save yourself an easy $15 by dropping one of the cards. Since both Visa and MasterCard are accepted just about equally in this country, it doesn't much matter which one you choose.

Paring the plastic in your wallet can save you money in another way, especially if you make lots of charges and extend your balances from month to month. In many states interest ceilings fall as balances rise, so you could get yourself a lower rate of interest by putting all your charges on one card instead of splitting them up.

As bank cards began to levy annual fees, they lost some of the edge they had enjoyed over travel and entertainment (T&E) cards—American Express, Diners Club, Carte Blanche—which have always charged fees.

If you're going to pay a fee anyway, would you be better off putting your money into a T&E card? Not if you've managed to get along perfectly well without one until now. Charges for T&E cards have gone up, too, so you'd still probably end up paying more than you would for a bank card. Besides, your decision about which kind of card to carry should depend as much on what you need it for as on what it costs.

T&E cards are still most useful for frequent travelers and business people who value the travel services these cards offer.

If you don't pay the month's bill in full, you're charged a late fee or interest, which has been rising along with the basic cost of the card.

Although you may be able to get more credit with T&E cards than with bank cards, bank cards are accepted by more merchants. T&E cards are accepted at many retail stores, especially pricier department stores and specialty shops in cities frequented by tourists, but travel-related services and restaurants are still their mainstays.

DEBIT CARDS

You may recall that MasterCard was once called Master Charge. The change in its name a few years back prepared the way for its use as a debit card. Debit cards can be used in much the same way as credit cards: The merchant runs it through a little machine and off you go without any cash actually changing hands. But that's where the similarity ends. When you use a debit card, the amount of your purchase is deducted from your account. It's useful to think of a debit card as a paperless check that, in some cases, clears immediately, with no grace period, no float.

The main use for debit cards is to get cash from automated teller machines, but devices known as point of sale (POS) terminals have been installed in an increasing number of retail outlets. Clerks at a store using a POS terminal can check a customer's account balance on the machine. If you offer a debit card for a purchase and your balance shows up as insufficient, the terminal will disallow the transaction unless you have an overdraft credit line.

A key fact to remember about debit cards is that, although they may look like credit cards, they aren't.

OTHER LINES OF INSTANT CREDIT

Credit cards are convenient, but they can also be expensive. There are other sources of "instant" credit, a few of which are available at bargain rates.

Overdraft checking accounts. This special setup, which allows you to write checks for more money than you have in your account, is one of the easiest sources of credit to use;

unfortunately, it is also one of the easiest to misuse.

As with credit cards, interest rates vary among banks. Because checks cost much less to process than loan applications, banks may offer lower rates on overdraft accounts than on personal loans, especially small ones.

You can lose the interest-rate advantage if the bank imposes a transaction fee each time you write a check. Even if the fee sounds small, it can have a significant effect. Suppose your overdraft account carries a 12% APR (1% per month) and a 50-cent fee for each check. And suppose you write a $100 overdraft check and pay it back one month later. You will have paid a total charge of $1.50 for the month—the same as an APR of 18%. Whatever interest is charged, it will be charged from the date of the transaction; overdraft accounts don't have grace days.

Be sure to find out whether your bank will advance you money in the exact amounts you request or only in multiples of $50 or $100. If it uses the $100-multiple system, don't write an overdraft for an amount like $210 because you'll have to pay interest on $300. It's cheaper to write a check for $200 and dig into your pocket for the extra $10.

Since the interest on overdraft accounts is usually less than the interest on credit card balances, these accounts can come in handy if you want to pay credit card bills in full but don't have the cash; you'll incur interest, but at the rate of perhaps 12% to 15% instead of 18% or more.

One potential drawback of overdraft credit lines is that there's often no compulsion to repay them in full right away. Some banks automatically deduct a minimum monthly payment from your checking account, but as with all minimum payments, you don't make much headway. You may find your supposedly revolving line of credit has turned into a permanent debt.

Credit card advances. Credit card cash-advance privileges have many of the same advantages and disadvantages of overdraft accounts. Interest rates may be lower than on charges, but as a rule they're assessed from the date of the transaction, with no grace period. And a low interest rate can be hiked considerably if there's a transaction fee.

Retail installment credit. When you buy a big-ticket item such as furniture, a major appliance or an expensive stereo, you often have the option of paying the retailer in equal installments over a set number of months. This kind of "closed-end" credit may sound convenient, but it can also be expensive.

Before you sign on the dotted line, see how the retailer's APR stacks up against what you would pay if you got a loan from a credit union, wrote a check on your overdraft account or used your revolving charge account or bank credit card.

BORROWING ON YOUR ASSETS

Your assets can give you leverage on a loan. Pledging security might help you get a bigger loan than you could on an unsecured basis, and maybe you'll get a break on the interest rate in exchange for giving the lender an extra hedge against the risk that you won't repay. Most lenders want only highly liquid assets as collateral, things that can easily be converted to cash if they must be used to pay off the loan.

Savings accounts. Cash in the bank is the epitome of liquid assets, and borrowing against savings will get you the most favorable rates. By law the rate must be at least 1% over the interest rate being earned by your passbook account. In effect, you're borrowing from yourself, with the bank or savings association serving as a middleman to make sure you pay yourself back. During the term of the loan, your savings account continues to earn interest but you can't withdraw the funds pledged as security. As the loan balance decreases, more of your savings is freed for your use.

Certificates of deposit (CDs), in which your money is tied up for a certain period of time, can also be used as collateral. Here, too, the interest rate can be as little as 1% above what your CD is earning. If a money pinch has you tempted to cash in a CD early, consider whether it might be cheaper to use the certificate as collateral for a loan rather than pay the penalty for premature withdrawal.

Stocks and Bonds. Borrowing from the broker who holds your securities account can be an especially good deal for two reasons. First, rates are comparatively low—usually one to three percentage points above the prime rate. Second, if you use the money to buy more securities, you can deduct the interest you pay as long as it doesn't exceed your net investment income. There's no requirement that you use the money to buy more stocks or bonds, but if you don't, the interest falls under the consumer-interest rules described in Chapter 21.

You can also use your stocks and bonds as collateral for a bank loan. If you want a loan to buy more stocks, neither a bank nor a broker can legally lend you more than 50% of your stock's value. On loans for other purposes, bank policies could depend on what kind of stock you use as collateral. For example, a bank might lend up to 70% of the value of stocks traded on the New York Stock Exchange, up to 60% for those on the American, and up to 40% on over-the-counter stocks. The same bank might lend up to 90% of the value of Treasury bills. Federal regulation prohibits the use of U.S. savings bonds as collateral.

If you pledge securities, the bank will hold them for the life of the loan and keep an eye on the market. If the value of your stock tumbles, the bank can require additional collateral and might call in the loan (make you pay in full) if you can't provide it. Same goes for the broker. That could force the sale of your stock at a depressed value.

Household goods. Your refrigerator, color television set and similar items can serve as collateral for certain loans. Some banks accept such security, but this sort of loan is really the province of consumer finance and small loan companies. The majority of the personal loans made by such lenders are secured by household goods. Even though the resale value may not cover the loan in case of default, lenders view security interests in household goods as evidence of the borrower's good faith and commitment to repay. Note, too, that when you buy something on the installment plan you are in effect using it as collateral for a loan, because the seller who is financing the deal can repossess the item if you default.

Home-equity loans. Tapping home equity for money can be done with a second mortgage, with refinancing of the existing first mortgage or through a home-equity line of credit. With refinancing you negotiate a new first mortgage, use part of the proceeds to pay what's due on the existing loan and pocket the difference. If the interest rate on your existing loan is low, a lender might let you refinance for less than the current rate just to get that old low-rate loan off the books. You pay the closing costs.

You may not like the thought of surrendering a low-interest loan. It would probably be better to keep it and borrow against your equity via a second mortgage, also called a junior mortgage. Transaction costs are often lower than for refinancing, but interest rates are higher.

Many banks, savings and loan associations and brokerage firms offer lines of credit secured by the equity in your home. Under a typical plan, you get a credit limit equal to 70% to 80% of the appraised market value of your home, minus what you still owe on the mortgage. You pay the appraisal fee and, in many cases, an annual fee to maintain the account. When you want to use it, you write a check or use a credit card for the amount you want to borrow. Interest may run 1% to 4% above the prime rate, adjusted monthly. You get from five to ten years to repay, at which time the loan is usually callable, meaning you have to pay the whole thing off.

Home-equity loans, in whatever form they take, should be approached with caution. If for some reason you can't repay, you could lose your home to foreclosure. The variable rates charged on such loans may have no caps, meaning the sky's the limit if interest rates soar. Their main advantage is that the interest is deductible as mortgage interest as long as the loan doesn't exceed $100,000.

Life insurance loans. Borrowing against accumulated cash values in your permanent life insurance is quick, easy and cheap. You can borrow up to 95% of the cash value at as little as 5% or 6% interest; on recently issued policies the rates are higher, and some companies charge floating rates on their policy loans. There is no set date for repayment of principal; you can even skip interest payments and have them added to the balance of the loan. Any balance due at your death will be deducted from the proceeds your beneficiary receives. Some life insurance loans have special tax advantages (see Chapter 10).

OTHER KINDS OF LOANS

Unsecured personal loans. These are common types of loans made by banks, credit unions and finance companies. They are based on your signature, and perhaps your spouse's, and your promise to repay. Usually, the top amount you can get fairly easily and quickly at a bank is a couple of thousand dollars or so, perhaps more from some specialized finance companies. Interest rates can run high; the length of time you'll have to repay normally ranges from 12 to 36 months.

You can arrange to pay back a personal loan in either fixed monthly installments or one flat payment at the end of a set term. There are advantages either way. Lenders usually prefer monthly installments, which enable you to climb slowly and steadily out of debt. On the other hand, if you can count on some future sizable lump-sum income, such as a bonus, you might prefer a single payment. The repayment plan selected may have a bearing on the interest rate you'll be charged.

Debt consolidation loans. There is nothing basically wrong with the idea of borrowing money to pay your debts as long as you realize that consolidating bills doesn't eliminate them. Used wisely, a consolidation loan can get you through a period of income reduction or an emergency that puts a sudden drain on funds that are normally available for debt payments. It can be a way to get back on course if you find yourself temporarily overextended. In fact, it might be a more convenient, even cheaper, way to pay off some debts.

But many specialists in personal credit say that taking a consolidation loan is a sign of money mismanagement, is habit-forming (many consolidation loans end up being refinanced) or, even worse, may be a prelude to bankruptcy.

If you must consolidate, figure out precisely what you need to do the job and borrow that amount—no more, no less. Aim for the lowest possible interest rate on an installment schedule that fits your situation. Don't take on bigger payments just to reduce the term of the loan, or you may end up as harried as before. Don't secure the loan with your car, furniture or equity in your home, and avoid interest-only loans with a final balloon payment calling for the principal in one lump sum. If you don't have a monthly payment obligation, you may be lulled deeper into debt.

If you find yourself too deep in debt and wondering if you can ever get out, you may benefit from the help of a consumer-credit counseling center. There are nearly 300 such nonprofit offices around the country. A counseling session may be free; debt rescheduling may cost a small fee, based on your ability to pay. You can get the name of a counseling center near you by writing to the National Foundation for Consumer Credit, 8701 Georgia Ave., Silver Spring, Md. 20910.

HOW LENDERS SIZE YOU UP

Imagine that you have just applied for a loan or a credit card. What's more important to your potential creditor: your income or whether you have a telephone? The age of your auto or an unblemished credit record?

The answers may surprise you. If you are being sized up by a computer rather than a loan officer, your income and credit history might not even be considered, but having a telephone in the house and a two-year-old car in the garage might weigh heavily in your favor. Because scoring by computer systems is being used increasingly to decide who will get credit and who won't, you need to know how it works.

In essence your application becomes a test, and how high you score depends on how many points you get for your answers to such questions as: time on job? own home or rent? number of credit cards? Owning a home might be worth 15 points, for example, compared with five for renting. If you score enough points on a dozen or so questions, you get the credit; if you don't, your application is rejected.

The questions that make up the test and the score needed to pass often depend on where you live as well as what kind of credit you want and the creditor's experience with previous customers. A computer identifies the characteristics that most clearly distinguish between customers who paid as agreed and those who did not, and it assigns point values to specific attributes. It then predicts the creditworthiness of applicants whose answers add up to certain scores. A score of 115, for example, might translate into a prediction that 95 of 100 customers will repay as agreed. As the score increases, so does the probability of repayment. The lender chooses a cutoff score that is expected to limit losses to an acceptable level.

One reason for the use of computer analysis as a basis for credit decisions is that the growth of credit markets to include nationwide retailers and credit card issuers has made it comparatively rare for a lender to know applicants or their references personally. With the loss of such firsthand information, the methods to winnow out bad credit risks have grown impersonal.

Moreover, federal law limits the criteria that can be used to decide who will get credit. The Equal Credit Opportunity Act prohibits discrimination on a number of grounds. A lender can program a computer to consider only legally permissible information and must apply the same standards to all applicants.

This does not mean that all credit scoring systems use the same criteria. A trait that is valuable in one system may carry little weight in another. A doctor, for example, might win high points for his profession from a bank but very few from a finance company. Commercial Credit Corporation, a nationwide consumer finance company, has used different scoring standards for different types of loans and for applicants under and over age 30. (Lenders are permitted to score age, provided that applicants 62 or older aren't penalized for their age.)

Although the way you've handled credit in the past is considered by most lenders to be the best predictor of your future performance, it might not be scored. Many creditors check with the local credit bureau only if a score falls in a gray area between automatic approval and automatic rejection. When it is considered, a bad credit record—several late payments, for instance—can knock down an otherwise passing grade. A good record might boost your score to the approval level.

What if you are denied credit? If a credit report helped tip the scales against you, you have to be told the name of the bureau that provided the information so you have an opportunity to find out whether outdated or erroneous data killed the deal. If you're turned down for credit, take the time to find out what the credit bureau is saying about you.

Call the local bureau to arrange for an appointment to go over your file or to learn how to authorize the bureau to discuss it over the phone or mail the record to you.

When you examine your report you should not see any negative information more than seven years old, unless you have been declared bankrupt. Federal law requires that most unfavorable reports be purged after seven years (ten in the case of bankruptcy) so that past financial problems won't haunt someone for life. Creditors are generally most interested in the last couple of years or so.

If you find any information in your credit record that's wrong, demand that the credit bureau investigate the report. It if can't verify the accuracy of the item, the information must be dropped from your file.

When unfavorable information is accurate, you may be able to minimize its damage by attaching to the report a short statement telling your side of the story. If you missed several payments during a period in which you were unemployed or ill, for example, an explanation of the extenuating circumstances might give you a better chance with the next potential creditor who calls up your report.

Assuming your report is changed after your review, either because negative information is dropped or an explanation is attached, you can have the credit bureau send the revised report to credit grantors who got the original version during the previous six months.

YOUR CREDIT RIGHTS

When you apply for and use credit you should expect a fair deal from the lender. Your credit rights are protected chiefly by three federal laws: the Truth in Lending Act, which requires the lender to disclose the terms of the deal in a way you can understand; the Equal Credit Opportunity Act, which prohibits unfair discrimination in the granting of credit; and the Fair Credit Billing Act, which is designed to prevent foul-ups on your bills and help straighten them out when they do occur. You could benefit from detailed knowledge of these laws.

The Truth in Lending Act. Federal truth in lending rules require that lenders express the cost of borrowing as the annual percentage rate, or APR (see page 47). This piece of information is essential for comparing the cost of loans. The APR and the method of calculating the finance charge must appear prominently on lenders' loan disclosure forms; otherwise, they are not in compliance with truth in lending rules.

The Equal Credit Opportunity Act. This says that you cannot be denied credit because of sex, marital status, age, race, color, religion, national origin, your receipt of public assistance income, or your exercise of your rights under truth in lending and other credit laws. Understand that neither this law nor any other guarantees anyone credit. There are many valid reasons for a creditor to deny credit. But the law does guarantee that your creditworthiness will be evaluated on the same basis as that of all other customers. The law contains a number of special provisions designed to protect women:

• When evaluating a joint application for credit of a husband and wife, creditors must consider the wife's income, even if it is from a part-time job, in the same way they consider the husband's in determining the couple's creditworthiness and allowable credit limit.

• If you want them to, creditors must count as income any alimony and child-support payments to the extent that they are likely to continue. If these payments are included as part of income on a credit application, then the lender can ask for proof that this income is reliable (copies of court judgments, checks and the like), and the lender is also entitled to check on the credit record of the ex-spouse if it is available under other applicable credit laws.

• Creditors must permit a woman to open and maintain credit accounts in her birth-given first name and married surname or combined surname, whichever she prefers, regardless of marital status. For example, Jane Doe married to Robert Smith has a right to obtain credit as Jane Smith or Jane Doe Smith.

• When checking on the history of any kind of account, joint or separate, used by a woman or her husband, late husband or ex-husband, the creditor must take into account any additional information she presents to show that the credit history being considered does not accurately reflect her willingness and ability to repay debts. This protects her from getting poor marks as a result of an unpaid bill that was solely her husband's responsibility or such things as a creditor's failure to clear the record on an account mixup.

• When creditors pass along information about your account to credit bureaus or other agencies, they must report all information on joint accounts in the names of both spouses if both use the account or are liable for it. This is to insure that both husband and wife get equal acknowledgment for the credit history of the account.

• If a lender denies credit or closes your account, you have the right to know the specific reasons so you can compare them against anything you might have been told that leads you to believe sex or marital-status discrimination was the reason.

• Creditors must not discourage you from applying for credit because of your sex or marital status, and they must not consider your sex or marital status in any credit-scoring systems they have for evaluating creditworthiness.

• They cannot refuse to grant husband and wife separate credit accounts if each is creditworthy without relying on the other's income or credit history.

• Whether a woman is applying individually or jointly, creditors cannot ask about childbearing intentions or capability, or birth-control practices.

• They cannot require a co-signature on your loan or credit account unless the same requirement is imposed on all similarly qualified applicants—that is, others whose income, existing debt obligations and credit history are comparable.

• They must not change the conditions of a credit account or close it solely because of a change in your marital status while you are contractually liable for it. However, they can require you to reapply for the credit when your marital status changes, if the credit was initially granted in part because of a spouse's income.

• They must not ask for information about a woman's husband unless he will be liable for or will use the credit account or loan, they live in a state with community-property laws, she is relying on alimony provided by him as part of the income listed in credit applications, or she is applying for a student loan.

• They cannot require a woman to use a courtesy title, such as Mrs., Ms. or Miss, even though these may be printed on the application forms. Courtesy titles are not part of anyone's legal name.

The Fair Credit Billing Act. The heart of the Fair Credit Billing Act obligates credit card issuers and firms that extend revolving-type credit to do the following:

• Credit payments to your account the day the payments are received at the address the company has specified, so that you don't run up finance charges after you've paid the bill.

• Mail your bill at least 14 days before payment is due, if your account is the type that gives you a period of time to pay before finance charges are assessed.

• Send you a detailed explanation of your rights and remedies under this law twice a year or, if the company prefers, enclose a brief explanation with every bill and send the longer explanation when you ask for it or when you complain about a billing error.

• Follow certain procedures in resolving complaints you may make about billing errors. Six common types of situations covered are:

1. An unauthorized charge on your bill, from which you received no benefit, or a charge that is for a wrong amount or a wrong date or is not correctly identified.
2. A charge or debt for which you want an explanation or clarification. (Example: You need to see the creditor's documentation before paying for an item.)
3. A charge for goods or services that were not delivered to you or were not accepted by you in accordance with your agreement with the seller. (Example: a charge for something that was delivered in the wrong quantity or wrong size.)
4. A failure to properly reflect a payment or credit to your account.
5. A computation or accounting mistake. (Example: computing finance or late-payment charges incorrectly.)

6. An additional finance charge or minimum payment due that resulted from the creditor's failure to deliver a bill to your current address. However, if you moved, you must have notified the creditor of your address change at least ten days before the closing date of the billing cycle involved.

If you run into any of those problems, here's what the law says you should do.

First, write to the creditor. Telephoning may not preserve your rights under the law. Include in the letter your name and account number, a description of the error, including an explanation of why you believe it to be an error, the dollar amount involved and any other information, such as your address, including zip code, that will help identify you or the reason for your complaint or inquiry. You have 60 days from the postmark on the questioned bill to get your letter to the creditor. The creditor must acknowledge your letter within 30 days of receiving it and resolve the matter within 90 days or explain in writing within that time why it considers that no billing error occurred.

While an amount on a bill is in dispute you needn't pay the disputed item. If you have a checking or savings account and a credit card account at the same bank and your payments are made automatically, you can stop payment on the disputed amount or have it restored if you notify the card issuer of the error at least three business days before the scheduled billing date.

During the dispute-settlement period the creditor must not dun you, sue you, report you to a credit bureau as delinquent, close your account, deduct money from your other accounts to pay the amount or otherwise hassle you about the disputed amount. It can, however, continue to include the disputed amount in your bills and levy finance charges against it, as long as it notes on the bill that disputed amounts don't have to be paid until the dispute is settled in the creditor's favor.

The law says your complaint has to be resolved in one of two ways: If your contention proves right, the creditor must correct the error and subtract any finance charges added as a result of it, then notify you of the correction.

WHERE SHOULD YOU TAKE YOUR FINANCIAL BUSINESS?

CHOICES, CHOICES, CHOICES

A quick look around the financial-services marketplace that has sprung up in the past few years is all it takes to kindle confusion in the minds of those who remember how things used to be. Savings and loan associations are offering car loans and checking accounts, services once available only at banks. Banks have set up brokerage departments for buying and selling stocks and bonds. And brokerage firms are offering packages of services that act for all the world like bank accounts.

The lines that once separated the functions of different kinds of financial institutions have been redrawn and in some cases eliminated entirely. The result is more competition for your business. That's good, but if you haven't reexamined your assumptions about who does what lately, you could be missing out on significant new opportunities to make your money grow. Although it is possible to take care of virtually all your financial business in one place these days, it may not be the smartest thing for you to do. Where you take your money should depend on considerations of convenience, price, service and safety. You won't always find the best of all four in the same place.

BANKS

Convenience. If location were all that counted, commercial banks would win on convenience hands down. With nearly 15,000 of them in the country (more than 47,000, counting branches), they are easy enough to find. In fact, it's probably safe to say that most people choose a bank on the basis of its location, picking the one that's closest to their home or job. Before you do that, however, drop into the branch you're considering to see how it handles its customer traffic during the peak lunch-hour rush, particularly on Fridays. Is there an express line for customers with simple deposits or withdrawals? Is there a single line that moves people most efficiently to the next available teller? Are there enough tellers? Are there automated teller machines? Would going an extra block or two take you to a more efficient bank and reduce the time you spend in line?

Price. There are two parts to price. One is the rate the bank pays you on the kinds of accounts you have in mind; the other is the fee structure the bank imposes on those same accounts and the rates it charges for loans. Shopping around is the only way to discover the best deal.

Banks can no longer count on the low rate paid to savers to subsidize the cost of other services. As a result, some are attempting to discourage small accounts by levying fees on accounts below a certain size or by charging savers for withdrawals exceeding a certain number within a specified length of time. Even if you are not in the small-saver category, you could find yourself paying fees for services that used to be free. The only way to make sure you're getting a good deal is to compare the interest rates and fee structures of banks you're considering.

In comparing competing savings accounts and certificates, remember that your real yield, usually referred to as the effective yield, depends on how often interest is compounded, how often it is credited to your account, and other factors.

For example, a 5½% nominal (stated) interest rate increases to a 5.66% effective yield if interest is compounded daily, as shown in the table below. What you gain on compounding, however, can easily be lost to infrequent crediting. If the interest isn't credited to your daily compounded account until the end of the quarter and you withdraw, say, $1,000 five days before the quarter ends, you usually lose all the interest earned on that amount up to that point.

The ideal account is one that pays the highest rate, compounds interest daily (or "continuously," a formula that yields fractionally more) and credits interest daily to the day of withdrawal. Many institutions offer these day-of-deposit-to-day-of-withdrawal accounts.

Compounding practices also affect the yield from certificates of deposit. Certificates are commonly advertised with their nominal and effective yields, so you can spot the differences fairly easily. The more frequent the compounding, the higher the effective yield, as this table shows.

STATED ANNUAL PERCENTAGE RATE	ANNUAL EFFECTIVE RATE	
	IF COMPOUNDED QUARTERLY	IF COMPOUNDED DAILY
5.25%	5.3543%	5.3899%
5.50	5.6145	5.6536
6.00	6.1364	6.1831
6.50	6.6602	6.7153
7.00	7.1859	7.2501
7.50	7.7136	7.7876
7.75	7.9782	8.0573
8.00	8.2432	8.3278

Services. The variety of services available from a bank these days is limited mostly by the ingenuity of individual bankers and the competitive environment in which the bank operates. You can find the following: safe-deposit boxes; telephone bill-payer accounts, which permit you to direct the bank by telephone to pay certain bills directly from your account; overdraft protection, which will automatically advance you a loan to pay for any checks you write that exceed the balance in your checking account; direct deposit, by which your paycheck or other regular income, such as a social security check, is sent directly to your bank account; stockbrokerage services, which permit you to buy and sell stocks and bonds through your bank at a discount from the rates charged by full service brokers. (Note, however, that banks are not permitted—so far, at least—to recommend purchases or sales; all they can do is take your order.) Some also have arrangements by which you can purchase car, home and life insurance.

With the exception of stockbrokerage, those are the kinds of things banks have been doing for their customers for years. Automated teller machines, which have sprouted more recently, are another service you might find useful. They permit you to withdraw cash, make deposits, check your balance, transfer funds among different accounts and perform a variety of other banking functions any time of the day or night. If you work in the city and live in the suburbs, local ATMs linked to your downtown bank give you easy access to emergency cash at night or on weekends and still let you make your deposits in person downtown.

Perhaps the most obscure of all bank services are the trust departments, not because what they do is that difficult to understand but because banks have not aggressively promoted them. Trust departments have traditionally been viewed, often by banks themselves, as preserves of the wealthy. However, many families who don't rate themselves as wealthy need trust services as part of their overall personal money-management plan.

For a fee, a trust department will help you manage your personal property. You can arrange to have the bank simply act as a custodian of your assets and follow your instructions in carrying out your investment decisions, or you can assign it complete management of your financial affairs. A trust department will also execute the terms of your will and manage your estate for your children.

Most larger banks will consider you as a trust customer if your estate is valued at more than $100,000. This includes the current value of your home and any other real estate, savings, stocks, bonds, business interests, life insurance and personal property, including stamp or coin collections or antiques.

If you are thinking about using trust services, ask your branch manager to introduce you to a trust officer of the bank. If nothing else, you will probably come away with good free advice on managing your finances. If you are seriously considering trust services, you should also consult your lawyer and an accountant.

Safety.   Most commercial banks and mutual savings banks are members of the Federal Deposit Insurance Corporation (FDIC). That means depositors' accounts up to $100,000 are fully insured by an agency of the federal government. That's about as safe as you can get, and in some circumstances accounts can be arranged so that the insurance covers far more than $100,000.

The limit applies, in the words of the law, to all accounts owned by an individual "in the same capacity and the same right." In effect, you can get more than $100,000 of insurance by opening different accounts in different capacities and rights in the same bank, and you can duplicate that coverage with accounts in other banks. For example, a couple could stretch its coverage to $500,000 in one bank with the following series of accounts:

husband, in his own name	$100,000
wife, in her own name	$100,000
husband-wife, joint account	$100,000
husband, in trust for wife	$100,000
wife, in trust for husband	$100,000

They could also get insurance for accounts opened in trust for their children or grandchildren. They can't extend the limits, though, by opening more joint accounts at the same bank. All of your interest in joint accounts at the same bank is considered as one. If you have $100,000 in a joint account with your spouse and another $100,000 in a joint account with your child, you are insured as an individual for only $100,000. (Money held in IRA and Keogh accounts is insured separately from money held in other accounts in the same institution.)

Although banks, savings and loan associations, and credit unions are insured by different agencies, their rules are essentially the same.

Suppose your institution goes broke? As long as it's federally insured and your balance is under the $100,000 limit, you won't lose anything except possibly a few days' interest. In most cases, a failing institution is merged with a healthy one, with no interruption in business. If an institution is shut down, you may have to wait a few days to get your money.

SAVINGS AND LOAN ASSOCIATIONS

Convenience. There are about 4,000 savings and loan associations in the U.S. Counting branches, the total number of s&l offices tops 25,000. Some call themselves federal savings banks. Finding a conveniently located place to do business shouldn't be a problem. But you should subject an s&l to the same kinds of tests described above for banks.

Price. Thrifts no longer enjoy a rate advantage over banks. As a potential customer, you should gather information about rates and fees on accounts you're interested in, then compare the figures before choosing a place to take your business.

Services. Like banks, s&l's can offer a variety of savings and certificate accounts, telephone bill-paying accounts, NOW accounts, credit cards, networks of automated teller machines and other services. The Depository Institutions Deregulation and Monetary Control Act of 1980 gave thrifts the authority to set up trust departments, but they seem to have moved into this area slowly. One of the most significant changes in the operation of savings and loan associations occurred in October

1982, when they were authorized to use up to 30% of their assets to make consumer loans, including car loans. That, coupled with the elimination of the differential on savings accounts and certificates, has considerably blurred the distinctions between s&l's and banks. For all practical purposes, you should consider them direct competitors for your business.

Safety. All federally chartered savings and loan associations and most state-chartered ones are members of the Federal Savings and Loan Insurance Corporation. FSLIC insurance covers up to $100,000 of an individual depositor's money and in some cases more, as explained above in the section on bank safety. Some states have their own insurance plans for state-chartered savings associations that aren't members of the FSLIC. Spectacular collapses of state insurance systems in Ohio and Maryland in 1985 should cause you to think long and hard before entrusting your savings to an institution that does not carry federal deposit insurance.

CREDIT UNIONS

Convenience. More than 57 million people belong to approximately 16,000 credit unions across the country. By law, members must have a common bond, such as working for the same employer, living in the same neighborhood or community, or belonging to the same church, club or fraternal group. Members of a food cooperative or employees of different businesses in the same complex, such as a shopping center, can band together to form a credit union. Offices are often located at the workplace.

Price. Because they are not concerned with making a profit, credit unions can often pay more on accounts and charge less in fees. They have a distinct advantage for NOW accounts, which they call sharedraft accounts, because they frequently pay more interest and impose no minimum-balance requirements. On the other half of the price equation—rates charged on loans and fees charged on accounts—credit unions often, but not always, offer the best deal available. Certainly if you are eligible to be a credit-union member, you should compare what it has to offer with what's being offered elsewhere.

Services. Because they are often small, credit unions usually don't have the resources to offer the kind of services provided by banks and savings and loan associations. Thus they are usually not all-purpose financial institutions. Their competitive edge comes chiefly from the rates they pay on savings and checking accounts and the rates they charge for loans.

Safety. Most of these accounts are insured up to $100,000 by the federally sponsored National Credit Union Administration.

BROKERAGE FIRMS

Convenience. Most small towns have a bank or two to call their own, but chances are their residents have to travel to the nearest city to find a stockbroker. That's a useful reminder that, no matter how much banks and brokerage firms have come to resemble each other over the years, they still serve largely different functions. Banks and s&l's are for savers and borrowers, brokerage firms are for investors. Most are open only during normal business hours, when the markets in which they trade are open.

Prices. It has been more than a decade since brokerage fees were deregulated, leaving brokers free to charge whatever they wish. Since then the business has divided into two distinct camps: so-called full-service houses, which maintain research departments and issue a constant stream of recommendations for their brokers to pass along to their customers, and discount houses, which do nothing but take orders to buy and sell, passing along the benefits of their bare-bones approach in lower fees to their customers. Merrill Lynch, Smith Barney, Dean Witter and Prudential Bache are a few well-known full-service houses. Charles Schwab, Fidelity Brokerage and Quick & Reilly are among the prominent discounters (see Chapter 15). If you want the research services, you should expect to pay for them. If you use your own sources for making investment decisions, there's no need to pay a brokerage firm for something you don't use. Either way, however, you should shop around. Call a number of firms and ask how much they would charge to perform the trade you have in mind. If you can't get a clear answer, take your business elsewhere.

Services. Most of the services offered by brokerage firms are designed for investors—that is, for buyers and sellers ,of stocks, bonds, commodities, shares in real estate syndicates and so forth. Those sorts of transactions are discussed in later chapters. What makes brokerage houses eligible for consideration as a cash-management tool is the development by many of them of some very attractive special accounts. They are packages of financial services known generically as universal accounts or asset-management accounts; each sponsor uses a different name. Merrill Lynch, which was the first to introduce the concept, calls its chief account of this kind the Cash Management Account and requires a minimum opening balance of $20,000 in cash or securities. Charles Schwab calls its account Schwab One and requires only a $5,000 minimum. Dean Witter calls its plan the Active Asset Account. There are others. Specific features, minimums and fees vary, but these are the plans' chief attractions: a money-market account in which idle funds earn interest at current rates; the ability to write checks based on the value of assets in your account; a substantial line of credit; use of a debit or credit card for making purchases or obtaining cash; a monthly statement showing all transactions plus current and previous balances.

Most of these components are available in other places, although not necessarily in a single package. Some banks and savings and loans are offering similar plans.

Comparison shop if you're in the market for one of these accounts. Take a look at different sponsors' required minimum opening amounts, annual fees, commission charges, margin loan rates, and how they handle debit- or credit-card transactions. Also check the other uses that can be made of the card, the time taken for sweeps into the money fund, and the completeness of information provided on monthly statements. Before you choose an account, study the sponsors' prospectuses and other literature.

Safety. The Securities Investors Protection Corporation (SIPC) is a federally chartered body that provides insurance for brokerage firms' customer accounts up to $500,000, with a $100,000 limit on cash. Some brokers purchase additional

YOUR KIDS AND YOUR MONEY

TEACHING KIDS ABOUT MONEY

Any family money-management plan with a good shot at success will have to include the kids—which is easier said than done. You can teach your 4-year-old to close the front door, but you can't expect him to understand that one of the reasons you insist on it is that you don't want to pay for air-conditioning the whole neighborhood. A teenager, on the other hand, should understand that and more. While lessons in financial responsibility must be geared to a child's age and level of maturity, there are general guidelines you can follow.

Give your child an allowance. Most child specialists agree that the best way for kids to learn about handling money is to have some to handle. An allowance is a teaching tool through which a child begins to learn about living within his or her means.

How big an allowance is reasonable? When should it be started and how often should it be given? The answers depend largely on the child and will be discussed later. For now, note this rule: Every allowance should include some money the child can spend however he or she wants. If every cent is earmarked for lunches, bus fares and the like, the child gets no experience in choosing among spending alternatives. Another rule: Don't come to the rescue every time your youngster runs out of money. The allowance should be realistic and determined by mutual agreement. If the child consistently spends fast and needs more, either the allowance is too small or spending habits are sloppy. Find the cause and act accordingly.

Don't use money to reward or punish a child. Giving bonuses for good grades or withholding part of an allowance for misbehavior may be an effective way to teach a youngster about an economic system based on monetary rewards, but many child specialists fear it puts family relationships on the wrong footing. Such actions mix love with money, and in the minds of the young the two concepts can become confused. A better approach is to reward good behavior by showing pride and affection and to punish wrongdoing with some penalty that fits the crime. Don't give kids the idea that money can be used to buy love or to buy your way out of a jam. Paying older kids for doing extra jobs around the house is fine, as long as they realize they also have regular family responsibilities that they should not expect to be paid for.

Remember that your own example is the best teacher. Your attitudes toward money, the way you handle it and discuss it, make an impression on your children just as surely as your attitudes toward religion and other personal matters. If you speak longingly of the neighbor's new car or television set, if you spend impulsively, if you often quarrel about money with your spouse, the children will take note. Your behavior reveals the place of money in your life. It's unrealistic to expect your children to develop an attitude toward money that's more mature than your own.

Those are general guidelines. The problems parents face are usually more specific. What can you do to encourage financial responsibility in children of various ages, and how much can you expect of a child?

Preschoolers. Children 3 and 4 years old aren't too young to start learning about money. At least they can be shown that money is something you exchange for something else. You might want to give your child a few pennies to spend on a piece of candy or fruit during a trip to the store. This will demonstrate the use of money, even though the relative merits of different purchases are still beyond the child's comprehension.

Giving an allowance probably doesn't make sense at this age because children's concept of time isn't developed enough to grasp the idea of receiving a regular income. Besides, what would they spend it on?

Nevertheless, there are a few specific money-related exercises that can benefit a preschooler. As your child learns to count, you can demonstrate the relationship between pennies and nickels, then dimes and quarters. Also, children like to play store with play money, acting as salespersons or customers. It's a good way for them to learn the role of money.

Situations that don't seem to be connected with money at all may be the most important influences. If preschoolers are encouraged to share things, to take care of their toys and pick up after themselves, their sense of responsibility will be reflected in the attitudes they develop about money. Psychologists generally agree that a person's attitude toward money is really an extension of attitudes toward other things. Thus, if children feel secure at home, are given freedom to explore their environment within reasonable limits—in short, given a healthy, happy start in life—then they are off on the right foot where money is concerned, too.

Elementary-school children. Most kids are ready for a regular allowance when they start school. Weekly is probably best. The amount depends on what you expect the child to buy. If he or she has to pay for lunch and bus fare, then the allowance must be bigger than if you paid those expenses yourself. Either way, remember the rule that kids need free money, money to spend or save as they see fit. Handing out exact change for lunch doesn't teach children much if they merely convey the money from your hands to the hands of a cafeteria cashier. With an extra dollar to spend each week, deciding what to do with it is a more valuable experience than just carting lunch money to school.

You have to be the judge of how much allowance your child

can manage. Start small, then increase responsibility for lunches and other expenses gradually as the child matures.

With a little extra money at their disposal, kids in the elementary grades become serious shoppers. Help them learn to compare quality and prices of similar items. Allow them to make small choices on their own, such as gifts for friends or toys for themselves. As they mature, give them more say in buying clothes for school and play, pointing out along the way why one purchase may be a better buy than another because of quality, appropriateness or price. This will equip them for making intelligent choices on their own.

Allowing kids to do their own shopping means you have to expect some mistakes. There will be a cheap toy that breaks the first day, or too much candy or a garment that doesn't fit. Allow your child to make mistakes. Then do your best to make it a learning experience, not simply an occasion to say "I told you so."

Including older elementary-school kids in a few family financial discussions is a good way to demonstrate the kinds of choices adults face. They needn't be in on every detail, but some financial decisions present natural opportunities for including the kids. For example, the cost of a family vacation depends largely on where you go. Would the kids rather spend one week at the beach or two weeks at grandma's house? Or say you're thinking of buying a dog. Even though a pedigreed animal may not be under consideration, you can point out how much more it costs than a dog from the pound. Including the kids in discussions of this type shows them how the relative costs of things affect buying decisions.

This is also a good age for children to begin learning to save money on their own. The simplest way to begin is for you to open savings accounts in their names. In fact, your child can open an account and have full control over deposits and withdrawals if he or she has reached the age of "competence." This is a subjective standard that depends on state law and the policy of each financial institution. It's almost always required that the child be able to write his or her name.

If you would prefer to have some supervision over your

child's account, work out an arrangement with the financial institution whereby you'll have to countersign any of your child's withdrawal slips. For an account in the name of a very young child, you, as parent or guardian, can make deposits and withdrawals on the child's behalf until he or she is able to act alone.

But don't be tempted to use such an account as a tax shelter for yourself. If you're in control of an account and you use it for your own benefit, then in the eyes of the IRS you are responsible for paying taxes on the interest income.

Teenagers. If you wait until the teen years to give your child money-management experience, you're waiting too long. Your influence is waning.

The allowance is very important at this stage of life—it is the teenager's ticket to independence. It can now be on a monthly basis to encourage long-range planning, and it should cover most daily expenses as well as discretionary income. Discuss your teenagers' expenses with them and arrive at a mutually agreeable figure. Then stick to the amount, giving it periodic reviews. Make the payments on time, without having to be reminded.

If a teenager takes a job to earn extra money, fine. This adds to the all-important feeling of independence. Don't penalize initiative by reducing the allowance, unless financial circumstances leave you no choice.

Teenagers' savings should be kept in banks, credit unions or savings and loan associations, not piggy banks. Introduce your youngsters to the services of financial institutions and let them see the advantages. You can't force them to save, but they should be familiar enough with the family's financial circumstances to know whether they'll have to pay for all or part of college themselves, or whether you can help with a car plus the expenses of gasoline, repairs and insurance.

Teenagers should participate regularly in family financial discussions. They still needn't know every detail, such as total family income or the size of the mortgage, but they should know what pressures are on the budget. Seeing how dramatically the car insurance premiums shot up when they became eligible to drive might encourage them to drive carefully. Participating in the decision to fix up the old car instead of buying a new one can be a valuable lesson in the importance of taking care of things. And purchases that involve them directly—a lawn mower they will use, for instance—provide opportunities for comparison shopping.

A couple of cautions about including kids in family financial affairs: First, don't expect them to shoulder the weight of a financial crisis. Second, don't make them feel guilty about costing you money. Show them how mom and dad cost money, too. Dad's golf clubs, mom's new typewriter—everybody incurs expenses and nobody should get the idea he or she is a burden. If financial setbacks occur that make cutting some expenditures necessary, deciding where to trim the family budget can be an educational exercise.

Eventually your kids will be on their own, worrying about how to teach their kids the financial facts of life. Between now and then, you can't teach them everything they need to know. But with your guidance, they'll learn how to use money properly. Your job is to see that they get easy lessons when they're young and don't have to learn the hard way later.

SAVING FOR THE CHILDREN'S FUTURE

The Tax Reform Act of 1986 severely curtailed the advantages of such long-range planning devices as Clifford Trusts and custodial accounts set up under the Uniform Gifts to Minors Act. Parents in high brackets used to be able to save a considerable amount in taxes by shifting income-earning property, such as bonds or savings certificates, to their offspring, so that earnings in such accounts were taxed at the child's rate rather than the parents'. In the case of a Clifford Trust, ownership of the property reverted to the parents after a specified time, usually ten years. The Tax Reform Act eliminated Clifford Trusts except in carefully prescribed circumstances that make them virtually useless to most people. (Clifford Trusts set up before the new law took effect may continue until their terms run out.) Furthermore, any income over $1,000 generated by any custodial account set up for minors is taxed at the parents' top rate until the child reaches age 14, when all earnings begin being taxed at the child's rate.

This hasn't eliminated entirely the advantage of shifting some assets to a child's name. After all, it takes a pretty big pile of money to generate $1,000 in interest or dividends in a single year. At 10% interest, it would take $10,000 to reach the threshold. In addition, the first $500 of unearned income—interest, dividends and other nonwage amounts—can be protected by the standard deduction. Thus, some sort of asset shifting can still pay off. (But if your child is close to college age already, shifting assets can backfire on you when you apply for financial aid, as explained later in this chapter.)

You can give as much as $10,000 a year to each of as many individuals as you like, including your children, without incurring the consequences of the gift tax; for you and your spouse, that makes a total annual exclusion of $20,000. For smaller amounts especially, the child's tax bill is likely to be smaller than yours, despite the Tax Reform Act. (Also, if done properly, gifts can result in reduced estate taxes and a saving in probate costs. For that sort of planning, you should consult an attorney.)

The Uniform Gifts to Minors Act. It's relatively easy to use the gifts-to-minors law. You choose a custodian to manage the account until the minor comes of age, but the asset is held in the child's name so that he or she is liable for taxes on its earnings. All you have to do is go to a financial institution or broker and arrange to open your gift account, which will be set up in a form similar to this: "(name of custodian) as custodian for (name of minor) under the (name of state) Uniform Gifts to Minors Act." Besides the possible tax advantage, you'll have the comfort of knowing that the custodian you name will control the account until the child reaches the age of majority.

All the income distributions from the account must be used for the child's benefit, but not for any purposes that are part of your legal obligations to support the child. To avoid any future wrangling, make sure to keep records of all transactions and consider appointing someone other than yourself as custodian to keep the value of the assets out of your estate (you can't appoint yourself custodian when giving bearer securities).

A gifts-to-minors account is particularly useful when you're giving securities. Although stocks and bonds can be registered directly in the name of a minor, trading in such an account can present problems. Brokers, bankers and others are understandably reluctant to deal with minors, who usually can't be held to contracts and who can revoke transactions when they reach majority. The role of the custodian solves this problem.

Just because the gifts-to-minors act is easy to use doesn't mean you should use it lightly. It has its limitations, notably:

• Your gift is irrevocable (you can't take it back), and the minor is legally entitled to receive the principal and any undistributed income when he or she reaches the age of majority. Then the minor is also entitled to use the money as he or she wishes, even if those wishes don't coincide with yours. (Some states with lower ages of majority have retained age 21 in their gifts-to-minors laws.)

• If you are both donor and custodian and die before the child reaches majority, your gift would be considered part of your estate for federal tax purposes. This is an argument for appointing someone other than yourself as custodian. The amount of a gift that exceeds the annual gift-tax exclusion would be considered part of your estate even if you weren't the custodian.

OTHER WAYS TO SHIFT TAXES

One way around the restrictions on asset-shifting is to put the money in accounts that defer taxable income until the child turns 14, to take advantage of his or her lower bracket. There are a number of ways to do it.

Savings bonds. Buy Series EE bonds in your child's name and you can defer paying taxes on the interest until the bonds mature or are redeemed. But be careful: If your child already has EE bonds and has chosen to report and pay taxes on the interest as it accrues year by year, he or she must do the same for new bonds. In such a case, you could redeem all the old bonds and buy new ones. Then you could choose the deferral option.

If your employer has an employee-investment program,

check to see whether your contribution can be put into a gifts-to-minors account on behalf of your child. If you buy Series EE U.S. savings bonds through a payroll plan, they can be registered directly in your child's name. Bear in mind that if they are, they can also be cashed in by the child when he or she is old enough to write his or her name and understand what's going on. If you want to maintain some control over use of the bonds, you'll have to place them in a gifts-to-minors account. You'll find a more detailed explanation of savings bonds in Chapter 16.

Municipal bonds. You could get tax-free income by purchasing municipal bonds in your own name, of course. But buying them in your child's name creates an additional tax saving if you stick to discounted issues—that is, bonds selling for less than face value. This happens to bonds when interest rates rise after they have been issued. The owner of such bonds receives face value at maturity and must pay tax on the amount of the discount. Here's how to take advantage of that: Purchase discounted municipals in your child's name, looking for maturity dates on or after the day the child turns 14. That will assure that the discount gets taxed in the child's bracket, which will presumably be lower than yours, tax reform or no tax reform. There's more on municipal bonds in Chapter 22.

Zero-coupon bonds. Zero-coupon bonds sell at a steep discount from face value. Interest accrues year by year but is not paid out until maturity. This no-interest-along-the-way feature makes possible dramatic discounts. For instance, a Treasury zero-coupon bond worth $10,000 in 1997 was selling for $4,500 in mid 1988.

You can see the appeal of zeros for college planning: You know exactly what you'll get when the bond matures, and you can schedule maturities to coincide with your need for the money.

The catch is, interest earned by zeros is subject to tax as it accrues, even though you receive nothing until maturity. But with a little planning you can minimize the tax bite.

Interest on zeros doesn't build up steadily each year. Because of compounding, the rate of accrual accelerates over the life of the bond, and you get less interest in the early years. This means that if you purchase a zero in the child's name, taxes owed in the early years will be relatively small, even if the child must pay at your rate. As the years go by and the rate of accrual gains momentum, the child may turn 14 and thus be taxed at his or her lower rate.

For example, say you want to fund your new baby's college education through zero-coupon bonds. For about $15,000, you can buy $60,000 worth of zeros paying 8% and maturing in 18 years. That means there will be about $45,000 in appreciation that someone is going to have to pay taxes on.

During the first 13 years, the bonds accrue interest at an average rate of $2,000 a year. If the child has no other income, about $1,000 will be taxed at your rate. In the final five years before maturity—after the child has turned 14—the average annual interest earned (about $3,900) will be nearly twice as much as in the first 13 years, but all of it will be taxed at the child's rate, not yours.

Life insurance. Life insurance policies with investment features—called whole life, universal life or variable life insurance—can be useful for long-range planning because earnings within the policy are generally allowed to accumulate tax-free. Single-premium whole life is especially attractive for this purpose because it permits more of your premium dollar to be directed into the investment account than other kinds of policies, thus hastening the growth of your cash value. Later on, you can borrow against that cash value without incurring a tax liability as long as you don't bite too deeply into the principal. But be aware: The tax-favored status of single-premium whole life policies is under almost constant fire from a Congress in search of tax revenues, and its future as a tax haven may be limited. See Chapter 10 for more information about life insurance with investment features.

Deferred annuities. These permit you to pay now for income later. Meanwhile, as long as you don't withdraw any money, interest on your payment accumulates tax-free. Such plans are usually paid for in a lump sum, in which case they are called single-premium deferred annuities, or with a series of contributions that may vary from year to year. Those are called flexible-premium annuities. In either case, you can schedule the payments to begin when the child reaches college age and needs the money. Note that there is a 10% penalty on withdrawals from annuities if they take place before the annuitant reaches age 59½. That restriction can put a damper on the money-saving possibilities of such plans for college bills. Whether it will pay off at all will depend on how the combination of the penalty and the child's tax bracket compares with the taxes you'd pay while the earnings accumulated in a non–tax-sheltered plan. In most cases, the annuity will probably not be worth the trouble. See Chapter 24 for more on annuities.

FINDING THE MONEY FOR COLLEGE

Read the numbers and weep: The average cost of four years away at a private college is running about $48,000 these days. The average for public colleges and universities is over $23,000. A few years from now costs will be even higher. If you didn't start planning for bills like that years ago, you're probably going to need help.

Fortunately for many parents and students, help is available. It comes from the federal and state governments, private agencies and the colleges themselves. But the money has a way of running out before everyone who wants some can get it. The best way to increase your chances of finding aid is to start looking early. Even if college is a couple of years or more away, it's not too soon to familiarize yourself with the possibilities and begin mapping your search.

Assessing your need. Most financial aid is awarded on the basis of need, and most aid programs rely on one or more of the standard need-analysis systems to sort out their applicants. At a minimum you'll have to complete either the Financial Aid Form (FAF), which is published by the College Scholarship Service of the College Board, or the Family Financial Statement (FFS), which comes from the American College Testing Program. The colleges to which your youngster applies will tell you which they accept. Along the way you may also have to fill out additional forms for specialized kinds of aid programs. Both the

FAF and the FFS are multipaged documents that demand detailed information about family income, expenses, assets and debts. The forms don't look alike, but they ask essentially the same questions and result in identical assessments of need. The high school guidance office or the financial aid department of any college can tell you where to get the forms.

How you come out in the need analysis will depend on how your finances stack up against others in the applicant pool. Computers process the information you supply and calculate a precise estimate of how much you'll be expected to contribute. Using that figure, financial aid officers at individual schools decide how much aid, if any, they can give you. Their decision will be based on the cost of the school, the amount of money on hand for financial aid, and the competition for funds. Applicants showing the greatest need generally get first crack at the money.

If you are going through need analysis to apply for aid, you may be better off with the family assets concentrated in the parents' name. If you take steps to shift income from these assets to your child to take advantage of your child's lower tax liability, you could run into this problem: Children are expected to chip in about 35% of their assets toward college costs. They do not get an asset protection allowance; parents do. Because of the way the aid formula works, parents contribute a maximum of about 5% of their net assets, not 35%. A $20,000 savings certificate could add about $7,000 to the contribution expected from the family if treated as the child's asset, about $1,000 if owned by the parents.

Although aid money comes from a variety of sources, the great majority of it is funneled through the colleges themselves, so the assessment forms and college financial aid offices should be the early targets of your efforts. If your need is judged great enough, you may not have to look further.

Successful aid applicants are commonly offered a package of aid, part of which is an outright grant, part a loan and part the opportunity for a campus job. If you don't survive the need test, or if you aren't offered enough money to make ends meet, your search for help gets considerably more difficult. That doesn't mean the situation is hopeless: Scholarships, loans and jobs aren't always tied to need. But because most of them are, let's examine need-based programs first.

Help that's based on need. The federal government is by far the single largest source of financial aid to college students. Aid from state governments, once paltry, has grown increasingly important in recent years. A look at the details of the major programs will give you an idea of whether you might qualify.

Pell Grants. These constitute the largest of the government's programs. Grants have ranged from $100 to $2,100 per year, and more than two million students qualify each year. The average Pell Grant in recent years has been about $1,300. It is based on the cost of the school and the financial resources of the student.

The income level at which a family qualifies for a Pell Grant has changed over the years. In general, families with incomes of up to about $25,000 are eligible for grants, although most of the money goes to students from families with less income than that. Special circumstances—several children in college at the same time, for instance—can make higher-income families eligible. That's why it is important to follow through on the application process, no matter what your expectations may be.

Supplemental Educational Opportunity Grants (SEOG). For students who have greater financial need than can be met by a Pell Grant, the SEOG program offers grants ranging up to $4,000 a year. Financial aid officers at each school decide which of their students get the money, which comes from the federal government.

College Work-Study Program (CWSP). Students from higher-income families have a better chance of getting a part-time job under CWSP than of getting most kinds of grants. Jobs can be on or off campus and commonly take about ten to 12 hours a week of the student's time. The school's financial aid office picks the workers. Pay is modest, usually about the federal minimum wage. Typical jobs: faculty aide, library clerk, cafeteria worker.

Perkins Loan Program (formerly called National Direct Student Loans). Eligible undergraduate and graduate students can borrow up to $4,500 during their first two years of undergraduate work and up to $9,000 for four years of study. Graduate students can borrow up to a total of $18,000, including undergraduate loans. Interest is below market rates. Repayment needn't begin until nine months after the student graduates, leaves school, or drops below half-time status, and it can be stretched out over ten years, with payments of as little as $30 a month.

Guaranteed Student Loans. Under the Guaranteed Student Loan program, students who can demonstrate need can borrow up to about $2,600 per year as freshmen or sophomores, and $4,000 a year as juniors or seniors, to a total of $17,250 as undergraduates. For graduate students the maximum is about $55,000, including undergraduate loans.

Loans carry a subsidized interest rate, and repayment needn't begin until the student leaves school. Loans are arranged through private lenders—banks, savings and loan associations, credit unions, even some colleges. Some lenders allow up to ten years to repay. Check with your school or ask local financial institutions for information on how to apply.

An important thing to remember about both the Perkins Loan Program and Guaranteed Student Loans is that the students, not parents, are the borrowers, and the students therefore are responsible for paying back the money.

State aid programs. Every state provides some sort of financial assistance to qualified residents. Most awards are based on need, although some are based on other criteria, including academic performance. Florida, Idaho, Indiana, Louisiana, New York and South Dakota, for example, have performance-based programs of aid. Generally, recipients of state awards or loans must be residents of the state and enrolled in a school within the state. A few states have reciprocity agreements with others. Check with high school counselors about such programs.

Private agencies. Labor unions, fraternal organizations, corporations, and other private agencies often sponsor scholarship and loan programs for the sons and daughters of people affiliated with them. Some programs, like the National Merit Scholarships, are open to everyone, with awards being determined on the basis of competitive examinations and financial need. A few programs rely on the results of competitive exams, projects or school records without considering need.

The amount of money available through private agencies is nothing to sneeze at, but the sources are so diffuse that it is perhaps the hardest to find. Check with employers and local, state and national organizations with which you or any member of your family may be affiliated, and watch high school bulletin boards.

Colleges and universities. Schools themselves support many different aid programs for students who need the money. If you start your search at the colleges' financial aid offices, you'll find out about such programs.

If you have ten or more years before college bills will start coming due, you might want to investigate some of the pay-now, study-later plans being offered by a number of colleges and universities around the country. Sometimes called the Duquesne Plan because Duquesne University in Pittsburgh is credited with originating the idea (although it suspended its program in 1988), these plans allow parents to buy a college education for a one-time payment of a few thousand dollars for a newborn, more for an older child. This idea works a lot like a zero-coupon bond: It assumes a certain level of earnings on the original payment and may or may not represent a good investment. It also assumes that your child will want to attend the school you picked out years earlier. A number of states have adopted similar plans for their public college and university systems.

Aid if you can't show need. Parents living on what they thought were modest incomes, especially compared with the size of college bills, are often surprised to learn that the standard need-analysis systems judge them too affluent to qualify for the bulk of financial aid. The fact is that the aid money peters out pretty quickly for families earning more than $25,000 a year. But it isn't gone completely, as an examination of the possibilities will show.

No-need scholarships. A growing number of financial awards are going to students for their academic achievements. At many colleges and universities, good high school grades and high test scores are being converted to cash to help pay the bills. Check with the colleges your child is considering and with your state's financial aid office.

PLUS program.   A law enacted in 1980 created this class of government-backed subsidized college loans. Parents may borrow up to $3,000 a year, up to a total of $15,000 per dependent undergraduate. Graduate students have the same limits, but independent undergrads can't borrow more than $2,500 per year. Graduate students and independent students can defer payment on the principal until 60 days after leaving school but must make interest payments in the meantime. Parents must begin repaying interest and principal 60 days after the loan is made. Financial need is not a criterion. Independent and vocational school students can borrow up to $2,500 a year to a maximum total of $12,500. Graduate or professional students are also eligible for PLUS loans of up to $3,000 a year ($15,000 total), irrespective of their dependency status. Check with local lenders or your state guarantee agency; these loans may not be available everywhere.

Commercial loans.   Sometimes institutions unwilling or unable to make guaranteed loans will lend money for college at regular commercial rates or under special programs they have set up for education loans. Interest rates will be higher than under the guaranteed loan program, and repayment periods are likely to be shorter. Shop for these loans the same way you would for an auto loan or a mortgage—by checking with several lenders and comparing rates and terms. Loans of this type are generally available only to parents, not students.

Stretched-out payment plans.   Commercial firms and some colleges offer ways to stretch out college payments in a way that gets you over the hump of the big bills that come due each semester. The Tuition Plan is perhaps the best known of the commercial plans. A subsidiary of Manufacturers Hanover Corp., it offers a number of options, including loans, lines of credit, and combination prepayment and repayment programs that let you spread out payments for as long as ten years. In considering this or any other commercial program, take into account the interest you earn on prepayments as well as what you pay for loans. Colleges can give you the names and addresses of firms offering such plans.

Part-time jobs.   Although many jobs are offered to students only if they need money, many others are available to whoever asks for them first. Pay for part-time campus work is generally at the minimum wage or above, and earnings of $1,000 or more during the school year are not unusual. Check with the college's financial aid and employment offices.

Part Two

THE ROOF
OVER YOUR HEAD

BUYING, SELLING AND RENTING A HOME

THE RENT OR BUY DECISION

W̶e Americans want to own our homes. Six out of ten households are homeowners, although for the first time since the 1930s the rate of ownership is falling. Would-be owners under age 35 have been especially hard hit. And the fact is that most first-time buyers, whatever their age, need two incomes to swing it.

Still, homeownership is an enduring part of the American dream. It is taken as a sign of independence, prudence, thrift and stability. With luck it may also be the path to some profit.

But it isn't right for everyone. The benefits also carry responsibilities and obligations you may not be ready—or able—to shoulder. In fact, a good case can often be made for renting.

You can probably get more space for the money. Usually you can rent an apartment or house for less than the monthly cost of buying it, and you don't have to lay out closing costs.

You're also freer to move. You have no long-term financial investment to consider. When you need to leave or you want a change, you can go. There's no waiting to sell out first, no agonizing about the housing market at your destination, no tax pressure to roll the profit from one home into another. You are freer, psychologically and economically, which can be a distinct advantage in some circumstances. For instance, suppose you anticipate being relocated in connection with a job promotion, or you want to try out a potential retirement community before buying. In such circumstances, renting can be a wise, relatively carefree alternative to homeownership.

Renting allows you to adjust to change more readily. If your fortunes improve, you can step up to a bigger place or into a more desirable neighborhood. If your fortunes decline, tightening your belt is easier. If you marry, or add a child to your family, moving to a larger apartment or house is simpler than expanding your home or buying a larger one.

Renters worry less than owners about property values. If housing values decline, the worst that can happen is that you pay too much rent until your lease expires. Then you're free to ask for a rent cut or move to where rents are more reasonable. The same decline could be a disaster for an owner.

As a renter you can resist spending. Home improvement is big business not just because owners must maintain their properties, but also because they often have an almost irresistible itch to make improvements. The renter, on the other hand, may spend money only on furnishings. In fact, the lease may even forbid other kinds of fix-ups.

Finally, renting may leave you with more money to invest elsewhere. Home buyers now spend, on average, more than $1,000 a month to carry a new home, $950 to own an old one. Such payments make it hard for many owners to start and maintain savings and investment programs for retirement, vacations and other purposes. As a renter, you probably will pay less for comparable shelter.

A common thread runs through these advantages: freedom—freedom from the long-term commitment homeowners make the moment they decide to buy.

THE CASE FOR OWNERSHIP

To some people, the sense of roots homeownership provides

is as important as the sense of freedom renters enjoy. But the financial arguments for owning are very hard to refute.

Homeownership is a hedge against inflation. In the period from the mid 1970s to the early 1980s, the cost of living rose about 70%. Home prices doubled in the same period. In most places, home prices haven't risen as fast, or at such a sustained pace, since then. But in general, home values continue to rise faster than the inflation rate, providing at least some investment benefit in most parts of the country.

Homeownership has substantial tax advantages. Prices may go up or down, but the federal tax rules still favor homeowners. Mortgage interest and property tax deductions by themselves constitute an enormous benefit.

Interest on up to $1 million of mortgage debt you take on to build or buy a home is fully deductible. That means that when figuring out how much house you can afford, you have to consider two figures: your out-of-pocket mortgage payments and your after-tax cost. In the early years of a home mortgage, nearly all of your monthly payments go for fully deductible interest. Take a conventional, 30-year, fixed-rate $100,000 mortgage, for example. Each year, interest and principal payments total $10,530. In the first year, $9,975 of that amount—95% of it—is deductible as interest. Even in the 15th year, 79% of your payments would be deductible.

The value of such tax deductions to you depends on your tax bracket. If you fall in the 28% bracket, for example, $1,000 in deductions saves you $280 in taxes. In other words, for each $1,000 of housing payments consisting of interest and property taxes, Uncle Sam pays $280 by reducing your federal income tax bill by that amount. Add to that any state income tax savings you'll pocket because of your deductions.

Fortunately, you don't have to wait until the following year when you file a tax return to cash in on the savings. You can immediately direct your employer to begin withholding less tax from your paycheck. Get a copy of the W-4 form from your personnel department or a local IRS office.

When you sell the place, you can defer taxes on the profit if you roll the profit over into your next residence. To qualify, you must buy and occupy another principal residence within a 24-month period. This so-called replacement period encompasses the two years before and the two years after the sale of your house. (If you are in the armed forces or living outside the U.S., you may qualify for a longer replacement period.)

Eventually, you get to keep up to $125,000 profit—tax-free. This is the icing on the cake. You qualify if you are at least 55 years old when you sell your home and have owned and lived in it for at least three of the five years leading up to the sale. If you are married and the house is jointly owned, you can qualify as long as either you or your spouse meets the age, ownership and residency tests (page 127).

Homeowners can also use the equity in their home as protection against the crackdown on the deduction of consumer interest. The Tax Reform Act of 1986 ordered a gradual phase-out of the right to deduct consumer interest, a category that includes interest on car loans, student loans, credit card accounts—just about every kind of loan except mortgages. You can deduct 40% of your consumer interest in 1988; 20% in 1989; and only 10% in 1990. From 1991 on, there will be no deduction at all for consumer interest. However, homeowners have a safety valve. You can borrow against your home—via either a second mortgage or a home-equity line of credit—and deduct interest on up to $100,000 of such loans, regardless of how you use the money.

Homeownership gives you leverage. Normally, you buy a home with some of your own money plus a mortgage. That use of borrowed money enables you to profit from price increases on property you haven't yet paid for. The larger your loan as a proportion of the home's value, the greater your leverage. Say you purchase a home for $100,000 with no mortgage and sell it three years later for $125,000. The $25,000 gain represents a 25% return on your $100,000 outlay.

Now look at the deal another way: Make a downpayment of $20,000 and get a mortgage for the rest. You still make a $25,000 profit after three years of ownership, but you've invested only $20,000 to get it. Your return: a spectacular

125% on your investment (ignoring for sake of simplicity the cost of the loan, tax angles, commissions and other costs).

HOW MUCH HOME CAN YOU AFFORD?

Once you decide you want to buy a house or apartment, you'll need to calculate how much you can afford: how much you can pay down and how large a mortgage you can carry.

Start your homework with the net worth statement in Chapter 1. This inventory of your assets and liabilities will help you come up with a realistic down payment. Then complete the worksheet on pages 102 and 103, which will show you how much of a monthly mortgage payment you can afford.

Lenders usually expect you to put down from 10% to 20% on the purchase price of the property. If you plan to buy with a down payment of less than 20%, you'll probably be required to buy insurance provided by a separate private mortgage insurance company. Private mortgage insurance (PMI) generally covers the top 20% to 25% of a first mortgage loan. This permits lenders to lend you up to 90% or 95% of the appraised value of a home while taking about the same risk they would assume in making a loan with a down payment of 30%. In addition, if you anticipate a gift of money from family or friends, you'll find that lenders generally will expect at least a 5% cash down payment from your own resources in addition to any funds you receive as a gift.

QUALIFYING FOR A MORTGAGE

Lenders today think twice about pushing home buyers to their financial limits. During the free-and-easy days of the early 1980s, you could almost overwhelm yourself with mortgage debt to buy your dream house, secure in the thought that inflation would raise your earnings and make the load less of a burden. Then living costs settled down, and lenders began to face foreclosures against overextended borrowers.

The days of skyrocketing home values are over in most parts of the U.S. No longer can you sit and watch your home grow more valuable by the minute. Lower tax rates tend to dampen the after-tax value of interest deductions, too.

Whether you agree that prudence is best or are determined

HOW MUCH CAN YOU SPEND FOR HOUSING?

I. Before you can know how much house you can afford, you need to calculate your other expenses. Do that in the blanks below, then subtract line B from line A to see how much you have available for housing (line C).

MONTHLY INCOME

Net pay (after taxes) _____	
Other income _____	
Total	**A**

MONTHLY NONHOUSING OUTLAYS

Food and household supplies _____	
Transportation _____	
Insurance _____	
Health care _____	
Clothing and cleaning _____	
Education _____	
Debt and installment payments _____	
Recreation and vacation _____	
Telephone _____	
Personal _____	
Taxes (not deducted from pay) _____	
Savings _____	
Charity _____	
Other _____	
Total	**B**

AMOUNT AVAILABLE FOR HOUSING

Monthly income (A) minus _____	
Nonhousing expenses (B) _____	
Amount available	**C**

continued

II. With the figure on line C in mind, plus a firm idea of the size of the down payment you plan to make, you're ready to begin assessing individual homes. Real estate agents or current owners can give you reasonably precise estimates for the categories of expenses listed below. Under "other" you might include any additional cost of commuting to work from that location or new expenses, such as community association fees. If you would reduce any of your current nonhousing expenses by buying a particular home, estimate your saving and subtract it from anticipated expenses. Then add up the housing costs and compare the total on line D with line C. If C is larger than D, you've probably found a place you can afford.

ANTICIPATED MONTHLY HOUSING EXPENSES

Mortgage payment _____	
Insurance _____	
Property taxes _____	
Utilities _____	
Maintenance and repairs (figure at least $\frac{1}{12}$ of 1% of the price) _____	
Other _____	
Total	**D**

to stretch your credit to the limit, you should know how lenders will evaluate your application. Thus armed, you can play by their rules—or maybe stretch them.

Today the guidelines used to qualify prospective home buyers are fairly standardized. They come primarily from Fannie Mae—the Federal National Mortgage Association. This for-profit corporation was formed by the government to buy up mortgages from lenders, repackage them as securities and then resell them to investors. In some respects, however, Fannie Mae knits straitjackets. To make its mortgage pools attractive to investors, Fannie Mae wants loans to conform to its rather strict standards, and that limits the flexibility of original lenders. Either they write loans as Fannie Mae specifies, or they risk being unable to sell them and thus replenish their supply of lendable cash.

Fannie Mae measures your borrowing power by matching your projected housing expenses to your gross household income, and the magic numbers are 28% and 36%. Monthly mortgage interest and principal payments, plus homeowners insurance and property taxes, should total no more than 28% of your gross monthly income, and your monthly house payment plus other long-term debts with ten or more monthly payments still outstanding (that could include an automobile or student loan) should total no more than 36% of gross income.

Income is what you and your spouse earn in before-tax wages. And it's pay for work that you have been doing for a year or longer, not the extra job you took a few weeks before applying for the loan. Other income—such as bonuses, commissions and overtime pay—must be averaged over two years to be considered wages. Count alimony and child-support payments as income if the payments will continue at least three years from the date of your loan application.

Not all loans get the straight 28/36 once-over. To qualify for certain adjustable-rate mortgages (ARMs), you must meet stricter requirements. Here we're talking about ARMs that represent more than 80% of the value of the home, extend beyond 15 years and rely on a so-called 2/6 cap, which allows a maximum increase of two percentage points in any one year and six points over the life of the loan.

Fannie Mae also has tightened up on mortgages with down payments of less than 10% of the purchase price. These loans are held to stricter 25% and 33% standards. For a $92,000 loan on a $100,000 house, your home payment should equal no more than a fourth of your gross monthly income and your long-term debt no more than a third.

Ratios are only guidelines, and 30% to 40% of the loans Fannie Mae buys exceed the guidelines because other factors can tip the scales your way. It counts in your favor if you have a good credit history, make a substantial down payment, possess liquid assets equal to at least three months of home payments or have in the past paid a large proportion of your income for rent or toward a mortgage. In such cases, the 28% rule can drift upward to 30% or even beyond.

The worksheet on pages 102 and 103 will help you assess your home-buying potential. If you anticipate sizable financial obligations, your employment outlook is uncertain, your down payment fund is low, your family is likely to grow, or you'll be needing money for improvements or furnishings, prudence suggests spending less per month than the calculations indicate you can afford.

FINDING THE RIGHT MORTGAGE

Shopping around for a mortgage can yield worthwhile dividends, both in the short and long run. A $100,000 loan that carries 1.5 "points" rather than 2 (a point is a fee—1% of the loan—that the lender will charge you up front) saves you $500. Likewise, a fixed-rate $90,000 mortgage with a rate of 9.25% instead of 9.75% lets you keep $33 a month. Over 30 years $33 a month adds up to nearly $12,000.

Shop around and compare. Hunt for the best loan—interest rate, points, processing costs, and in the case of adjustable mortgages, the most favorable adjustment features. Don't focus your attention on the firm that lends you the money. It's often just as easy to deal with an out-of-town lender as one in your community.

Mortgage reporting services make the job easier. These firms survey the major lenders in a given metropolitan area every week or two and publish information sheets on who is offering what loans on what terms. You can get the names of such firms from real estate agents. Some agents will show you their fact sheets for nothing, but even if you have to buy the current sheets, it's still a bargain because of the time and trouble you'll save. The cost is usually about $25.

Here are several firms that cover lenders in more than one state:

HSH Associates
Ten Mead Ave.
Riverdale, N.J. 07457
201-831-0550; 800-873-2837
Surveys more than 2,000 lenders in more than 30 states and many metropolitan areas.

Gary Myers and Associates
20 W. Hubbard St., Suite 500
Chicago, Ill. 60610
312-670-2440
Reports mortgage rates weekly for Boston, Chicago, Cincinnati, Dallas, Detroit, Houston, Kansas City, Los Angeles, New York City, Norwich, Conn., Phoenix, Rochester, Minn., Washington, D.C., and York, Penn. It also provides rate information to some 200 newspapers in more than 44 states.

National Mortgage Weekly
P.O. Box 18081
Cleveland, Ohio 44118
216-371-2767
Covers the metropolitan Boston, Cleveland, Columbus and Detroit areas.

Peeke LoanFax Inc.
101 Chestnut St., Suite 200
Gaithersburg, Md. 20877
301-840-5752
Provides mortgage reports for the Washington, D.C., area, including northern Virginia and suburban Maryland; Baltimore; and one for Dade, Broward and Palm Beach counties in southern Florida. The Florida report includes Miami and Fort Lauderdale.

If there isn't a reporting service in your area, begin the search with your own bank or savings & loan. Ask real estate agents for names of s&l's, banks, mortgage companies and mortgage brokers, but don't depend entirely on them to find you the best deal. You have to go (or telephone) and ask the questions yourself.

The costs of borrowing. Mortgage lenders charge you for the use of their money in two ways: through the interest charges you'll pay each month over the life of the loan, and through points. Each point is a one-time sum of money equal to 1% of the loan amount. Points are paid up front, at settlement.

Points are prepaid interest charges that raise the effective yield to the lender without raising the interest rate on the note, and they are factored into the annual percentage rate, or APR. Whether called a discount point, loan origination fee, or something else, it's really prepaid interest.

Use the annual percentage rate to compare loans. APR is the cost of your mortgage loan expressed as a yearly rate. It reflects the effect of origination fees, points and (if applicable) mortgage insurance by calculating them as if they were spread out over the term of the loan. Lenders may advertise a loan by the simple interest rate or monthly payment, but they are required by law to divulge the APR as well.

Fixed-rate loans. In this sort of mortgage, the interest rate—and your monthly payments—remain the same for the life of the loan. The most familiar is the long-term loan of 20, 25 or 30 years. Interest rates on this type of mortgage usually run higher than starting rates on adjustable loans, and you may have to pay more points. (While your mortgage payment remains level over the term of the loan, monthly outlays still will increase as property taxes and insurance costs rise.)

Intermediate-term mortgages. Ten- and 15-year fixed-rate loans have become popular forms of financing for home buyers who can afford them. Principal balance is reduced more rapidly than with longer-term loans, and interest rates usually are a half to one percentage point less than on 30-year, fixed-rate loans. The 15-year loan, for example, lets you own your home free and clear in half the time and for less than half the total interest cost of a 30-year fixed-rate loan. The catch is that higher monthly payments can be burdensome, especially for first-time buyers. On a 15-year, $75,000, 10% note, monthly payments are $805—$119 more than for a 30-year, 10.5% note of the same amount.

Bi-weekly mortgages. You make your mortgage payment every other week instead of monthly, which speeds up repayment to about 18 to 20 years and reduces total interest costs. Such loans can usually be converted to a 30-year fixed-rate mortgage without penalty.

Reduction option loan. One of the newest mortgages around is the so-called reduction option loan, or ROL. This works like a typical fixed-rate loan but allows a one-time opportunity to reduce the mortgage interest rate if market rates go down. The cost of locking in the option is ¼% of the remaining balance, plus an additional $100 processing fee—a bargain compared to the costs involved in refinancing a traditional fixed-rate long-term loan. Borrowers may exercise the reduction option when the index to which the mortgage rate is pegged drops by at least two percentage points and that drop occurs after the first year of the loan and before the end of the fifth year.

Growing equity mortgages. With a GEM, your payments increase each year for a set number of years and then level off. The mortgage is designed to be paid off more quickly than usual by requiring the systematic payment of more principal than a normal amortization schedule would require. This shortens the loan term—usually to 12 to 17 years—and increases the monthly outlay.

Graduated payment mortgages. These are designed primarily for younger homebuyers who expect their incomes to increase. GPMs start out with lower payments than normal amortization would require. Payments rise gradually (usually over five to ten years) and then level off for the remaining years of the loan. Lower initial payments let buyers qualify for larger mortgage loans than they otherwise would.

What are the drawbacks of GPMs? For one thing, you pay more interest. That's because reducing the principal takes longer with the smaller payments. The outstanding balance increases over the period when payments do not completely cover the interest actually due. This is a process known as negative amortization.

Few mortgages run their course. But because the principal of a GPM loan increases or is reduced so little in those first years, your payments will not increase your equity as fast as payments under a standard loan. That means you will get less cash when you sell, perhaps not enough for a down payment on the next house you want to buy. If you sell after only a few years, you could actually end up owing more than you borrowed in the first place.

GPMs also entail more risk of default. If your income fails to increase as you anticipated, or if it declines because you or your spouse stop working, you might be unable to keep up with the rising payments.

Adjustable-rate mortgages.   Adjustable-rate mortgages (ARMs) have an interest rate that changes periodically as market interest rates move up and down. Common adjustment periods are one, three and six years. The one-year ARM usually will get you the most house because initial rates—and thus monthly payments—are one to three percentage points lower than on a long-term fixed-rate loan.

The key considerations in signing up for an ARM are the initial interest rate, the interval between adjustments, the index on which the adjustments will be based, and the margin the lender tacks onto the index at adjustment time.

Rate changes occur at the end of each adjustment period. The adjustment schedule is stated in the mortgage contract. The size of the change will depend on the level of the index at the time your rate is recalculated—typically one to two months before the anniversary date of your loan.

Many ARMs are linked to the rates on one-, three- and five-year Treasury securities. Ask what index will be used in any ARM you are considering. Find out how quickly it responds to changes in interest rates and how it has performed in the past and how you can follow it yourself.

The margin—the additional amount the lender adds to the index rate—is typically one to three percentage points. The index rate and the margin rate combine to create the new interest rate on your mortgage at each adjustment date.

Most ARMs have limits, or caps, on rate changes. When interest rates are rising rapidly, caps protect you from extreme jumps in your monthly payments. Most ARMs have both periodic ceilings (limiting the increase from one adjustment period to the next) and lifetime ceilings (limiting the overall interest-rate increase over the term of the loan). Typical limits are two percentage points on annual increases, with a lifetime cap of six points.

ARMs with payment caps limit your monthly payment in-

HOW MUCH WILL
THE MORTGAGE COST?

This table shows the monthly payment required per $1,000 of mortgage amount at various interest rates for four common mortgage terms. The numbers shown include principal and interest only; insurance and property taxes would be additional. To determine the monthly payment for a mortgage you're considering, multiply the appropriate amount in the table by the number of thousands of dollars involved. Example: A 30-year loan of $80,000 at 10% would be 80 × 8.78 = $702.40 per month for principal and interest.

INTEREST RATE	15 YEARS	20 YEARS	25 YEARS	30 YEARS
6%	8.44	7.17	6.45	6.00
6¼	8.58	7.31	6.60	6.16
6½	8.72	7.46	6.76	6.33
6¾	8.85	7.61	6.91	6.49
7	8.99	7.76	7.07	6.66
7¼	9.13	7.91	7.23	6.83
7½	9.28	8.06	7.39	7.00
7¾	9.42	8.21	7.56	7.17
8	9.56	8.37	7.72	7.34
8¼	9.71	8.53	7.89	7.52
8½	9.85	8.68	8.06	7.69
8¾	10.00	8.84	8.23	7.87
9	10.15	9.00	8.40	8.05
9¼	10.30	9.16	8.57	8.23
9½	10.45	9.33	8.74	8.41
9¾	10.60	9.49	8.92	8.60
10	10.75	9.66	9.09	8.78
10¼	10.90	9.82	9.27	8.97
10½	11.06	9.99	9.45	9.15
10¾	11.21	10.16	9.63	9.34
11	11.37	10.33	9.81	9.53

continued

11¼	11.53	10.50	9.99	9.72
11½	11.69	10.67	10.17	9.91
11¾	11.85	10.84	10.35	10.10
12	12.01	11.02	10.54	10.29
12¼	12.17	11.19	10.72	10.48
12½	12.33	11.37	10.91	10.68
12¾	12.49	11.54	11.10	10.87
13	12.66	11.72	11.28	11.07
13¼	12.82	11.90	11.47	11.26
13½	12.99	12.08	11.66	11.46
13¾	13.15	12.26	11.85	11.66
14	13.32	12.44	12.04	11.85
14¼	13.49	12.62	12.23	12.05
14½	13.66	12.80	12.43	12.25
14¾	13.83	12.99	12.62	12.45
15	14.00	13.17	12.81	12.65
15¼	14.17	13.36	13.01	12.85
15½	14.34	13.54	13.20	13.05
15¾	14.52	13.73	13.40	13.25
16	14.69	13.92	13.59	13.45

crease at the time of each adjustment, typically to a certain percentage of the previous payment. They can result in negative amortization when rising interest rates would dictate payments higher than the cap permits. The difference in such cases is added to the loan principal. As a result, payment caps are rarely offered today.

Convertible ARMs. Some ARMs can be converted to fixed-rate loans. You may want the right to do this down the road— say after two or three years—if you can lock in a lower rate. If the cost is the same, you should always pick a convertible ARM over a nonconvertible one. However, there typically are costs connected with the convertible ARM (conversion fees and interest rate differentials, for example), so it takes study to determine which of the two ARMs is the better deal.

FHA loans. The FHA (Federal Housing Administration) insures a wide variety of mortgages. The maximum loan amount varies somewhat from one geographic area to another. Because they are insured, FHA loans often carry an interest rate a bit below the going market rate. Down payment requirements can be as low as 3% for buyers who will live in their homes. For investors, however, loans are limited to 75% of a property's value. The buyer must pay the cost of FHA insurance, and processing the application can take longer than for a conventional loan.

VA loans. The Veterans Administration guarantees lenders against losses on mortgages taken out by eligible veterans. No down payment is required by the VA unless a veteran is obtaining a loan with a graduated payment feature or the loan amount requested is more than the VA thinks the property is worth.

Interest rates are set by the VA. If the VA rate is below the market rate, the seller will have to make up the difference by paying points, and you may find the seller trying to recoup those points in the price.

The VA collects from the buyer a one-time funding fee of 1% of the amount of the loan amount at settlement. This pays for the VA guarantee. In addition to the 1% funding fee, veterans are not required to pay more than a 1% fee to the lender.

VA loans are available in most places, and you can find out whether you qualify by calling or writing the nearest VA office. It will ask for your military service number, social security number, birth date, date of entry into the service, date and place of separation, name of the unit you were with when discharged and the type of discharge.

CREATIVE FINANCING FOR TIGHT MARKETS

When interest rates get so high that few people can afford a mortgage, how can buyers and sellers of homes still manage to strike deals? Often they do it with "creative financing"—unusual loan arrangements that most homeowners would shun in ordinary times. The seller provides some form of interest-rate subsidy for the buyer, making possible a sale when rates are prohibitively high.

Take-back mortgage.   This is a form of seller financing in which the seller accepts a mortgage from the buyer for part of the purchase price. Take-backs often bridge the gap between the price of the property and the combined amounts of the down payment and first mortgage. They can be attractive to sellers who don't need the entire proceeds from the sale right away and to buyers trying to work out a contract with terms they can handle.

The seller's interest is protected by a lien on the property that is subordinate to the primary lender's lien. If the buyer defaults and a foreclosure results, the second mortgage holder will get reimbursed only after the first mortgage holder gets its money. If the foreclosure doesn't yield as much as the original sale price, the second mortgage holder could lose money on the deal.

Payments on seller take-backs may be figured as though the loan would be paid back over a 20- or 30-year period, but the loans are often due in full—with a balloon payment—three to ten years after the sale. That means the buyer will probably have to sell or refinance.

Purchase-money second mortgage.   Here the seller agrees to finance part of the buyer's down payment through a second mortgage, usually of three to five years. The primary mortgage lender should be told of such an arrangement because the payments on the second mortgage may affect the buyer's ability to meet payments on the first.

Wraparound mortgage.   This sort of deal involves an existing mortgage, plus additional financing to complete the purchase. Say a house is selling for $100,000. The seller has an assumable mortgage with an outstanding balance of $40,000. A buyer makes a down payment of $20,000. He finds a lender, often the seller, who gives him a new mortgage for $80,000—enough to cover the old loan balance plus an additional $40,000. The buyer makes payments on the wraparound loan to the lender, who then uses part of the money to make payments on the old mortgage. The rate on the "wrap" is higher than the rate on the old mortgage, and the lender profits from the differential. Thus, by "blending" the rate on the original $40,000 mortgage with the rate on the new $40,000 mortgage, the lender can afford to offer a rate on the wraparound that is lower than prevailing rates. If you are looking for a wraparound, be sure that the underlying older mortgage contract permits a seller/lender to make that kind of deal. Most contracts forbid it.

Land contract.   Also known as a conditional sales contract or contract for deed, this is actually an installment sale. The buyer doesn't get title to the property right away but must wait until some point agreed upon in the contract—usually years down the road.

The main advantage in such deals belongs to the seller. If anything goes wrong during the course of the contract, the seller still owns the property. And much can go wrong. As part of the deal, the buyer may agree to take over payments on the seller's existing mortgage—an arrangement that may violate the "due on sale" provision in most mortgage contracts. Lenders who find out about it may be able to foreclose on such mortgages, leaving the buyer with nothing to show for the payments except a worthless contract. Neither buyer nor seller should draw up a land contract without legal help.

Shared equity.   In a typical shared-equity arrangement, the home buyer is paired with an investor—frequently a parent, relative or friend—who supplies the down payment, while the home buyer occupies the property and pays either all or some share of the carrying costs. At some future point, when the property is sold or refinanced, the investor gets back the down payment money plus a share of any appreciation that has taken place. The owner/occupant may buy out the investor and stay put, or sell and use the proceeds for a down payment on another home.

Shared-equity arrangements can run into trouble if there is disagreement between the parties over when to sell, how much to sell for or how to treat the value of improvements made by the owner/occupant. A shared-equity arrangement should address such issues in the agreement—for instance, by specifying that an appraiser will arbitrate disputes over what is a fair price.

Buy-downs.   A buy-down is a mortgage loan that carries a below-market interest rate because the seller of the home has paid the lender a fee to make such a loan. When new homes are hard to sell, builders are willing to subsidize buyers with this and other creative techniques. The low-interest feature usually lasts two or three years, then is adjusted to the market level or some other preset rate. The cost of a buy-down may be passed on to you in the form of a higher home price. On the other hand, a buy-down can bridge the "affordability" gap for families and first-time buyers. Just make sure you measure the trade-offs and read the fine print.

The FHA offers an insured buy-down mortgage that works like this: A borrower gets a 10% mortgage but is qualified using an 8% interest rate. The builder buys down the first year's rate to 8% and the second year's to 9%, thereby reducing monthly loan payments for the first two years of the loan, giving the buyer's income time to catch up with the payments that will be based on a 10% rate starting in the third year.

Balloon loans.   In a balloon-payment contract, a borrower agrees to make a lump-sum payment of the loan balance at the end of a certain period, typically two to ten years. In the meantime, periodic payments are set up as though the loan were going to run for much longer. Some require payment of interest only until the date the loan is due. This arrangement keeps current payments down and gives the borrower an opportunity to sell the property or refinance the loan before the balloon comes due.

Balloon-payment contracts can be useful, but they also can be dangerous for the unwary. Before you sign such a loan be sure you know exactly when the balloon payment will be due, how large it will be and whether there is any escape clause if for some reason you can't come up with the money.

A lender, especially an individual, will want to schedule the balloon payment to coincide with his or her future financial needs. But for the borrower, the further away the due date, the better. Seven years should be long enough to assure an opportunity to sell or refinance before the balloon falls due.

USING A REAL ESTATE AGENT

It's important to know the ropes when dealing with a real estate agent. Both buyer and seller face a major financial decision. A buyer wants the most home for the money; a seller wants the most money for the house. A good real estate agent can guide events toward a mutually beneficial conclusion. A bad one, through inexperience or ineptitude, can make an already stressful situation worse.

If you ever buy, sell or rent any kind of real property, you confront these questions: What can I expect an agent to do for me? Do I really need one? How much should I pay? What recourse do I have if something goes wrong?

Before looking at the answers, it's helpful to review the nomenclature. Agent is a popular term for a salesperson who is licensed to work for a real estate broker. A broker is licensed to conduct a real estate business and to negotiate transactions for a fee. Both may properly be called agents, because they act as agents for clients. Not all brokers and agents may be called Realtors. A Realtor (note the capital R—it's a trade name) and a Realtor Associate (who works for a Realtor) are members of the National Association of Realtors, a trade and lobbying organization. Realtists are members of the National Association of Real Estate Brokers, a smaller group.

Tips for buyers. Unless you hire your own agent (called a buyer's broker), an agent works for the seller and is paid by the seller. Remember that as you start each shopping trip. It is always true, even though an agent may spend hours and hours working with you, the buyer. As the seller's agent, he or she cannot represent your interests aggressively in the contract negotiations, and consequently, it is not in your interest to divulge your strategy or the top price you would be willing to pay.

A seller's agent can help you with information about market conditions, neighborhoods, schools, public facilities, tax rates, zoning laws, proposed roads and construction, and other essentials for evaluating your purchase. No agent can know everything about a property, but an honest one will tell you about problems he or she is aware of. And an agent could be held accountable for providing wrong information on something he or she ought to know about. (A buyer could also sue an owner who conceals known defects.)

Do you really need an agent? A house hunter on his or her own is at a disadvantage. Unless you are thoroughly familiar with a given area, you'll miss an agent's knowledge and resources. Just as significant, you'll have no access to the computer multiple-listing service (MLS) of houses for sale. Through these services, participating brokers share information on listings, giving them the widest possible exposure.

Suppose you'd like an agent's undivided loyalty, or you're buying into an unfamiliar area, or you just need some special counsel and guidance. Consider hiring your own agent. Someone you employ and pay is obliged to get you the best possible price and terms. And you'll know who is working for whom. (A buyer's broker can negotiate for you, and if the fee you agree to pay a buyer's broker is not tied to the selling price of a property, there is no possible conflict of interest.)

Some buyer-broker's fees are tied to the sale price of a house, just like sales commissions. Study the contract and satisfy yourself that it covers all the bases. It should set out how the agent will be paid; specify the retainer fee and incentive commissions, if any are involved; minimum and maximum fees; how conflicts of interests will be handled; exactly what services will be provided; and how disagreements will be resolved.

Tips for sellers. You're paying, so be choosey. Ask friends, neighbors or business contacts which brokers and agents are most active in your area. Check the local newspaper ads. Select one or two brokerage firms with good reputations and proven track records. Then interview at least two successful agents in each firm. Look for experience, professionalism and compatibility. Choose someone with whom you can be frank and open. If an agent's personality or selling style grates on you, get someone else.

The overwhelming majority of brokers charge commissions of 5% to 7% of the selling price of residential property and 10% for vacant land and farms. By law the amount is negotiable, but you won't get very far negotiating a lower rate unless special circumstances make your property more economical to sell than others.

An agent who stands to receive a regular commission from you should:

• Obtain a full description of the property, plus information about tax and utility rates, mortgage balance, the neighborhood and nearby facilities, such as parks and public transportation.

• Brief you on things you can do to make the place as appealing as possible, such as painting, making repairs, tidying up the yard, and seeing that appliances are working.

• Help set the price. You should be provided with "comparables" (recent selling prices and current asking prices of similar properties).

• Prepare forms for prospective buyers giving detailed information about the property and terms of sale.

• "Sit" on the property—that is, be there or have another agent there to receive prospects, at least one afternoon a week. Hold your house open on specified Saturdays or Sundays.

• Be available to show the property during regular business hours and some evenings and weekends.

• Know where mortgage money can be obtained and provide prospects with information about rates and other terms.

• Screen prospects to find out whether they're financially able to make the purchase.

• Promptly present you with all offers to purchase and advise you of any problems with them.

• Assist in the settlement of the transaction as your representative. You also should have an attorney because real estate agents aren't supposed to give legal advice.

If this sounds like a lot, remember that the salesperson and broker stand to collect a good sum at settlement—perhaps $6,000 or more on a $100,000 home, for example.

Listing the property. When you've made your choice, you'll have to decide how the property should be listed. These are the principal ways:

• *Exclusive right to sell.* This arrangement, the most widely used, provides that a commission will be owed to the listing broker no matter who sells the property. Because the broker is sure to benefit from this agreement, you should get the best possible service.

• *Exclusive agency.* This is similar, except no commission is owed if you sell the property yourself. If you sign an agreement like this you are, in effect, competing with your own listing agent, who, because there may be no commission at all, has somewhat less incentive to work hard on your listing.

• *Open listing.* With this agreement, you can list your property with several brokers at the same time. You agree to pay a commission to the first agent to produce an acceptable buyer—typically half the standard 6% or 7%. This type of listing is used where there is no computer multiple-listing service available. It also is used by sellers who want to do most of the selling work themselves but want the cooperation of agents in finding buyers. No commission is owed if the owner makes the sale.

A listing agreement is a legally enforceable contract. It sets forth the kind of listing and other specifics, including a description of the property, the price, the terms of sale and the fee or commission.

Contracts often run from 30 to 90 days. You can extend a listing beyond its original life, so don't lock yourself into an initial contract that binds you for too long. Some contracts provide for an automatic extension of the listing period. If you encounter such a provision, have it changed.

Some agreements provide that the commission will be payable when a purchaser is produced who is ready, willing and able to buy on the terms provided, whether or not settlement occurs. That means if your agent produces a willing buyer, you could be obliged to pay a commission even if you change your mind about selling or are unable to sell for some reason during the listing period. Real estate professionals say that in practice the provision is seldom invoked. Nevertheless, it has been enforced in the past. For your protection, ask that it be stricken. Your agreement with the broker, like the commission itself, is negotiable.

What if you have a grievance? If the broker doesn't resolve it to your satisfaction, take it up with the state real estate commission and, if the company is a member, the local real estate board.

TAX ANGLES OF BUYING AND SELLING

Buying or selling a home can serve as a startling introduction to the often baffling world of tax planning. Uncle Sam is a generous partner in your purchase, first by subsidizing your mortgage payments and then by winking at the profits you make when you sell it—so long as you invest the money in your next principal residence. But this generosity has a price, and a misstep on your part can have expensive consequences. Following are some answers to the kinds of questions that come up when people buy and sell homes—and while they own them.

Is there a limit on the amount of interest a homeowner can deduct? If so, what is it?

All the interest on debt you take on to build or buy a principal residence and second residence is deductible on loans up to $1 million. The $1 million ceiling on first mortgages includes money you borrow to renovate your home.

What are the rules for deducting interest on home-equity loans?

Interest on home-equity loans is deductible up to $100,000 no matter how you use the money. Prior to 1988, your tax-deductible borrowing—via either a second mortgage or a home-equity line of credit—could not exceed the cost of your home plus the value of any improvements, unless you used the money for improvements, education or medical expenses.

We've completely paid off the mortgage on our home, which is now worth $200,000. We want to take out a new mortgage to renovate the kitchen and add a small wing to the house for guests. The estimated cost will be $110,000. In addition, we intend to borrow $10,000 for a car. Since I'll be borrowing more than $100,000, will the extra $20,000 debt be nondeductible?

No. Interest on the entire loan is deductible. The $110,000 borrowed for renovations is considered acquisition debt, subject to the $1 million ceiling. The $10,000 for the car qualifies as home-equity debt and counts against the $100,000 limit.

We refinanced our mortgage and were told that because of an IRS crackdown we wouldn't be able to deduct all the points we paid. Somehow we're supposed to write it off a little at a time. Will the proper amount be included in the interest the bank reports we paid each year, or is there a special way to figure it out?

It's an extra deduction and you have to figure it out yourself. The IRS considers points paid to refinance a mortgage to be prepaid interest and says they must be deducted proportionately over the life of the loan. If you paid $3,000 in points on a 15-year mortgage, for example, $200 would be deductible each year. If you refinanced around midyear and made six payments, your first-year deduction would be $100. Don't include the amount as part of the mortgage interest deduction. Line 10 of Schedule A for itemized deductions is reserved for points.

How do I figure the "adjusted basis" I'm supposed to use to determine my profit or loss when I sell my home?

Start with the cost basis, which is the price of the house plus certain settlement charges. Over the years the basis can be adjusted—up to reflect the cost of permanent improvements that increase the value of the property, or down because of casualty losses or depreciation deductions you take if you use your home for business or rental purposes.

Be sure to keep records to substantiate your home's basis and any adjustments to it. You need the purchase contract and settlement papers, plus receipts, canceled checks and other evidence of improvements.

When you sell your home, the profit for tax purposes is the difference between the adjusted basis and the amount realized on the sale. The amount realized is the selling price minus certain expenses, such as commission and advertising and legal fees.

Which settlement charges can be added to the basis of my home?

State and county transfer taxes, appraisal fee, assumption

fee, attorney's fees, credit report fee, mortgage origination fee, notary fees, property inspection fee, recording fee, title examination fee, title insurance premium, utility connection charges, and amounts owed by the seller that you pay, such as part of the selling commission or back taxes and interest. (You can't deduct taxes and interest owed by others even if you agree to pay those bills yourself.) If you qualify, you may be able to deduct settlement costs as moving expenses.

Why worry about profit on the sale? Don't you escape taxes as long as you buy another home?

Not really. Basically, what the law allows is deferring taxes on the gain if within 24 months before or after the sale you buy and occupy a home that costs as much or more than the adjusted sales price of the old home.

You can do this any number of times, delaying taxes on each transaction. But you don't escape the tax completely. The liability for it remains.

Here is how deferral works. Say you sell a house for $100,000, an amount that includes a $30,000 profit. Within the replacement period, you buy a new home for $125,000. Rather than pay tax on the $30,000 profit, you reduce the basis of the new home by that amount. Its adjusted basis thus becomes $95,000. If you later sell that home for $150,000 ($25,000 more than you paid), you would actually have a profit of $55,000—the $30,000 gain on the first sale plus the $25,000 profit on the second. You could put off the tax bill again by buying another home that costs $150,000 or more.

If you buy a replacement home that costs less than the one you sell, you will owe tax on the built-up profit to the extent that the adjusted sales price of the old home (the actual price minus certain expenses, such as an agent's commission) exceeds the cost of the new one. Once you or your spouse reaches age 55, however, you may be eligible for the once-in-a-lifetime opportunity to escape taxes on up to $125,000 profit on the sale of your home, as described later in this chapter.

Is it true that I can't take advantage of those tax-deferred

provisions if I sell my house before I've lived in it for 24 months?

Generally, you can't postpone tax on the profit from more than one home sale within a 24-month period. Assume, for example, that you sold a house in March and deferred the tax by buying another principal residence in the same month. Then, in April of the following year you sell that home and buy a third. The 24-month rule would prohibit you from postponing tax on the gain from the sale of the second house. However, if the third home is purchased within 24 months of the time you sold the first one, profit from the first house is considered reinvested in the third, and therefore the tax is deferred. You'd owe tax only on the profit that accrued during the months you owned the second home.

If you are in the armed forces or living outside the U.S., you may qualify for a longer replacement period allowing you up to four years after the sale of one home to buy and occupy a replacement.

We sold our home for $110,000. That's $84,000 more than the balance on the mortgage. We put only $36,000 of it down on our new $165,000 home and used the rest of the cash to buy into a business. Can we postpone paying tax on our gain even though we didn't reinvest all of it in the new house?

Yes. What matters is that the new home cost more than the adjusted sales price of the old one.

I just sold a house in a depressed market and took a $3,000 loss. Since Uncle Sam would demand a share of my profit if I had made one, will he share my loss by letting me deduct it?

No. Losses on the sale of a personal residence are not deductible, nor do they affect the cost basis of the next home you buy.

When we bought our home, there was a broken-down wooden fence around the back yard. Last summer we replaced it at a cost of nearly $2,000. Can we add that amount to the basis of the house?

Yes, because the fence is a capital improvement. The law

draws a line between repairs, which are considered nondeductible personal expenses, and improvements, which, though nondeductible, are added to the cost basis. It's an important difference because expenditures that qualify as improvements cut the taxable gain when you sell the house. In other words, Uncle Sam helps pay for improvements but not repairs.

To qualify as an improvement, the expense must add value to your home, prolong its life or adapt it to new uses. Adding a bathroom, putting in new plumbing or wiring, and paving a driveway are examples of improvements that increase the basis.

Repairs, on the other hand, merely maintain your home's condition. Replacing a broken window pane or painting a room would be considered repairs. However, the cost of some work that would ordinarily be a repair—such as painting a room—can be added to the basis if done in connection with a remodeling project. Also, some major repairs, such as extensive patching of a roof, may qualify as improvements.

The IRS doesn't have a list of what qualifies as an improvement and what doesn't. It's often a judgment call, and two IRS agents could disagree over any specific expenditure. So it's important to keep detailed records of any expenses that might affect your home's basis. If you think it might qualify as an improvement, keep the receipt.

Our refrigerator gave up the ghost last winter, and we replaced it with the latest deluxe model. When we sold the house during the summer, the new refrigerator went with it. Do we count the $1,245 it cost as an addition to basis?

It depends on whether local law considers the appliance a fixture that must be sold with the house (your real estate agent should know). If so, its cost is added to the basis. But if the refrigerator is considered personal property, its cost is not included. However, the refrigerator's value when you sell (as distinguished from its cost when new) does cut your profit.

Here's an example of how to handle buying and selling a home when the price covers personal property as well as real estate: Say you bought your home five years ago for $85,000, a price that included a stove, refrigerator, washer and dryer—all of which are considered personal property rather than fixtures where you live. You estimate that at the time of purchase the appliances had a fair market value of $1,800. Subtracting $1,800 from the purchase price gives the home a basis of $83,200.

Shortly before selling you replace the stove and refrigerator; the estimated value of the appliances sold with the house is now $2,400. You sell the house for $100,000, but for purposes of determining your profit, use the figure $97,600 ($100,000 minus the $2,400 attributable to personal property). Your gain is the difference between $83,200 and $97,600, or $14,400.

After arduous negotiations we agreed to pay half of the real estate commission owed by the couple who was selling us a home. It cost us $2,910. Can we deduct it?

No, but add that amount to the basis of the new home.

My sons and I spent the last two summers building a garage. It cost $7,400, but if we'd hired all the work out, I'm sure the price would have been twice as much. When calculating the addition to the basis of the property, how do I figure the value of our labor?

Sorry, you don't. The addition to the basis is the actual out-of-pocket cost of the improvement to you. If you hire workers, you can include their wages, but you get no credit for your own time.

A job switch this year meant moving my family from Kansas to Texas. We sold our home and bought a new one in Austin. Which of the buying and selling costs are deductible as moving expenses?

You must meet several tests before you can deduct moving expenses. For example, the move has to be related to a full-time job—which you must hold for at least 39 weeks during the 12 months before the move—and your new place of work must be at least 35 miles farther from your old home than your former workplace was. (People who move to take their first job can also qualify.) Since you are apparently eligible to take these deductions, you can write off many expenses that would ordinarily only affect the gain on the sale of the old house or the basis of the new one.

Selling costs that can be written off as moving expenses include real estate commissions, attorney's fees, title fees, escrow fees, points or loan placement charges, state transfer taxes and similar expenses. Purchasing expenses that can qualify include the settlement charges listed in the answer to an earlier question (see page 121). There is a $3,000 limit on such "indirect" deductions. The direct expenses of the move—transporting your household goods, for example—are fully deductible.

We recently inherited some money, enough to pay off the mortgage on our home. If we do so, we'll be stuck with a prepayment penalty. Would it be deductible?

Yes. Prepayment penalties are treated as interest and may be deducted in the year paid.

We sold our home for $97,500 and the real estate commission took $5,850 of it. Can we deduct this charge?

No, but the commission does reduce the amount realized on the sale and therefore cuts the profit by $5,850.

After several years in Washington, D.C., we moved to Indianapolis. We discovered that we'd have to buy a mansion here in order to reinvest the $198,000 we received for our modest home on Capitol Hill. The house we bought cost $150,000, leaving us with $48,000 we didn't reinvest. Here's our question: The house has a garage we could convert into a guest house. If we spend $30,000 remodeling it, can we count that as part of our investment for purposes of figuring how much of the gain from the old house we can postpone paying taxes on?

Yes, as long as you complete the work within 24 months of the time you sold the Washington home. The purchase price of a replacement residence includes costs for reconstruction, extensive rebuilding, capital improvements and additions.

We sold our house and deferred the tax on our profit by reinvesting all of it in a new home. Even though there's no tax payable, do we have to report the sale to the IRS?

Yes. You should attach a completed Form 2119 to your tax return. And you should be aware that since 1987, the settlement agent for the sale of homes has been required to report the transaction to the IRS.

HOME SWEET TAX SHELTER

When you turn 55, the tax law gives you a valuable birthday present: The chance to escape taxes on up to $125,000 of profit from the sale of your home. This break can be worth thousands of dollars, money to make your retirement years more financially secure. It also adds new flexibility to your retirement planning.

To be eligible, you must be 55 or older when you sell your principal residence. The exclusion applies only to a principal residence that you have owned and lived in for at least three of the five years preceding the sale. If you're married, only one spouse needs to meet the age, ownership and residency tests. You can take the exclusion only once in your lifetime. For purposes of this limitation, married couples are treated as one; if one spouse used the exclusion before marriage, the other spouse forfeits his or her right to use it later on.

The $125,000 limit is not cumulative. If you exclude $45,000 of the profit on the sale of one home, for example, the other $80,000 is forfeited. You can't carry an unused portion forward to be applied against the gain on the sale of another home. You can use the exclusion in conjunction with the part of the law that lets you defer taxes on profits that are reinvested in another home. If you realize a $150,000 gain, for example, the exclusion will let you escape the tax on the first $125,000 of it. And you can postpone tax on the rest if you buy a new home that costs at least what you sold your house for, minus that amount of excluded gain. The gain you roll over into the new home will not be taxed until you sell it and fail to replace it with a more costly house.

To illustrate the savings offered by the exclusion, consider the case of a married couple, ages 57 and 54, who've been living in their present home for 14 years. The kids are grown, and the couple have decided the house is too big and too expensive to maintain. They want to sell and rent a smaller house or an apartment. The couple's taxable income is $50,000.

They figure that if they sell their house and make a $100,000 profit, taxes will be about $30,000. However, if they use their once-in-a-lifetime exclusion, the couple can sell the house and not have to pay taxes on any of the profit.

This tax break confronts many taxpayers with questions about how to make the best use of it.

What if you meet the age and residency tests and want to sell your home but your profit is only $40,000?

Using any part of the exclusion uses it all up. If you don't intend to buy another house, you don't really lose anything. If you do plan to buy another, more expensive home, you should roll over your gain rather than exclude it. As the new house appreciates and your profit grows toward $125,000, so will the value of your exclusion. But say you want to buy a less expensive home and therefore can't roll over all your profit. Should you use the exclusion now to shelter the $40,000 of gain, even though doing so means forfeiting the unused $85,000 worth? If you don't take the exclusion, you'll have to pay tax on the gain you don't roll over. On the other hand, using the exclusion now means any profit on your new home will be taxed when you sell it. Since you can't be certain what your tax bracket and the amount of taxable gain you'll realize will be at that time, it's difficult to compare the benefits of using the exclusion now with the advantages of saving it for later.

What if you put off taking the exclusion and defer the gain by buying a more expensive home, but then decide to sell the new house and move into an apartment before you meet the residency test to qualify anew for the exclusion?

As long as the tax return for the year in which you sold the old home is open to amendment, which it is for at least three years after its due date, you can retroactively elect the exclusion. That would eliminate up to $125,000 in taxable profit on the first house. The cost basis of the second home, which had to be reduced when you deferred the gain, will be increased by the amount of the newly excluded gain.

What if you're 54 and want to sell your home and move into an apartment or small home?

You can still take advantage of the exclusion by renting out your house until you're 55. Make sure that when the house is sold, you still qualify for the exclusion by having lived in the house as your principal residence for three of the five years preceding the sale. If you need the proceeds from the sale of your home to buy a retirement place, consider taking out a second mortgage against the equity in your house to make a down payment, then waiting until you're 55 to sell it.

CONDOMINIUMS AND COOPERATIVES

Despite some important differences in their legal forms of ownership, life in condos and co-ops is quite similar, and much of the advice in this chapter can be applied to both. First, though, it's vital to understand the differences.

WHAT IS A CONDOMINIUM?

A condo is a legal form of ownership, not a special type of structure. In a condo, the owners of individual dwelling units in a housing development hold title to their own units and own a proportional interest in the land and common areas. Garden apartments, high-rises and townhouses are the most common types of condominiums, but the genre can also include detached houses, beach houses, offices and warehouses.

The common property usually is conveyed by the developer to an owners' association after a period of time or after a specified percentage of units have been sold. Thereafter the development is controlled and operated by directors of the condo owners' association, often through a hired manager.

Condominiums can be purchased with conventional and

government-backed mortgages, meaning you can deduct mortgage interest and property taxes from taxable income.

WHAT IS A COOPERATIVE?

In a cooperative, residents own shares of stock in a corporation that owns the development; they do not hold title to their individual units but are, in effect, tenants of the corporation entitled to occupancy by virtue of their ownership of stock.

Cooperative ownership normally cannot be financed with a mortgage. In the past, buyers paid cash or took out personal loans, usually with short terms and at rates higher than the going rate for mortgages. This made co-op ownership possible mainly for upper-income buyers.

In 1984 another kind of financing became widely available when the Federal National Mortgage Association began buying and packaging "share loans," which are secured by the cooperative's stock and accompanying occupancy rights. Share loans offer co-op buyers terms similar to those of mortgages. You pay back the loan and make separate monthly maintenance payments to the cooperative corporation, which pays for the mortgage on the building, the real estate taxes, and general upkeep. As a partial owner of the corporation, you deduct on your tax return your proportional share of the corporation's mortgage interest and taxes.

ADVANTAGES AND DISADVANTAGES

Many condos and co-ops have amenities that few residents could afford as individuals—swimming pools, saunas, game rooms, squash courts, even golf courses. In most projects residents don't have to mow lawns or rake leaves.

Condos and co-ops often cost less than detached houses in comparable locations. You have a say in how the project is run. The value of your unit may rise.

On the other hand, all this comes at a price. You will be required to pay your share of the operating costs, which can exceed the projections you get when you buy. You can't put off paying monthly fees or special assessments as you can postpone maintenance or repairs on an individual home. You probably have less space than in a conventional house. You can't enlarge your unit. You are subject to strict rules adopted by the majority of owners. Certain activities and hobbies, such as gun collecting or amateur radio, may be banned or restricted. The same may be true of pets.

Prospective owners of apartment-style condos and co-ops should pay particular attention to potential problems with reserves and assessments, and that means wading through detailed legal documents.

Insufficient reserves can have wrenching financial consequences. Find out whether the condo or co-op has accumulated adequate reserves to pay for major repairs and to replace obsolete or worn-out equipment. As buildings age, residents must be prepared for such expenses as a new roof, upgrading the electrical system or replacing the boiler.

Monthly assessments can be expected to go up gradually over time. Look for a record of reasonable increases. Assessments should be large enough to cover routine maintenance and still permit reserve buildup. Some condos and co-ops choose to deal with big repair bills by imposing special assessments rather than accumulating the necessary cash in a reserve fund. If you buy into a building where residents have postponed needed work, remember: It lies ahead—at your expense.

A GUIDE TO THE DOCUMENTS

Condo and co-op buyers face a pile of often incomprehensible documents. Take each one slowly enough to digest it and refuse to be rushed into a decision. Answers to many questions will be in the documents, which you should be given if you start getting serious about buying.

Sales contract or purchase agreement.   This basically is similar to other real estate contracts, but there are differences. In signing you may acknowledge receipt of other documents. Check for conditions under which you could back out of the deal, such as your inability to get mortgage money. If the contract doesn't give you the right to withdraw within a specified period, don't sign until you have studied it and the other papers with legal assistance. There should be assurances, if appropriate, the project will be completed as promised, and you should have the right to make an inspection prior to settlement. It definitely would be advantageous to you to have your deposit placed in an escrow account, preferably one that pays interest.

An enabling declaration. Also called the master deed, plan of ownership or corporation, or declaration of conditions, covenants and restrictions, this is the most important instrument. When recorded, it legally establishes the project as a condominium or co-op. It also, among other things, authorizes residents to form an operating association and describes individual units and commonly owned areas.

Bylaws. These spell out the association's authority and responsibilities, authorize the making of a budget and the collection of various charges, and prescribe parliamentary procedures. They may empower the association to hire professional managers or may contain other special provisions. The bylaws may also set forth insurance requirements and authorize the imposition of liens or fines against the owners who fail to pay monthly charges.

House rules. They state what owners can and can't do. Any restrictions on pets, children, decorations, use of facilities and such will be found here. The rules may be incorporated in the bylaws or set apart in a separate document.

Other papers. These could include a copy of the operating budget, a schedule of current and proposed assessments, a financial statement on the owners' association, any leases or contracts, a plat, or drawing of the project and your unit, and an engineer's report if one was done. One of the financial documents should show how much money has been reserved for unforeseen and major projected outlays, an important consideration. A few states require developers to give each potential buyer a prospectus that details all the important facts about the offering. Read it carefully; information that may be buried in small print or obscured by legalese in the other papers may be readily understandable in the prospectus.

CAUTIONS FOR CONDO BUYERS

Some states regulate condo sales as such, and broader consumer protection measures in others may apply (antifraud statutes, for instance). Your state may not require the delivery of documents to prospective buyers before a contract is signed. Even so, you should insist on time to examine these papers. For information about condo regulation in your state, contact the attorney general's office, a real estate board or a consumer protection agency.

In the past, leases on condo recreation facilities provoked numerous complaints and lawsuits. In some projects the developer retained ownership of one or more of the amenities, such as the pool. These facilities were then leased to the owners' association for up to 99 years, and monthly charges could be—and sometimes were—raised using an arbitrary formula that did not reflect actual increases in operating costs. Thousands of residents maintained that they had no idea when they bought their units that the facilities belonged to the developer and not to the condo owners.

Be on the lookout, too, for "sweetheart contracts"—long-term agreements that obligate the condo owners' association to obtain management services or do other business with firms designated by the developer.

After you become an owner, you will need insurance on your unit and its contents; the development should also be insured. You should also be protected from claims arising from damage you do to others, which could occur if, for example, water from a leak in your kitchen seeped into the apartment below.

If you become a director of the association, you will need liability insurance in case negligence or damage suits are brought against the board.

IF YOUR RENTAL APARTMENT GOES CONDO

When rental buildings convert to condominium ownership, tenants usually have only two choices: buy or move.

You could rent another place, but it might cost you more. Besides, there's the cost and inconvenience of moving. Yet if you buy, you'll assume some risk, and odds are your monthly costs will jump.

Those are the negatives. The brighter side is that here's your chance to stop collecting rent receipts and start building equity.

If you like the place and the price is right, you may have a golden opportunity.

The rules for sizing up a converted rental unit for possible purchase are the same as for other kinds of condos. Naturally, you should ask your fellow tenants whether they plan to buy. If many of them say no, it could be a bad sign. Find out why.

If you don't want to buy or move, check out your legal rights. The owner probably can't throw you out until your lease expires. In some areas condo conversions are permitted only if certain conditions are met. It may be necessary for a certain number of tenants to give their assent before a conversion can take place. And find out whether the owner will continue to rent some unsold units. You may be able to stay put at least for a while.

HOW TO SHOP

Generally, the best locations are residential areas where you see a good mix of quality apartment buildings and homes in the middle to upper price range and where property values are rising. Convenience to stores, hospitals and parks is a big plus, of course.

Try to visualize the neighborhood in ten or 20 years. Could your view be obstructed by a future high-rise? Could a shopping strip or highway be built nearby?

Check the vacancy rate and the supply-demand situation in the area. A glut of empty units or a high percentage of renters can affect property values in a general area or in a particular building.

Buying into a new development. It's obviously less risky to buy into an unfinished project when it is at a late stage of construction and organization than when it is in the early stages. Never buy into an uncompleted project unless you are provided with site drawings, floor plans, maintenance cost projections and other descriptive material. Model apartments are sometimes built larger than those to be sold. What's more, some developers have used scaled-down furniture to make rooms look larger. Measure them yourself if you have doubts. Another thing to find out about: Will you have any recourse if the project isn't finished when you're ready to move in?

Buying into an older project. This may be the safer route because you may be able to obtain an evaluation of the project's construction and can judge the competence and experience 'of the owner's association. You also can talk with residents and walk through the building and grounds to get a feel for atmosphere and general upkeep. What you won't get is the faster-than-average appreciation that may occur early in the months before the project is sold out, or soon after.

Whether the form of ownership is cooperative or condominium, learn all you can about the building's structure and equipment. Some states require that buyers be given such information in writing. Warranties should be provided in a condo purchase; be sure to ask whether you'll get them on common property as well as your own unit.

If the building has been renovated before it was put on the market, make sure improvements aren't merely cosmetic. Getting an appraisal of the entire development would be too costly for individuals, but if a lender has agreed to finance purchases of units, you may be able to obtain a copy of its appraisal.

Make a special effort to estimate the expenses you'd incur as an owner. They may be considerably higher than the rent you're paying. When the property is reclassified on the tax rolls as a condominium, real estate taxes could go up sharply because of new assessments. Of course, the additional expense could be partly offset by the federal income tax deduction for mortgage interest and property taxes.

SPECIAL CAUTIONS FOR CO-OP BUYERS

You need to ask many of the same questions you'd ask as a prospective condo buyer. Is the corporation financially sound? Are reserve funds adequate to pay for major replacements and repairs? How old is the building, the heating, cooling, plumbing and electrical systems?

Cooperative corporations whose shares can be bought using share loans must meet Fannie Mae's minimum standards for structural soundness, restricted commercial use and appropriate management. In addition, approved projects must have adequate cash flows and monthly assessments sufficient to meet current operating costs and build reserve funds.

Before buying into a cooperative you'll need to study the following documents:

Articles of Incorporation. The corporation's purpose, powers and obligations are described in the Articles of Incorporation, which will vary according to state law.

Bylaws. Just as in a condo, these lay out the duties and responsibilities of shareholders, officers and directors.

Shares, stock or membership certificate. You'll receive these as proof of ownership in the corporation.

Proprietary lease or occupancy agreement. This specifies the number of shares allocated to your unit (the more expensive the unit, the larger your share of ownership in the corporation) and spells out the terms under which you occupy the apartment. It also obligates you to pay your share of the corporation's expenses, including real estate taxes, operating costs and debt. Rules on using your unit, subleasing and maintenance are also in the agreement.

Recognition agreement. This sets out the rights of the share loan lender and the corporation's responsibilities and obligations to the lender. A cooperative may have recognition agreements with more than one lender.

Security agreement. In this document, the share loan borrower (that's you) assigns the lease or occupancy agreement and pledges his or her stock, shares or membership certificate to the lender in return for a loan.

As a prospective co-op buyer, you may be asked to meet with members of the co-op's board of governors. You could be asked to submit personal references. But no matter how selective the co-op residents are, federal law and many state statutes prohibit them from rejecting or discouraging prospective buyers on the basis of race, gender, creed or national origin.

Contact the Share Loan Service Corporation (1630 Connecticut Ave., N.W., Washington, D.C. 20009) for help in locating a lender and for additional information on buying into a cooperative.

MOBILE AND
MANUFACTURED HOMES

Despite their name, most mobile homes aren't in the least mobile. Almost all of them—more than 90%—stay put on their original sites. This fact, plus changes in design and construction methods over the years, means that as you shop you may hear the term "manufactured home" used interchangeably with the more familiar term "mobile home." Manufactured housing encompasses both those units that start out with wheels on them and models that were never designed to have wheels in the first place. Built in factories and assembled in the plant or on site, manufactured homes make ownership possible for many families and individuals who might otherwise be priced out of the market.

Before you buy such a home, you must decide whether you will place it on land you own or on land you rent or lease. The decision is important because if you later regret your choice of a homesite, you may find the only practical solution is to sell.

The majority of buyers put their manufactured homes on land they own. It's best to select a lot before you buy the home. While some of the zoning restrictions that kept mobile homes out of residential neighborhoods have been eased, many have not. Nevertheless, there are well-designed, attractive subdivisions to choose from, and you may be able to buy land in a ready-made community, complete with swimming pool, recreation center, and nearby school and shopping. A good subdivision developer should help you select a lot that will suit the home you have in mind.

If you plan to rent the land on which your home will be situated, you must be prepared to have certain of your activities controlled by park management on the one hand and a group of your neighbors on the other. If you move into an established community, you will rent a small piece of property and have your house installed at your own expense. A written lease may or may not be involved. There generally are rules and regulations, but they may not be given to you in writing. In most cases you will rent your space month to month or on a yearly lease.

In a new development, on the other hand, the management may also be the mobile home dealer, and you can get into the park only by buying a home from the dealer. This arrangement is not entirely sinister. It allows management to enforce strict standards for the homes that go into its park. When you select a lot, you get to pick a home from the listing of models approved by the management. You will be shown catalog and price information, and in some developments the management will encourage you to go to the factory to custom design your model.

New developments and those still under construction are often promoted on the basis of such amenities as swimming pools, shuffleboard courts and recreation halls that don't yet exist. If you move into such a park, you may discover—to your dismay—that the landlord lets the amenities wait while funds and space are devoted to developing more sites for homes. To add insult to injury, you may be asked for a substantial entrance fee, although some states have outlawed such fees.

Keep in mind that if you lease a site rather than buy it, you will be in a particularly vulnerable situation. You will own a valuable piece of property located on someone else's land. In a dispute with the landowner you may have no recourse but to sell your home or move it. It is very costly to move a single-section home even a short distance. Including necessary dismantling and reassembly, you can pay thousands of dollars to move a luxury multisection home less than 50 miles. Because of the expense and the damage that can result from vibration and road shock, you probably will decide to sell, possibly at a loss, and be faced with the prospect of buying another home elsewhere.

SELECTING A SITE

Whether you intend to buy or rent a homesite, visit several developments. Stay a few days if you can, to sample the neighborhood and meet the residents. Familiarize yourself with each community's rules and regulations. In condominium developments, for example, residents own part of the common facilities as well as their own units and lots. Try to determine how much turnover there is and how the majority of residents view their community. Is your lifestyle compatible with that of your potential neighbors?

Check on security, fire protection and trash collection. Remember that the complexion of a rental park can change more rapidly than a community of landowners. As a tenant there may be little you can do if a park is sold or the management becomes lax.

Study the purchase contract or lease, bylaws, rules and regulations, and all other pertinent documents. Do not commit yourself to a lot or a home until you've had time to consult with an attorney. Don't sign anything you don't understand.

COST AND QUALITY

You might pay around $18,000 for a single-section unit, $31,000 for a multisection. Those were average prices for new single and multisection units in the late 1980s. The purchase price usually includes some furniture, major appliances, draperies, carpeting, and delivery from the manufacturer to a homesite.

"Single-section" or "single-wide" mobile units may give you up to 1,000 square feet of living space. You can join two or more single-sections together. The most luxurious multisection models—featuring wood siding, pitched roofs, cathedral ceilings, fireplaces, bay windows, drywall interiors and the like—can be hard to distinguish from their conventional site-built counterparts.

Questions of quality. Manufactured homes are not subject to local building codes. Units built after June 14, 1976, are covered by the National Mobile Home Construction and Safety Standards Act and must display a permanent label saying that the manufacturer has conformed with the standards.

The standards do not apply to units made before then, nor to multifamily mobiles or special units for the handicapped. The Department of Housing and Urban Development (HUD) has overall responsibility for enforcement, but inspections are conducted by approved state or private agencies.

Judging quality yourself can be difficult, because the innards of a mobile home are hidden from view. Nevertheless, a careful inspection can be revealing. Signs of good construction include a floor that is level and firm; windows and doors that open and close smoothly; walls that do not give excessively when pushed; a firm ceiling; a chassis with two parallel steel I-beams ten to 12 inches high that are reinforced over the axle area; and three axles if the unit is 60 feet long or more.

Look for a 2-by-4-inch aluminum label—located at the taillight end of each section—indicating that the home conforms with HUD standards, and a data plate near the main electrical panel or in some other visible location. The plate gives the name and address of the manufacturer, serial number, model and date of manufacture, as well as other information about appliances, the design approval agency, and the wind and snow loads for which the unit is designed. You should also get a booklet giving specifics about the unit.

Single-section mobile homes are more prone to wind damage from hurricanes, tornadoes and severe thunderstorms than site-built homes. Multisection units, though, are quite stable and require only frame ties. Evidence indicates that when properly tied or attached to a permanent foundation, they are no more vulnerable than ordinary houses. A significant number of structural problems have been traced to improper installation of units on their sites, which HUD does not regulate.

FINANCING THE PURCHASE

You may be able to finance your home with a conventional

mortgage if the unit is permanently set up on land you own or on land you will finance along with the unit. Manufactured houses also are eligible for a number of government-backed loan programs. But most homes still are financed like motor vehicles with personal property, or chattel, loans, and mobile home dealers and park and subdivision developers still arrange most financing. Interest rates are higher and payback periods shorter, as a rule, than for mortgages on site-built homes.

Interest on debt you take on to buy or renovate a manufactured home (or home and land together) is fully deductible for federal tax purposes, so long as you use it as your principal residence or second home.

When you find a unit you like and know how much you want to borrow, ask as many lenders as possible about rates and terms. A few phone calls just might save you a lot of dollars.

Mobile home loans are subject to the federal truth-in-lending law, which means you must be informed in writing of the finance cost expressed as an annual percentage rate (APR). If somebody quotes you an unusually low figure, it's probably an "add-on" or "discount" rate, neither of which reflects the true cost. (see Chapter 3.) Always insist on being told the APR, as the law requires, and make sure that it is the figure in the contract. With add-on loans the interest is added to the amount borrowed before payments begin. If an interest rebate formula called the rule of 78s is used on prepayment or refinancing, you could actually owe more than you borrowed even after making payments for several years.

Two FHA programs are available for financing mobile homes. FHA Title I insures loans of up to $40,500 for terms of up to 20 years if the home meets HUD standards. FHA Title II covers homes on permanent foundations sold with the land as real estate. Such loans are insured up to $54,000 with a maximum 20-year term for single-section homes and a maximum 25-year term for multisections.

The VA guarantee for mobiles is $20,000 or 40% of the loan, whichever is smaller, for up to 23 years. A 5% down payment will be required.

Part Three

PROTECTION
AGAINST CATASTROPHE

SORTING OUT YOUR
INSURANCE COVERAGE

Y̲ou buy insurance, regardless of type, for two reasons: to protect you and your family from the consequences of a financial loss—affecting your health, your car, your home, your belongings or your life—and to make good on your obligations to others who might suffer injury or loss caused by you or your property.

What you get for your money is a promise to pay if the event you hope never happens does happen. In most cases, if the dreaded event doesn't happen, about the only tangible thing you have to show for your money is the policy document, maybe a card you carry in your wallet, and a stack of canceled checks. Unfortunately, far too few people treat insurance as the big-ticket purchase it is.

THE PARTS OF THE POLICY

The policy is probably pockmarked with legalese. Sentences and paragraphs may be studded with terms such as "incontestability period" and "nonforfeiture values." Language like that should make the point: An insurance policy is a legal contract. Court interpretations over the years have attached specific meanings to certain terms and, taken together, those terms spell out your rights and obligations as well as those of the insurance company. Unless your policy expressly calls for the payment of a certain benefit upon the occurrence of a given event, you won't be paid, no matter what a salesperson or other representative may have told you. If the fine print takes away what the big print appears to bestow, that's your tough luck. What's worse, the marketplace is in flux: increasingly complex offerings, changes in coverage, soaring—and wildly varying—rates, distracting discounts. In short, insurers are not only writing new policies but they are also rewriting the fine print of yesterday's.

Difficult and time consuming though it may be, you should do to your policies what most insurance buyers fail to do: Read them. Read each and every one, new or renewal, from front to back with a dictionary at your elbow and perhaps the phone numbers of your agents near at hand. Understand what's behind the sizzling policy titles. In recent years some insurance companies have undertaken laudable campaigns to make their policies more understandable. But mostly you're on your own. Here's a rundown on how typical policies are organized and the kinds of insurance coverage available.

LIFE INSURANCE

Whether it's some kind of term coverage (unembellished death protection up to a certain age or for a span of years) or some form of whole life (meaning you're covered as long as you continue paying premiums, which generate a cash value that can be borrowed on), a life insurance policy can be broken down into three parts.

The summary. This gives the essential details of the two-way deal between you and the company. For your part, you agree to pay, on a regular basis, a stipulated premium based primarily on your age. If the policy was issued on a participating basis, you'll receive or be credited with dividends at regular intervals; if not, you won't. In return for your premiums the company promises to pay a certain amount, less any unpaid loans and interest, to someone you have named, provided the policy is in force at your death. This section also commonly describes two additional benefits you may or may not have elected: waiver of premium (the company itself pays the premiums if you become totally disabled) and an accidental death rider (the benefit usually doubles if you die as the result of an accident).

The details. Here you'll learn about such things as the due date (when premiums are to be paid); the grace period (how long you have, usually a month, to pay the premiums without penalty); lapses (how soon the policy expires if you don't pay); reinstatements (how you can put the policy back in effect); nonforfeiture and surrender values (the money you have coming under a cash value policy if you give up or let lapse the protection); extended term and reduced paid-up options (ways you can use the cash values to provide continuing coverage without further payments); and settlement options (how you or the beneficiary can choose to have the proceeds paid).

The application. This section reflects what you told the company about yourself when you applied for coverage—age, occupation, health, other life insurance you carry and whether the activities you engage in could be considered dangerous—and how you wish to exercise the rights you have under the policy. For example, if you haven't assigned ownership to someone else, you can change the beneficiary arrangements and you can determine how the dividends and cash values are to be used. Dividends can be taken in cash, used to reduce premiums, left with the company to earn interest or be invested, or used to buy more coverage; cash values can be earmarked to reimburse the company for any premiums you fail to pay.

If you are insured by a solid company and pay your premiums on time, there isn't much that can go wrong with a life insurance policy. Note, though, that if your age is misstated on the application, the company may pay whatever death benefit would have been called for by the correct age. While the suicide clause is in effect, usually during the first two years, the beneficiaries of those who take their own lives are entitled only to a return of premiums.

HEALTH INSURANCE

Because they are written in so many different forms, health

insurance policies can't be readily categorized. The major types of traditional health insurance have been hospital/medical/surgical coverage (the basic protection that pays, up to specified limits, for room and board in a hospital and the services of physicians and surgeons while you are a patient there); major medical (backup coverage that provides substantial reimbursement for the costs of a lengthy illness, often up to catastrophic amounts); and catastrophic medical (protection that picks up where other coverages stop for serious illnesses involving long confinements). Increasingly, these forms of insurance are packaged together into single policies.

More prevalent than ever are the cost-conscious alphabet-soup providers. HMOs (health maintenance organizations) come in two versions: a staff model providing a range of prepaid services under one roof; and IPAs (individual practice associations), which have doctor-affiliates usually treating patients in their own offices. PPOs (preferred provider organizations), steer patients to certain doctors and hospitals who agree to keep costs low.

Disability income policies pay a percentage of your regular income when you are unable to work because of illness or injury. And long-term-care policies are designed to help pay for nursing home stays and certain home health services for the elderly.

Some policies contain far more liberal language than others, and that fact can determine whether your particular problem is covered or not. Here are a couple of examples of the difference a few words can make, cited by Herbert S. Denenberg when he was insurance commissioner of Pennsylvania. If, in defining which sicknesses are covered, a policy says this means "sickness or disease which is first manifested after the effective date of this policy," you must have had symptoms or known you were ill when the policy took effect for the coverage to be denied. By contrast, if your problem is defined as "sickness or disease contracted and commencing after the policy has been in force not less than 30 days," it is necessary only that you had the disease when the policy took effect, whether you knew it or not, for your claim to be disqualified. If injury is defined as "bodily injury sustained directly and independently of all other causes" rather than "accidental bodily injury sustained while this policy is in force," it increases the chances that the company will be able to deny the claim on the grounds that the injury was related in some way to other causes, such as a medical condition.

AUTO AND HOME INSURANCE

Most automobile and homeowners policies are set up along similar lines. Some companies are even packaging them together, offering a discount if you buy both.

Declarations. This section gives the personal information you supplied to the agent, such as your name and address. It spells out how long the policy is to run, the premiums and the deductible amount that applies. (The deductible is the sum you have to pay before the insurance cuts in.) The location of your dwelling or a description of the vehicle being protected is included in this section, along with a rundown on the kinds of coverage you have chosen: benefits to replace the house, other structures and personal property following a loss, money to help tide you over in temporary quarters, personal liability coverage (some even cover libel and slander) and medical payments coverage for others under homeowners plans; liability, medical expense, uninsured and/or underinsured motorist, collision, comprehensive, rental expense, total disability and accidental death indemnity insurance under auto policies. The dollar limits for each kind of coverage are also specified.

In your auto insurance policy, be careful to differentiate between single and split limits. Under single limits, the policy pays up to a total amount for all claims resulting from a single accident. Split coverage provides separate limits per accident for injuries to each individual, a total amount for bodily injuries and yet another sum for property damage.

Insuring agreement. To be covered, the event involving loss usually must be listed in this section, which is the company's promise to pay. This promise, however, is very broad, and payments for some mentioned occurrences may be limited by the language in other parts of the policy.

Exclusions. Some risks, such as damages or injuries a policy-holder inflicts intentionally, are not covered at all. They are listed in this section. Other risks are only partially excluded, giving you the right to limited coverage under certain circumstances. In still other cases, a particular risk is considered to be so out of the ordinary that it is thought best to have it covered by a special endorsement rather than have all policyholders pay for it under a standard contract.

One exclusion under auto policies prohibits coverage of a car while it is hired or used to carry people for a fee. (Shared-expense car pools don't come under this ban.) A typical home policy excludes coverage of flood damage and earth movements. Home insurance companies now exclude communicable diseases from the standard clause that extends homeowners liability coverage to "bodily harm, sickness and disaster." (The exclusion, covering new policies and renewals, was devised after a woman won a $25,000 settlement under the bodily harm provision after she contracted herpes from the policyholder!)

Conditions. This section clarifies the rights and obligations of both the policyholder and the company. Some of the provisions tell what you must do following a loss in order to get paid. For example, if you're involved in a hit and run accident, you may have to report it to the police or the motor vehicle department within 24 hours and file a statement made under oath with the company within 30 days. If you fail to notify your agent within 30 days after trading in your car for another one, the new car may not be covered.

Endorsements. These attachments are used to tailor the broad policy format to individual needs, perhaps by adding boat and trailer coverage to auto insurance or specific protection for jewelry and furs under a homeowners plan. However, the policy and its endorsements are considered as a unit, the latter having as much heft as the former. Make sure that the endorsements don't unduly limit or reduce the coverage spelled out in general terms elsewhere.

UMBRELLA LIABILITY INSURANCE

Auto and homeowners insurance can provide pretty good

protection, but in light of the millions of dollars that sometimes constitute the settlements in personal liability cases, a policy that stops at $300,000 or $500,000 may strike you as inadequate. (Jury awards for injured knees alone averaged $295,380 in 1986, more than twice the amount of two years earlier.)

Suppose someone sues you for a million? Fortunately, you can buy extended personal liability coverage in the form of what's called an umbrella policy. It picks up where your existing coverage leaves off and protects you to whatever limit you choose—typically a million dollars. A typical umbrella policy covers accidents involving your home, motor vehicles, boat and other property, and slander and libel (provided you're not a professional writer).

Umbrella coverage costs less than you might expect because it works largely on an "excess" basis, meaning it pays for claims not completely covered by your other policies and doesn't cut in until that coverage is exhausted. You can get $1 million in umbrella coverage for a family with one home and two cars for about $150, plus the money you may have to pay to upgrade your existing coverage to meet the umbrella's sometimes stiff "deductible." If you're considering buying such coverage, check with a few of the leading property insurers. Rates and conditions differ significantly; some umbrellas are bigger than others. Make sure you know the exclusions. Take into account not only the cost of the premiums but also any extra premiums needed to raise your underlying insurance to the umbrella policy's required limits.

With that quick tour of insurance policies under your belt, you're ready to concentrate on getting the most coverage for the least money. The next four chapters are designed to help you with that task.

MAKE YOUR MONEY GROW 10

INSURANCE ON YOUR LIFE

Do you really need life insurance? If your death would cause financial hardship for your spouse, children, parents or someone else you want to protect, then insurance is a must. But not everyone fits the description. Our need for life insurance tends to follow a pattern, starting with little or no need when we are young, progressing to greater and greater need as we take on more and more responsibility, and finally beginning to diminish as we grow older.

Little or no need. You're a student, 22, unmarried, with parents who are financing your education. Financially, your death would create no problems. An insurance agent might nevertheless remind you that your parents would have to pay funeral and other final costs. On the other hand, they would no longer have to pay your school expenses, so that's not a convincing reason for buying the insurance.

The agent's strongest argument may be that you should buy a policy now while you're young and rates are low. It's true that younger people pay lower rates. But consider the interest you could earn by saving your money instead of spending it on insurance premiums. What's more, those rates are low for a reason: They reflect the fact that you're less likely to die in your younger years, and thus less likely to collect on the policy.

Moderate need.   You're half of a married couple with no children. Together you earn $50,000 a year. The death of either of you would not be financially catastrophic; the other could presumably survive on his or her own income. Still, there would be a strain. Perhaps your home couldn't be maintained on a single income, or maybe you have big debts. Also, there would be funeral costs. It could be argued that you need insurance, but a modest amount would probably suffice.

Great need.   You're half of a couple living in a one-income household. You have two young children. This is the stereotypical insurance situation. There are four people dependent on one breadwinner for their total support, so insurance on that life is vital. And if the nonearning spouse should die, the other would have to pay for day-care for the children—a very expensive proposition that argues for insurance on both lives.

Diminishing need.   You're retired, the kids have grown and are on their own. You have accumulated considerable assets that can be used to generate income should you die. In circumstances like this, you clearly don't need as much life insurance as you once did.

HOW MUCH DO YOU NEED?

Deciding whether you need life insurance is pretty easy. Figuring out how much you need is not easy at all. Many people just pluck some figure out of the air that seems reasonable and settle on that. Some lean on an old rule of thumb that says you need four to five times your annual income. That's better, but you really should approach the problem more scientifically. You can arrive at a reasonable estimate of your life insurance needs without getting too technical, and the worksheet on the opposite page will help you do it.

The first step is to estimate the income your dependents would need to maintain their standard of living if you were to die tomorrow. Then subtract from that figure the income they could expect to receive in social security survivor's benefits (to find out how to calculate that, call the Social Security office listed in your local telephone book), salaries they now earn or could earn, investments and other sources. The difference is

FIGURING YOUR
LIFE INSURANCE NEEDS

A. SURVIVORS' ANNUAL EXPENSES

Annual expenditures from Cash-Flow worksheet (Chapter one, page 18) _____	
Minus your own living expenses _____	
Total Annual Expenses	**A**

B. SURVIVORS' ANNUAL INCOME

Salary _____	
Interest from savings _____	
Investment dividends _____	
Rents received _____	
Annuity income . _____	
Social Security benefits _____	
Veterans' benefits _____	
Payments from pension plan _____	
Income from trusts _____	
Other income _____	
Total Annual Income Available	**B**

C. ANNUAL AMOUNT NEEDED FROM INSURANCE

Annual expenses *minus* annual income (A minus B) _____	
Minus annual benefits from existing life insurance policies _____	
Annual income required from additional insurance	

Use the tables on pages 416 and 417 to convert the annual need
into a policy amount.

the amount of income your life insurance should provide.

You have to make a number of assumptions in the course of
this exercise—complex assumptions that scare many people

away from the task. For instance: What will inflation be? What rate should you use when projecting how much income your family will need in the future? Will the family live on the earnings generated by the proceeds of the policy and leave the principal alone, or should they expect to gradually use up the capital as well? What rate of interest can you safely assume the money will be able to earn? Will your spouse take a job if he or she doesn't have one now? Will that require a period of training? How much can he or she realistically be expected to earn?

You can see what makes this task so difficult. Insurance companies will be happy to perform the calculations for you; most have developed computerized programs for the purpose. These can be helpful, but they amount essentially to broad, educated guesses.

Eventually you will have to pick some total insurance figure that seems a reasonable compromise between what you'd like to have and what you can afford, using the companies' estimates for reference. The key point to remember is that what you buy today will be worth less and less in purchasing power as the years go by. You can get an idea of how much less from the tables at the end of Chapter 24.

LIFE INSURANCE CHOICES

Life insurance companies are good at dreaming up new kinds of policies. But whatever name they may give them—universal life, variable life, Irresistible Life, Irreplaceable Life, The Champion, The Solution—in fact they're all variations on the two basic kinds of life insurance: term insurance and cash value insurance (also called permanent or whole life).

Term Insurance. This is as simple as life insurance gets, and the easiest to understand. You insure your life for a fixed period—one year, five years or more—and pay an annual premium based on your age. The older you get, the more it costs. Many companies won't sell term policies that run past a certain age, say 65 or 70. But by that time term insurance is very expensive anyway, because life expectancy is comparatively short. Besides, as we've seen above, your need for insurance often diminishes as you reach retirement age.

A term insurance policy has no savings or investment features built into the rates, making it the purest form of life insurance and thus the cheapest for a given amount of coverage. Term insurance comes in several varieties.

Annual renewable term. This is the most common form. You buy a series of one-year policies and the insurance company guarantees you the right to renew the coverage each year without having to undergo an additional medical exam. As you grow older, your premium rises.

Level term. Coverage remains fixed for the life of the contract.

Declining, decreasing or reducing term. Coverage periodically drops according to a fixed schedule over ten, 15, 20 or more years. Mortgage insurance policies, which pay the loan balance when the policyholder dies, are a common form of decreasing term.

Term riders. These policies are sold as supplements to cash value policies.

Convertible term. For a higher premium, the policy can be converted into a cash value policy without your having to meet medical standards at the time of conversion. Most companies offer policies that are both convertible and renewable up to specified ages or for fixed periods.

Cash value insurance. With a basic cash value policy, you pay the same premium, based on your age when you sign up, for as long as the policy remains in force. Because the premium remains level as you grow older, it is set to exceed the company's cost of insuring your life during the early years. The surplus and interest it earns go into a reserve fund, part of which pays the agent's commission and the company's administrative costs. The rest gets credited to your account. After a couple of years your reserve begins to build, creating a cash value you can draw on.

You can use your cash value by borrowing against it while the policy stays in force; by directing the company to use it to pay your premiums; by directing the company to use it to purchase a paid-up insurance policy; or by surrendering the policy and taking the money. When you die, the company pays your beneficiary the policy's face amount (less any policy loan balance), not the face amount plus cash value.

Insurance companies offer cash value policies in a bewildering variety of forms, ranging from the standard whole life policy (sometimes called straight or ordinary life) to specially designed contracts in which the premiums or face amounts change according to a set schedule, investment results or some other factor.

PICKING THE RIGHT POLICY

When you set out to buy life insurance, odds are an agent will steer you toward a permanent policy. Term may be shrugged off as temporary insurance, good for filling the gap until you can. afford to buy a whole life policy, or okay for supplementing a whole life policy but not substantial enough to constitute your entire life insurance program. Don't believe it. A whole life policy may indeed make more sense than term for some people in some circumstances, but the comparisons of relative costs depend so heavily on assumptions about future performance of cash values that they are not especially dependable. Besides, insurance agents are only being human when they stress cash value insurance, since those policies pay much higher commissions than term.

If you're stretching your finances to buy enough insurance, term should be your first choice. The primary purpose of life insurance is to provide dependents with income they would lose by your death. Term almost always gives you the most protection for your money.

As mentioned before, term premiums can be extremely high in your later years, but the need for insurance late in life is sometimes exaggerated. At 70, for instance, it's likely that the only person depending on you will be your spouse. If he or she will be adequately protected by your pension, social security and other sources of income, you should be able to reduce or drop your insurance then. In any case you can leave your options open by starting with a term policy that is convertible as well as renewable.

It's true that cash values could add to your financial resources, but insurance can be a poor way to save. You can get your hands on the cash in the policy's fund in only two ways: You can collect the entire cash value by surrendering the policy, thereby terminating the coverage; or you can borrow against the cash value and keep the policy in force. Any unpaid loan balance will be deducted from the face amount if the insured person dies. To keep the face amount up, the loan will eventually have to be repaid, just like any other loan.

And you should know that borrowing against your life insurance policy isn't the bargain it used to be—and is sometimes still advertised to be. Several years back, when interest rates were in double digits and policy loans were commonly available at 5%, insurance companies were flooded with loans. This forced them to take a lot of money out of lucrative investments to make it available to policyholders. At the same time, each policy's dividends and cash values stayed the same, loan or no loan. This was a bonanza for policyholders but an expensive headache for insurance companies.

Today companies protect themselves in a couple of different ways. Some charge variable rates on policy loans so that the interest they collect reflects the current market. Others reduce dividends to reflect the amount of the cash value encumbered by the policyholder's loan, an approach called direct recognition. Under direct recognition, in effect, the more you borrow the less your policy earns. Either of these approaches, coupled with the phasing out of the tax deductibility of interest on such loans, makes them more expensive than they appear, and certainly more expensive than they used to be. Make sure you get a clear explanation of the loan provisions of any policy you're considering.

Insurance companies also sell cash value policies in various combinations with term. "Family income" plans, for example, combine a whole life policy with a decreasing-term policy in such a way as to provide beneficiaries with a fixed income for a certain period.

Whatever the relative merits of the two types of insurance over the long run, many people simply can't afford enough insurance unless they start with term. Still, the answer to the question of which kind of policy to buy isn't always clear-cut. You get more insurance per dollar with term, and by investing what you save you may be able to beat the return you'd get from paying higher premiums for a cash-value policy. On the other hand, some of the newer cash-value products, with earnings wedded to changing interest rates, have produced excellent returns in recent years.

What to do? You can always compromise by buying both term and whole life, either separately or through a package plan. Another way to add term to your whole life insurance is to use your policy dividends to purchase one-year term additions. Many companies allow you to buy an amount equal to the current year's cash value. Some let you buy as much as the dividend will cover.

Before deciding, familiarize yourself with the principal varieties of whole life insurance being sold today.

UNIVERSAL LIFE INSURANCE

Universal life offers yields on the cash value portion that can be substantially higher than those on basic whole life policies. What's more, rates of return are disclosed in advance. Although the rates the company guarantees to pay are generally low—4% or so—there is a possibility of earning considerably more. The low guaranteed return keeps premiums down; the opportunity to earn more keeps interest among buyers up.

Still, flexibility is universal's primary appeal. Generally, you can raise or lower the face amount, or death benefit, as circumstances change, with no need to rewrite the policy. You can vary the premium payments. If you can't make a payment, you can use money from the accumulated cash value to cover it. You can borrow against the cash value. You can cash in the policy at any time and collect all or most of the savings.

As with other cash value policies, only part of your premium payment is used to pay for the cost of insuring your life. The rest is invested in low-risk financial instruments—after deductions are made for sales commissions, administrative costs and profits. You can, within limits, designate how much you want used for insurance and how much for investments.

The company establishes the rate of return from savings or ties it to some financial index. Every company has its own formula, which may base the return on the Treasury bill rate or some other index.

You get annual reports showing the amount of insurance protection, the cash value, costs of the insurance, company fees, the amounts credited to savings from premium payments, and the rates of return from savings.

Picking a universal life policy.   Universal life is a complex form of insurance requiring special considerations.

• First, check the loads, or fees, carefully. They vary quite a lot and are imposed in different ways. There may be a lump-sum deduction of several hundred dollars from the first-year premiums plus deductions from future premiums. You can eliminate loads by buying so-called no-load universal life through a financial planner or someone else to whom you pay a fee. For a list of sellers in your area, contact the Council of Life Insurance Consultants, P.O. Box 803653, Chicago, Ill. 60680-3653.

• Find out how the rate of return is calculated and how long the initial rate is guaranteed. Check the projected cash value at the end of the first year and compare it with the first year's premium. Bear in mind that the advertised rates are paid on the money that goes into savings after load charges and the cost of insurance are deducted. Moreover, some companies pay less than the advertised rates on the initial money paid in premiums, such as the first $1,000.

• Ask about surrender changes, if any. They can make it especially expensive to cancel the policy in its early years.

• Find out if there are any medical requirements for increasing the policy's face amount.

• If a company sells more than one universal life policy, compare them carefully. Many companies sell two generic types. In one the death benefit is limited to the policy's face amount, which includes the cash value. In the other the cash value is added to the face value. Still other types are offered.

VARIABLE LIFE INSURANCE

Straight whole life and universal life pay interest rates based on fixed-income investments. Variable life lets you invest part of your cash value in stocks and other securities, usually through mutual funds run by the insurance company. Both the death benefit and the cash value of a variable life policy depend on the performance of those securities funds, meaning they can go down as well as up.

You decide how much of your net premium—that is, the amount left after such expenses as commissions are paid—is to be invested in different areas: stocks, bonds, short-term money-market instruments. Policyholders' investment funds are segregated from the insurance company's general accounts, so that they reflect the actual experience of the investments chosen. Because you decide where your money is invested and because you bear the risk of those investments, variable life is considered a security and is the only kind of life insurance sold by prospectus.

Just like their whole life brethren, variable policies have loan privileges, optional riders, and surrender and exchange rights. They may be participating (in other words, pay dividends) or nonparticipating (no dividends). The first year's premium is largely consumed by one-time administrative costs and the agent's commission. Thus, significant cash values take several years to accumulate even if the investment portion of the policy does well.

As mentioned above, both the total death benefit and the cash value of a variable policy rise and fall with the results of the investment accounts. A minimum death benefit—the policy's face amount—is guaranteed, but the cash value is not. If your investments perform poorly over a long period of time, it's possible your policy could end up with a cash value smaller than what you would have achieved with a traditional whole life policy. If you keep a poorly performing policy in force, it would represent an extremely expensive form of pure death protection if you die after paying premiums for many years. On the other hand, good performance in the investment account could increase the death benefit above the guaranteed level or create a substantial cash value.

Details of variable life policies are spelled out in their

prospectuses, which you can get from the agent or the company. This is a complex product, so read the prospectus carefully. Also, a variable life policy must be watched closely after you buy it. It will be up to you to change your investments in order to get the best return.

SINGLE-PREMIUM WHOLE LIFE INSURANCE

Single-premium whole life is just what it sounds like: a policy you pay for once, up front, rather than over a period of time. The minimum premium is $5,000, the maximum can be as much as a million, and with it you can choose either a whole life or a variable life policy. The advantage is that your money starts working faster to build cash value than it does in a conventional pay-as-you-go policy. Your earnings accumulate tax-free, as they do in other cash value policies, and you can borrow against the cash build-up at a rate likely to be promoted as "interest free" or "zero net cost," but which may not be quite free by the time the fees are paid. Remember these points about single-premium whole life insurance:

• As insurance, it's expensive. Recently, a $10,000 premium would buy about $52,000 worth of life insurance for a 35-year-old nonsmoking male at a time when the same man could purchase $100,000 of whole life coverage from the same company for a beginning annual premium of about $1,500.

• As a tax shelter, it's precarious. The immediate access it provides to tax-free borrowing of part of the original premium has caught the eye of a revenue-hungry Congress, and attempts to slap a tax on the internal build-up of cash value occur yearly. As this book went to press, such policies were alive but tottering.

• As an investment, it may not always be what it seems. The proper way for an agent to quote yields on such policies is "net"—that is, after commissions and fees have been deducted. Occasionally agents have quoted "gross" rates of return to unsuspecting purchasers.

• In the first few years of the policy's life, substantial surrender fees can make it very expensive to change your mind and get out. In the later years, cashing in the policy and taking out the principal will trigger immediate tax on the earning accumulated in the policy plus any amounts you might have borrowed while the policy was in force.

• Because most policies base their rates of return on the performance of the insurance company's investment portfolio, choosing a company with a solid record of performance is especially important.

FINDING THE LOWEST-PRICED POLICIES

The obvious way to compare costs of various life insurance policies is to compare the premiums charged by different companies for the same coverage. Unfortunately, it's not that simple. Dividends, cash values, interest you could have earned elsewhere and the number of years a policy is kept in force also play an important role in determining the actual cost.

Insurance industry analysts have tried to incorporate all these considerations into formulas that produce a couple of esoteric numbers called the interest-adjusted net cost indexes. The "interest-adjusted surrender cost" is a measure of the true anticipated cost of keeping a policy in force for ten or 20 years and then surrendering it for its cash value. The "net payment index" attempts to measure the cost of holding onto the policy until you die. Most states require agents to provide these numbers for cash value policies if you ask for them. Interest-adjusted costs vary according to the type of policy and your age at purchase. Armed with these numbers, you have another means for comparing the costs of different policies within the same company and among different companies.

Ask the agent for the ten- and 20-year interest-adjusted surrender costs per $1,000 of face amount for the specific policy being recommended. Ask also for comparable data for the same kinds of policies issued by two other companies. The agent doesn't have to furnish information on competitors' policies but should be able to obtain approximate figures for some companies from manuals widely used in the insurance business. If the agent won't or can't help, call other companies yourself.

The interest-adjusted net cost indexes are useful, but be aware that they, too, are not an invariably accurate guide. They are based on the assumption that the cash values will earn a certain amount per year. When interest rates are higher or lower than that, the relationships between premiums and cash values are thrown out of whack, especially in the later years that the policy is assumed to be held. But the distortions affect all policies, so you can still use the indexes as a relative measure of comparative policy costs over the years, provided the issue dates and death benefits are the same.

MAKING SURE THE RIGHT PEOPLE COLLECT

Most people don't run into beneficiary difficulties with their life insurance, perhaps because their lives generally follow the anticipated course. A husband designates his wife as beneficiary; he dies; she receives the money as he intended. However, you can't be sure that even well-conceived beneficiary arrangements won't be upset by later events. To avoid problems, take stock of these essential points.

Naming beneficiaries.   A policy owner can name anyone he or she chooses as beneficiary—relative, friend, business associate, charity. You can also change beneficiaries unless you have previously named someone as the irrevocable beneficiary. In that case you must obtain the beneficiary's permission. Irrevocable designations develop most often from divorce and separation settlements.

Customarily, beneficiaries can be changed merely by filling in a company form and sending it to the company. Some older policies require that the change be made on the policy itself.

If you die without having recorded a living beneficiary with the company, the proceeds will be paid into your estate or sometimes to surviving children, depending on the terms of the policy.

Primary and secondary beneficiaries.   The normal procedure is to name a primary beneficiary and a secondary, or contingent, beneficiary in case the primary should die before you do. You can select a third beneficiary to receive the money in case both the primary and secondary beneficiaries don't survive you.

If you name two or more beneficiaries in the same rank, the funds will be divided equally unless you provide otherwise. Two primary beneficiaries, for example, will each receive 50%.

Leaving it to your spouse. To avoid confusion, a wife or husband should be identified by his or her given name. Mrs. John Nelson, for example, should be described as Mrs. Jane Nelson or Jane Nelson, wife of the insured. For further specification, her premarital surname could be added—for example, Mrs. Jane Smith Nelson. If a woman has kept her premarital surname, then of course the policy should use it.

Leaving it to the kids. "My children" or "children of the insured" or some similar collective designation usually suffices because it usually covers all present and future children, including adopted children. However, a broad description might have to be modified to cope with a specific situation, such as step children.

Per capita or per stirpes. These Latin terms refer to two significantly different ways of distributing insurance proceeds, as well as other estate payments.

Under a per capita plan, all beneficiaries share equally. A per stirpes arrangement distributes according to family generational lines.

Assume a mother names her two sons as equal beneficiaries of $120,000 in insurance. If both survive her, each will receive 50%. However, suppose the mother wants to be sure that if either son dies before she does, shares will be distributed to his children. Suppose that son B dies, leaving three children. Then the mother dies. Son A has no children at the time of his mother's death. If she stipulated that the proceeds were to be allocated to her issue per capita, the figures on the left in the table below show how much each living beneficiary would receive. A per stirpes arrangement would produce quite a different result, as shown by the figures on the right.

PER CAPITA		PER STIRPES	
Son A	$30,000	Son A	$60,000
Grandchild 1	$30,000	Grandchild 1	$20,000
Grandchild 2	$30,000	Grandchild 2	$20,000
Grandchild 3	$30,000	Grandchild 3	$20,000

Payments to minors. When you name a child as beneficiary, legal problems may arise if the proceeds of your insurance have to be paid while he or she is still a minor. To protect itself against future claims, the insurance company will want a valid receipt for payments, and a minor may not be considered legally qualified for that purpose. State laws vary considerably, but in some cases the court may decide to appoint a guardian to receive and take care of the funds.

To avoid those difficulties, you can appoint a trustee to accept the insurance money and administer it for the child's benefit while he or she is a minor. The trustee could be directed in the trust agreement to pay the child any funds remaining at the time the child reaches his or her majority. You can also appoint a successor trustee to take over if the first becomes unable to serve.

If you both die.   Somewhere in the beneficiary forms you should find mention of common disaster, a situation in which both the husband and wife die in the same accident or later from the effects of the accident.

Common disasters sometimes create tax and legal difficulties when one spouse survives the other briefly. This is something to think about when you are deciding on settlement options. An option providing for the insurance company to keep the policy proceeds and pay them to the primary beneficiary—the wife, for example, as she wants them—with any funds not drawn out by her going directly to her husband's contingent beneficiaries upon her death, would be one way to meet the problem of a common disaster. Ask the agent for a detailed explanation of the plans suggested by his or her company.

The tax angles. A beneficiary receiving the death proceeds of a life insurance policy is given three substantial tax breaks:

• No income tax generally has to be paid on the money.

• The funds don't have to go through the time-consuming and possibly expensive probate procedures required for assets transferred by a will.

• The state may exempt part or all of the money from death taxes.

Life insurance proceeds may not be completely tax-free, because the money is included in the estate of the insured when estate taxes are figured. But it's possible to move life insurance out of your estate. One way is to assign to the beneficiary all "incidents of ownership," including the right to surrender the policy for its cash value or to change the beneficiary. Another method is to transfer ownership of the policy to an irrevocable living trust (a trust set up while you are living and whose terms normally can't be changed).

By taking either of these steps, you in effect make a gift of the insurance to someone else (the beneficiary of the trust) and may have to pay a gift tax. If you think you need estate tax planning, don't try doing it on your own with ready-made forms. Consult an experienced attorney, and see Chapter 25.

HOW SHOULD THE PROCEEDS BE PAID?

Life insurance proceeds are usually paid out in a lump sum. But insurance companies also offer several alternative arrangements known as settlement options. As a policy owner, you can select one of those plans for your beneficiary. If you make no choice, the beneficiary can elect one within a certain period after your death. These are the options commonly available:

Interest only.   The funds are left on deposit with the insurance company, which guarantees a minimum rate of interest but normally pays more. Interest is paid to the beneficiary, who can be given the right to withdraw principal as desired.

Installments for a fixed period.   The proceeds are paid out in equal amounts for as long as the money lasts. Again, the company usually adds extra interest to its guaranteed rate.

Life income.   The beneficiary is guaranteed a lifetime income based on his or her age and on the amount of the proceeds. The company may allow the beneficiary to use the proceeds to buy one of its regular annuities at a discount.

Installment and annuity plans may be useful in providing for a beneficiary who doesn't have the experience to manage a large sum. But it may not be wise to choose a settlement option for your beneficiary in all cases. A beneficiary often needs cash immediately for burial and other expenses. Furthermore, the beneficiary can often invest the money safely at a better rate than the insurance company offers.

REASONS NOT TO INSURE YOUR KIDS

Just about anyone with any knowledge of life insurance will advise you that insuring your children is not a very good idea. Whatever money you have available for premiums should be spent on insurance for breadwinners, those whose death would reduce the family income. Until they are adequately insured, why should you buy policies for the kids?

Year in and year out, though, parents insure their children for billions of dollars, often in mistaken solicitude for the child's welfare. The arguments for insuring kids go like this:

"It costs relatively little to insure a child, so you would not really be burdening your budget."

Counter argument: One reason you pay less for children, of course, is that the chance of death in the near future is low. In the case of a whole life policy, insurance companies have a longer time to accumulate the reserve fund needed to cover the heavier mortality costs of the later years.

If you want, you could settle for a small amount of protection and buy a term policy. The starting premiums for term are much lower than those for cash value policies.

"By buying a whole life policy for a child at an early age, you lock in the low premium rate, thereby making it easier for the child to carry the policy later. Moreover, you might pay less in premiums over a long period."

Counter argument: Consider the last column in this cost tabulation for a hypothetical $10,000 nonparticipating policy, the type that does not return part of your premiums as dividends:

AGE AT PURCHASE	ANNUAL PREMIUM	PREMIUM PAYMENTS THROUGH 65
16	$102.20	$5,110
20	115.40	5,308
24	130.90	5,498

The premium payments through age 65 appear to indicate

that you could get several years of insurance coverage for nothing because the 16-year-old wouldn't pay as much as the 24-year-old. To see the gap in that reasoning, let's add another column showing the amount you would accumulate by 65 if you merely deposited the annual premiums in a 5¼% savings account instead of giving them to the insurance company.

AGE AT PURCHASE	EQUIVALENT SAVINGS THROUGH 65 AT 5¼% INTEREST
16	$24,413
20	22,036
24	19,884

In effect, the extra interest you could earn on the early age premium payments would go to the insurance company. It stands to reason that the company must charge something for insuring your child's life for those years.

"Later in life your child might take a job or suffer a health impairment that would make him or her ineligible for insurance or for insurance at regular rates. You can guard against that danger by insuring now."

Counter argument: Relatively few people are turned down by insurance companies or charged a high risk premium. Probably fewer than 10% of applicants must pay higher than usual premiums and fewer than 5% get turned down. That includes applicants of all ages, including the older years when people are more likely to have health problems. Your child will probably be buying insurance in his or her late twenties or early thirties. The odds strongly favor your child's being able to get all the protection wanted at standard premiums.

"A child's policy will help defray burial expenses."

Counter argument: The overriding problem in a serious illness is not the burial but the potentially catastrophic cost of medical treatment. The money spent on a life insurance policy might better be used to beef up medical coverage.

Conclusion: The decision to insure a child must overcome

several impressive objections before it becomes justifiable. But in considering ways to help your children, you don't want to limit yourself to cold economic calculations. What seems unwarranted on a cost basis might make sense when viewed as a gift.

That doesn't mean you must accept all the claims made for juvenile insurance or buy any kind of policy. If you want to build up an education fund, you'd still be wiser to save on your own.

On the other hand, you can accomplish some important long-term objectives by insuring your child early in life.

• You can start off his or her adult career with a low out-of-pocket expense for life protection he or she is bound to need. The lifetime premium cost may be more, but that extra cost represents your present to your child.

• You can protect your child against the risk, however small, of not being able to buy insurance at standard rates.

• By carefully selecting the kind of insurance you buy, you can give children a base on which to build their own insurance programs later. With inflation constantly eroding the value of each dollar of insurance bought now, they will need a good start.

MAIL-ORDER LIFE INSURANCE

It seems to be getting harder and harder to turn on the television or open the mail without discovering that by virtue of some sort of affiliation or another, you're eligible for a special deal on life insurance. You may have a credit card or a mortgage or an alma mater or a profession that puts you in the select group eligible for the special rates.

In theory, buying insurance through the mail should save you money by cutting out the middleman—the life insurance agent who must be paid a commission for the work he or she puts in on your policy. Well, sometimes insurance sold through the mail is indeed cheaper. But mail-order or TV-sold policies don't necessarily deliver on the promise, and in fact very often they don't.

Some mail policies are sold to professional, fraternal and trade associations, who may choose to use sales commissions from their insurance programs to raise funds for the organization instead of passing on lower premiums to their members.

The size of the first year's premium isn't the only consideration. A large number of mass-marketed plans are offered by brokerage firms that specialize in mail-order sales of life, health and other types of insurance. If you buy directly from such a company, you get an individual policy, just as you would if you bought one from an agent. If the insurance comes through an association or sponsored group, your coverage is governed by the seller's master contract with the insurer or the broker. That distinction has two very important ramifications for the buyer.

First, individual policy rates are guaranteed; association and group plan rates are not. All term policies are renewed periodically, and rates are stepped up in line with the policyholder's age. Renewal premiums for individual policies can't be increased any faster. With association plans the insurer reserves the right to raise the rates beyond those normal increases. Of course, your premium might never be increased, but you can't be sure of that.

Second, if the individual policy is automatically renewable each year, as most are, you can keep the insurance in force up to the ultimate termination age simply by paying the premiums. With association and group plans the insurance normally stops if you leave the group, and the coverage can be maintained only by converting the term policy into a higher-premium cash value policy.

Mail vs. regular rates. Putting aside those considerations for the moment, do the claimed economies of selling by mail or TV actually produce savings for the buyer?

Sometimes. The National Insurance Consumer Organization, an independent watchdog group, has cited USAA Life Insurance Co. of San Antonio as one company whose term policies are sold directly (without an agent) to the public at very competitive rates. The rates charged by GEICO Annuity and Insurance Co., another direct seller, have also compared favorably. But it would be virtually impossible to examine the huge number of mail-order plans on the market and compare them with agent-sold plans. In the absence of a blanket rule, you can get some clues to the competitiveness of the charge by the company's attitude toward the medical qualifications of its applicants.

Medical qualifications. For policies issued subject to medical qualifications, the application form requires answers to a few questions that the company uses to evaluate your acceptability. Your replies will probably be cross-checked against data that may be on file with the Medical Information Bureau, through which companies swap information. You may be asked to have a medical examination at the company's expense.

However, some plans are sold without any medical conditions: You are guaranteed acceptance if you pay the premium. To avoid being swamped by deathbed or other high-risk applicants, the insurers may employ several safeguards:

• The full face value isn't paid for deaths that occur during the first two years the policy is in force, maybe longer.

• The premium may be set considerably above rates for medically screened plans sold through agents.

• The policy may be offered only during limited enrollment periods.

• Only a modest amount of insurance may be available for purchase.

Mail-order insurance companies set premium rates on the basis of sales costs as well as actuarial considerations. Only 1% to 2% of the people solicited by mail actually buy the insurance, and that is often regarded as a good return. Therefore, the rates have to take into account the costs of mailing to the other 99% or 98% who fail to respond to the first solicitation. Association plans may produce a higher response because of the sponsor's endorsement, but the insurer has to figure in fees to brokers and others involved in the deal. The same sort of situation applies to policies marketed by television: TV time is expensive, and the company may be sharing part of the revenue from each order with the television stations on which it advertises.

Plans for which there are no medical qualifications must be priced to cover the additional risks the companies assume, so there's no point in buying that kind of policy until you're sure you need it. Try first to obtain regular insurance, either by mail or through agents, at standard premiums.

The lack of premium and other guarantees in many mail-order

policies suggests that it's best to regard them as potential supplements to your individual insurance, not as the core of a family protection program.

CREDIT LIFE INSURANCE

Credit life is one of several kinds of insurance sold through lenders—banks, auto dealers, finance companies, retailers—in connection with their loans and charge accounts. (Others are credit accident and health insurance, which covers your payments if you become disabled, and credit property insurance, which covers the items you buy on credit.)

Although it's usually legal for a creditor to require you to have insurance as security for a debt, state laws generally make it illegal for the creditor to require you to buy it from him or her or someone else he or she names. You have the option of pledging an existing policy or buying coverage elsewhere. If the lender requires the insurance and you buy it from him or her, its cost has to be included in the loan's finance charge and annual percentage rate.

If the insurance isn't required but you decide to buy it anyway, the lender doesn't have to include its cost in the finance charge. Instead, the charges will be set out in a separate statement you're required to sign and date, acknowledging that you're buying the coverage voluntarily. This arrangement allows and even encourages lenders to pressure their customers to buy credit insurance (or at least suggest that they buy it) without actually requiring it: That way, they don't have to reflect the cost of the insurance to the consumer in the annual percentage rate. The price of credit life, which is usually decreasing term coverage, is generally expressed as cents per $100 of initial coverage per year of the loan.

One big catch is that the premium for credit life insurance is usually added to the loan and financed at the same rate, so you end up paying to insure not only the loan principal but also the insurance premium and all finance charges. You are actually insuring the insurance.

Let's say that you're borrowing $6,000 for four years at 13% APR and that credit life costs 75 cents per $100 of coverage.

You'd end up buying insurance not on $6,000 but on $8,036.01. That breaks down like this:

loan principal	$6,000.00
interest on loan	1,725.60
credit life premium	241.08
interest on premium	69.33
total coverage	$8,036.01

This decreasing term policy would cost you $310.41, or $6.47 a month. When credit accident and health premiums are added in, as they usually are, the insurance charges will be two to three times higher. Any way you slice it, that's expensive insurance.

Is credit life ever a good insurance buy?

● Not if you're in your twenties or thirties and eligible for other kinds of life insurance at better rates.

● Not if you're single with no heirs to worry about. Credit life is supposed to protect your surviving family from claims against your estate; if you have no family, you end up protecting the creditor.

● Not if you already have enough insurance to cover the debt.

● And not if your main reason for wanting more insurance is to beef up your overall coverage. Depending on your age and health, you can usually buy long-term policies in large enough amounts for a much smaller unit cost than you can buy credit life.

On the other hand, if you want to insure a small, short-term loan—say $2,000 for two years—credit life may be your only choice.

Credit life also might be a reasonable buy if you can't meet the health requirements for other insurance coverage or if at your age other policies cost even more than credit life. Some creditors deal with more than one insurer, so rates available to you may vary. Ask.

INSURANCE ON YOUR HEALTH

$\mathbf{H}$aving enough health insurance protection should be one of your top priorities, particularly in this age of fast-rising medical costs and treatments with tabs that can easily exceed $100,000. What would happen to your financial well-being if you or someone in your family came down with a prolonged serious illness? Without adequate insurance, how quickly would snowballing medical bills wipe you out?

Questions like these make it obvious that you should have as much health insurance as you can reasonably afford. But your options are more complex than ever. Rising costs have led to new efforts to control them, changing both what is being delivered and how. On top of that, employees are being asked to pay for a bigger portion of their companies' health insurance bills and insurers are trying to steer beneficiaries to providers who have agreed to plans to hold down costs, giving you less say in choosing the hospitals and doctors you can use.

Whether you have an individual policy, use a health maintenance organization (HMO) or have coverage provided where you work, it's more important than ever to sort through and understand your various options. Once you do, chances are you can put together enough coverage at an affordable price.

POPULAR KINDS OF COVERAGE

Unless you have prepaid care in an HMO, you have what's called fee-for-service coverage, which offers a package of protection through group and individual policies. Hospitalization, surgical and medical coverage are often referred to in policies as "basic" coverage and typically pay for bills up to $2,000 or so.

Hospitalization. This will cover you for daily room and board and regular nursing services while in the hospital. You'll also be covered for certain hospital services and supplies, such as X-rays, lab tests, and drugs and medication.

Surgical. This coverage pays for certain surgical procedures in and out of the hospital.

Medical. It covers you for doctors' visits in and out of the hospital. In addition, some plans cover such services as diagnostic tests and various laboratory tests. Some exclude physician coverage for routine physicals and well-baby care and pay only if an illness is diagnosed.

Major medical. Increasingly packaged together with basic coverage, this provides backup coverage that picks up where basic leaves off. Major medical pays the bulk of the bills in case of a lingering illness or serious injury, often protecting you against medical bills of up to $250,000.

Comprehensive major medical is a policy that combines basic and major medical insurance in one plan so that there are few gaps in coverage. Increasingly, both employer-sponsored and private plans combine coverage into comprehensive plans.

Excess major medical. This coverage protects you from the risk of a long-term serious illness. If both you and your spouse have severe heart attacks, for instance, the protection generated by an excess major medical policy could keep your family afloat financially. If you already have health insurance, buying excess major medical lets you increase your coverage without changing policies.

Disability. Disability insurance offsets earnings lost because of an accident or sickness. You can get coverage for both long-term and short-term disability in the form of salary continuation at work or disability insurance, or a combination of the two.

Long-term health care. This relatively new form of health insurance is intended to partly offset the huge costs of nursing home care and, increasingly, reimburse for care in homes for chronic illnesses. The policies are relatively expensive because most are sold individually and group rates aren't widely available. Premiums depend on the amount of the benefits, the number and type of restrictions, and the age of the purchaser.

HOW POLICIES PAY OFF

Having the right kinds of protection doesn't necessarily mean that you are well covered. Most every policy, no matter how good it is, limits the benefits it will pay. The trick is to make sure the benefit limits you choose keep pace with the ever-rising cost of medical care.

There are two basic types of benefit payout methods:

Actual costs. This pays a percentage of the fee for each covered service. The plan may limit coverage to "medically necessary" treatments and to "usual, customary and reasonable" fees for the community. Some services may be fully covered within these guidelines, others only partially covered. For example, 100% of your hospital bills may be paid, but only 75% of your medical and surgical costs might be covered. And if your doctor's fee should be above the usual range for your area, you'll have to make up the difference. Benefits are paid directly to the doctor or hospital.

Predetermined costs. An indemnity, or scheduled, type of policy pays specific dollar amounts for each covered service according to a predetermined schedule or table of benefits. These schedules tend to become out of date even before the ink is dry on the policy. That means you could wind up digging deeper into your pocket to make up the difference between what the insurance company pays and what the doctor or hospital charges.

With either type of policy you can't be sure that you're adequately insured unless you know exactly what's covered, and that may not be completely clear to you. Some health insurance companies are trying to use plain language in their policies, but there are plenty of cases in which you'll want a company to spell out exactly what a term means.

For instance, what does coverage for a preexisting condition really mean? Are you covered for a preexisting condition you didn't know about when you took out the policy, or just for known conditions that the insurance company agrees to accept? How long after a policy is in force will the insurance finally kick in for a preexisting condition? And how broadly does a company interpret such terms as "not medically necessary" and "not reasonable and customary?" As for disability insurance, are you covered if you can't perform any job your education or training prepared you for, or only if you can't perform your normal job? In the case of a long-term care policy, what restrictions define when care can begin? For instance, is a stay in a hospital or a skilled nursing facility necessary before you can claim other benefits? If so, how long is the required waiting period between discharge and entry into a nursing home?

DEDUCTIBLES AND LIMITATIONS

Conceivably, you could buy health insurance to cover the expense of bandaging a cut thumb. But who needs that kind of insurance? You can pay those bills yourself. Insuring such commonplace and financially insignificant needs, or even routine visits to your doctor, would only make your health insurance more expensive.

Catastrophic illnesses are something else. You want insurance to help you pay for dire eventualities precisely because you couldn't afford to pay for them yourself. And naturally you want the protection to be as cheap as possible because the cheaper the protection is, the more of it you can afford.

That's why health insurance is sold with a system of deductibles and coinsurance. A deductible is the amount you pay—say, anywhere from $100 to $1,000 in a year—before the insurance company makes any payments. Coinsurance, or the copayment, is the percentage of the bill you pay above the deductible, with the insurance company paying the rest up to the policy limits. For instance, you may pay 20% to 30% in coinsurance up to $2,500 or so, after which the company takes over up to the maximum.

The higher your deductibles and coinsurance, the lower your premium. You should try to match the deductible on your major medical coverage to the limits of your basic coverage. That way your major medical policy will pick up right where your basic policy leaves off. If you're getting comprehensive coverage from your employer, you may not be able to match the coverage precisely but you may still be able to select from various mixes of copayments, premiums and deductibles for the arrangement that best suits your needs.

Deductibles can vary within a policy, with certain services having higher deductibles than others. Deductibles that apply to the family as a whole are usually preferable to individual deductibles for each family member. With the former, once one or two members have met the family deductible, any illness or injury striking other family members is covered immediately.

Various limits and exclusions are written into the policy, too. For instance, there may be a limit to how many days you can stay in the hospital and still be covered. There is also a limit to how long you have to combine deductibles to reach the point at which the insurance begins to pay. If you don't reach that point within a stated time, often a year, you have to go back to square one and start counting toward the deductible sum all over again.

Similarly, there is usually a limit to the benefits payable. You may have either a maximum limit for each cause of illness, or an annual or lifetime maximum for all illnesses. For family coverage, an annual limit of $500,000 or $1 million may be worth a few more dollars a month in premiums than a policy with a $100,000 limit. Many plans also dictate the hospitals or doctors you can go to, or require you to pay more for visiting a provider not under contract with the policy; but most cover you in full anywhere in the U.S.

You are excluded from coverage for care in government hospitals and for illnesses and accidents covered by workers' compensation.

Renewability. A group plan is renewable as long as your employer pays the premium and the insurance company chooses to keep the policy in force, but you have to be careful about the renewability terms of an individual policy. Some companies sell optionally renewable policies, which gives them the right to end coverage when your policy period is over. Your best bet is a noncancelable type of health policy that will cover you at the same premium and benefit level up to a certain age— 65, for instance—as long as you pay the premiums. This plan gives you the broadest guarantees.

Your next best bet is a guaranteed renewable policy. It's like a noncancelable policy in that the company can't refuse to cover you as long as you pay your premiums and no acts of fraud are involved. But it differs in that premiums can be raised if the entire class to which you belong—meaning your occupation, age or gender—gets a premium increase.

MAKING SURE YOU HAVE ENOUGH

How much basic protection should you have? There are a variety of opinions about this. A study conducted by Pracon, Inc., a research firm, under a grant from Roche Laboratories, concluded that the "minimum adequate benefit package" should cover hospital care and medication for at least 15 days; physicians' services, including hospital, office and home visits; X-rays and laboratory work; prenatal care; inpatient psychiatric care; outpatient services; and nursing home care. The insurance should pay 80% of the costs except for psychiatric care, for which any inpatient benefit is considered adequate.

What should you have in the way of major medical? For individuals, the Pracon study recommends coverage that would pay at least $250,000 in benefits over your lifetime and also provide stop-loss, or cost-sharing, protection, an all-important safeguard that puts an annual limit, often $1,000, on your share of costs.

Most major medical is 80/20: The company pays 80% and the policyholder pays 20% of costs above a deductible, which is also paid by the policyholder. Deductibles range from $100 to $2,500 or even more.

As health care costs spiral upward, so do those out-of-pocket expenses. Once, if insurance covered 75% of your costs, that seemed adequate, but today it's very easy to run up a $100,000 hospital bill. With 75% coverage you'd have to pay $25,000.

But not if you have stop-loss protection. No matter how high the bills run up, or for how long, you pay no more than the stipulated amount in any one year.

Here's how such a plan works: After the policyholder pays a $100 deductible, the insurance company pays 80% of the first $5,000 of covered expenses during a five-year benefit period. The company pays 100% of any additional expenses up to $1 million. The policyholder's obligation would be capped at $1,100—the $100 deductible plus 20% of $5,000.

Insurers offer various choices of stop-loss limits. As with deductibles, the higher the limit, the lower the premiums.

FINDING A POLICY YOU CAN AFFORD

Most health insurance is provided by employers, who pay the premiums themselves or pass along the benefit of group rates to their employees. But if you're on your own, the job of finding affordable care gets tougher.

• If you're in good health, you're generally better off with a policy that has a low deductible and high copayments. A higher deductible makes more sense for a person in poor health; it means lower copayments for more frequent visits.

• Because group insurance is cheaper than individual policies, find out whether you're eligible for a group plan through membership in a club, professional or fraternal society, or other organization. If you are not, consider joining some group that offers a group plan.

• If you're in between jobs or starting one but coverage doesn't begin immediately, consider a temporary or short-term policy. They run for three, six, nine or 12 months and are fairly affordable because the policies are either nonrenewable or renewable just once.

• If you leave a job that provided insurance and aren't soon to be covered under new employment, see whether the coverage can be continued or converted to an individual policy. (See stop-gap policies.)

• If you're self-employed and have one or two others on the payroll, look for a local agent who sells group policies to people in similar occupations. Called multiemployer trusts, some policies may require you to provide the health benefits and may link coverage with life insurance.

• Pay close attention to the stop-loss protection, which insures your payments wouldn't exceed a certain amount. You want to keep your expense within reason.

• Try to get a guarantee that you can renew the policy either indefinitely or until you qualify for medicare. This is a decided plus.

The more policies you examine and compare, the better your chances of finding a good buy. Note carefully all conditions, restrictions, exclusions, waiting periods and other terms. Be sure you understand just what is covered and what isn't. Get as much protection as your budget will allow.

For a list of companies that sell major medical policies to individuals, write to the Health Insurance Association of America, 1025 Connecticut Avenue, N.W., Washington, D.C. 20036.

HEALTH MAINTENANCE ORGANIZATIONS

These prepaid medical practices have been billed as a convenient and cost-conscious alternative to traditional fee-for-service medicine and have grown tremendously in recent years. Nearly 30 million people are enrolled in more than 650 HMOs across the country. If forecasts hold up, almost half of the population could be under prepaid care by 1995.

HMOs are booming partly because the government has encouraged their growth. By law, if you work for a company with 25 or more employees that has a health plan and the company is approached by a qualified HMO, the company must not only offer the prepaid option but also kick in at least as much of the premium as would be contributed to alternative insurance. The employees must also be given a reasonable explanation of how the HMO works and how it compares with the company's plan.

How an HMO works. With traditional fee-for-service medicine, you go to your doctor when you believe you have a problem. He or she may decide that you should see one or more specialists or go to a lab or the hospital for special tests. You set up appointments in various locations and fill out insurance forms so that you can be reimbursed for your payments.

In contrast, at an HMO you pay in advance for guaranteed care. It handles just about all your medical and hospital needs—but without the blizzard of paperwork and with hardly any deductibles or copayments. The idea is to make services easily available, often in a clinic-like setting, and to encourage you to come in soon enough to prevent a minor condition from becoming serious.

How they differ. HMOs differ in how they are organized and how they deliver services and pay doctors. In one type, doctors are paid a salary regardless of how many patients they see or treatments they prescribe. Because there is no incentive to give unnecessary service, it is reasoned, the organization incurs fewer costs and patients' premiums can be held down.

When comprehensive services are provided in this fashion and given under one roof, the HMO is called a staff model. Care is provided by a primary-care physician or a nurse practitioner who hears your medical complaints first and then decides whether you should see a specialist or be hospitalized.

In a second type of HMO, called an individual practice association (IPA), doctors earn a fee based on services rendered, usually in their own offices. Because IPAs often allow patients to keep their own doctors, they are gaining favor. The prepaid premium does away with bills and insurance forms, just as in a regular HMO, but because care is usually not centralized, you and your doctor still have the obligation of locating medical facilities as they are needed. Still, as with a traditional HMO, the amount you pay should not depend on the level of services you use.

IPA physicians are paid from premium income, usually less than their standard fee. The difference goes to cover the plan's expenses. If sufficient economies are realized, the cash pool or parts of it may be distributed to participating doctors. If the plan runs short of cash, payments to physicians may be reduced so that members don't have to make up the deficit with higher premiums.

Should you join? A number of studies seem to support the claim that HMO care is more economical. In one government-sponsored study conducted by the Rand Corp., researchers found that a Seattle HMO delivered care on a par with the quality of the fee-for-service system, but for nearly 30% less. Other studies indicate that HMO members' health care bills are smaller on the average and that members tend to go to the hospital less and lose less time from work than patients under traditional care. But it's not clear whether the difference is due to wiser planning or to a tendency of HMOs to attract people who are healthier to begin with.

Increasingly, HMOs have found their record and performance fair game for criticism. The same Rand Corp. study suggests that patient dissatisfaction with medical care has increased along with HMO efforts to hold down costs; 15% of the patients randomly assigned to the Seattle HMO had nothing good to say about their care, compared with a 10% dissatisfaction rate in the traditional fee-for-service setting. The main reasons for favoring conventional pay-as-you-go doctoring over HMOs: shorter waiting time for appointments, easier access to specialists and hospitals, and usually more stable relationships between patients and their physicians.

If you have the option of joining an HMO, forget about the worry that you might have to deal with just any doctor who happens to be on duty when you have a medical problem. The choice of doctors is limited to those on staff or under contract, but you or members of your family will usually have a choice of which doctor you see first when you have a medical complaint. However, in many instances, patients see a nurse practitioner first. He or she prescribes treatment or refers you to one of the staff specialists; your doctor will hospitalize you when necessary, using one of the hospitals associated with the group. You may have to accept a stand-in in an emergency or if your own doctor is off duty, but this happens in private practice, too.

In a well-run HMO you are encouraged to come in for periodic checkups and to make doctor appointments whenever justified. Most plans cover routine visits, checkups, major illnesses requiring hospitalization, anesthesia, lab work, X-rays, children's immunizations, and physician and surgeon services. But details vary among plans.

Because of the economies achieved in HMOs through preventive medicine and cost control, there is additional cash, at least in some of them, to expand preventive and support services. These include courses in prenatal care, physical fitness, weight control and smoking cessation. Some groups provide guidance in reducing the risk of chronic ailments or controlling such disorders as high blood pressure and diabetes.

Before you join. HMOs are not for everyone. You may not be eligible for HMO protection as part of a benefits package offered by your employer or a group. If so and the HMO idea appeals to you, find out whether the HMO accepts single applications. Some do, but only during a once-a-year enrollment period.

Eligibility for medicare could affect your benefits under an HMO. Not all HMOs accept medicare patients, but those that do could fill in the gaps in your coverage. At least 150 HMOs in 33 states offer health care and hospitalization to medicare beneficiaries who enroll by taking out part B doctors' coverage and paying an extra premium. Because no health screening is required, this prepaid program covers most preexisting conditions with few or no copayments or deductibles. Depending on the particular HMO's benefits, enrollees can limit or do away with so-called medigap insurance along with the bother of filling out insurance forms.

If your employer offers the HMO option, listen to the explanation, read the written information and try to find out whether joining would be a good idea. Pinning down the benefits you can count on is important, but you should also find out when you can get back into your company's conventional insurance program without loss of coverage if you become disenchanted or for any other reason.

A new hybrid HMO product may make such concerns obsolete, however. Called an open-ended HMO, it extends conventional fee-for-service coverage to members. Enrollees get all the benefits of prepaid care but also have the option of going outside of the plan to see another physician, typically under another insurer, and paying for the privilege in copayments. The idea is catching on; at least 400,000 people are enrolled in open-ended HMOs.

Even though some HMOs are responding with more flexible plans, choosing among the ones available still requires your careful consideration. Here are some tips.

Know what you're giving up. To some people, the main drawback of an HMO is having to give up their present doctor, along with easy access to specialists and hospitals outside of the plan, then having to pick a new one from the HMO's list. That may sound like a fair trade-off for lower costs, if you understand the rules from the start. But a lot of people don't. Although HMOs reimburse for emergency care out of town, coverage for outpatient nonemergency care outside the geographical area of the plan is usually not covered. If the plan has no reciprocal arrangement and you travel a lot, consider other health care setups.

Some HMOs assign nurse practitioners and medical aides to deal with routine complaints, which could make you feel uncomfortable if you prefer to have a physician handle your medical concerns. To keep costs under control, most HMOs require you to see doctors within the plan unless some special care is unavailable or your HMO doctor can make a referral. If you want a second opinion, you'll probably have to pay for the privilege yourself.

Weigh your choices. The makeup of your family and how extensively an HMO covers services that are important to you are key considerations. A family with two children needing vaccinations and care for common childhood illnesses and a mother requiring obstetrical and gynecological checkups might find an HMO worthwhile. But a couple in their twenties with no kids could find that a simple indemnity plan is better for them. Someone else who expects to go for extended psychiatric treatment might think twice about an HMO; they generally limit mental health therapy to ten to 20 visits and only if the HMO primary-care physician approves it.

Consider convenience. Most HMOs tend to be concentrated in metropolitan areas. Be sure the HMO you're thinking of joining is within reasonable distance of your home or office.

Size up the quality of care.   Look for HMOs with open houses and tour them during these periods, noting the condition of facilities. If it's an IPA-type, set up a get-acquainted meeting with one or more of the primary-care physicians. Find out whether physicians as a group have been willing to stay for a considerable period with the HMO. Most HMOs provide doctors' biographies listing their specialties and credentials. About 62% of all doctors with active practices are certified in their specialties by national boards. There is no reason to expect a smaller proportion in an HMO. The higher the percentage, say some experts, the better the HMO.

Check out the plan's health.   Ask the HMO for the names of members who can tell you how it rates with them. Be wary of any that refuse. To get and keep its designation as "federally qualified," an HMO must provide a prescribed list of services, assure financial solvency and meet certain standards for staff and facilities. More than half of all HMOs can call themselves federally approved, but the absence of approval shouldn't automatically rule out a group. Reliable prepaid practices existed long before the government got into the act. And responsible plans comply with HMO rules in their state. Ask the state agency, often the department of insurance, for the track record of the HMO or, if it's just starting, whether it's seeking federal approval.

Assess the plan's costs.   In the mid 1980s, family premiums in HMOs averaged $196 monthly, with a low of $153 and a high of $240, according to InterStudy, a Minnesota-based health-policy research firm. Members generate some out-of-pocket costs. They averaged about $400 per family per year, about half of what fee-for-service patients laid out in another survey. Note that additional fees in a federally qualified HMO can add up to no more than 200% of the premium's cost.

Understand the complaint system.   HMOs usually have staff members handle problems or complaints. But there should also be a formal grievance procedure designed to have unresolved differences reviewed at a higher level. At a federally qualified group plan, provision is supposed to be made for appeal as high as the government office that regulates the HMOs. Your employer should be able to tell you whether there are any major complaints outstanding against the HMO it is doing business with.

A booklet, *Choosing an HMO: An Evaluation Checklist,* by the American Association of Retired Persons, contains helpful tips for anyone considering prepaid care. For a free copy, write to Fulfillment Section, AARP, 1909 K St., N.W., Washington, D.C. 20049.

PREFERRED PROVIDER ORGANIZATIONS

Preferred provider organizations started up in the 1970s and are now changing the rules of fee-for-service care. Increasingly popular with employers, PPOs steer employees to cooperating doctors and hospitals who agree to a predetermined plan for keeping costs down. They have caught on where there are doctor surpluses or HMOs already competing for business. If you have PPO coverage, you agree to use providers that your insurer and employer have contracted with at discount rates. You can usually use any doctor you want under a PPO, but you'll probably pay the difference between the nonmember provider's bill and the PPO discounted rate. Even if your doctor accepts the PPO rate, your plan may make you pay extra if he or she is not a member of the plan.

Because a PPO usually does away with deductibles and coinsurance, joining could save you money if you stay with its list of approved providers. But a PPO could complicate a decision to use a specialist or facilities outside. Check any such deals to make sure you're covered without a penalty if you get sick or injured in another town.

TRIPLE OPTION PLANS

A fairly recent program, called triple option, makes it possible for you to switch among PPO, HMO and regular fee-for-service plans as your needs change, and without waiting periods for preexisting conditions. Insurers may charge a higher deductible for the traditional plan than for an HMO or PPO, but you may be willing to trade higher premiums if you need to see a specialist. Triple option plans may have óne premium payment regardless of which setup you pick, or the premium may rise or fall as you float among options. Periods during which you are locked into a given option may vary from three months to a year.

EMPLOYER-RUN PLANS

Soaring health insurance costs have led some employers, primarily large corporations, to establish group coverage in the form of self-funded health plans for their employees. The employer provides health benefits funding to employees and may contract with an insurance company for additional coverage or for such administrative services as processing claims.

Some employers are also giving workers breaks on deductibles and premiums if they participate in company-sponsored wellness programs aimed at helping them adopt healthful lifestyles. Programs vary widely, often including blood pressure monitoring and aerobics classes.

DISABILITY INSURANCE

Disability insurance, which pays you when you can't work because of illness or injury, can be crucial to you and your family. Millions of people have some form of disability coverage from private or employer-sponsored programs. But only a fraction of those people have long-term coverage, which pays benefits generally up to age 65. The social security disability income (SSDI) program also offers disability insurance, but only for severe, long-term disability. Seventy percent of SSDI claims are rejected.

Disability programs vary so much and are so riddled with technicalities that you should assume you don't have adequate coverage until you dig into the detailed provisions.

The protection you get from any plan depends to a large extent on how strictly it defines disability. The plan may dictate, for instance, that you're not entitled to benefits unless you are totally disabled. And that can be severely interpreted to mean unable to perform every duty pertaining to a specific occupation or unable to engage in any other type of paid work as well.

A plan that covers partial disability, on the other hand, requires only that you be unable to perform one or more functions of your particular job. However, many policies won't pay benefits unless the partial disability is preceded by a period, commonly a year, of total disability.

You will have to shop around if you want to buy an individual, private disability policy to supplement whatever coverage you may have from other sources. The premiums for these plans can be exorbitant, ranging from a few hundred dollars a year to more than $2,000; they are being pushed higher by the AIDS scare.

Insurers won't cover your entire salary because they want you to have some incentive to return to work. Generally, the higher your salary, the smaller the proportion of it you can protect. If you make $50,000, you can probably insure around two-thirds of your gross income. But unlike benefits paid under an employer's plan, those paid under a private plan are tax-free.

If you're at least partly vested under your company's pension plan, find out whether it would provide some income to reduce your need for individual coverage. Then check with several insurance companies, because premium rates and policy provisions differ considerably. Before you start contacting companies, take the time to familiarize yourself with these essential terms:

Guaranteed renewable. Insist that the policy be guaranteed renewable, which means the insurance company can't cancel your insurance as long as you pay the premium. But most companies will cancel your policy when you reach age 65. And the rates can be increased, depending on a company's experience with those in your class—determined by such factors as age, occupation and income level.

Guaranteed future insurability. This feature permits you to hike coverage to match future salary increases without having to pass a medical exam.

Noncancelable. Don't buy any plan that can be canceled flat and leave you without coverage.

Waiting, or elimination, period. This is the time you have to wait for payments to begin after the onset or diagnosis of an injury or disease. The longer the delay, the lower your premium will be. Waiting periods generally are 14, 30, 60, 90 or 120 days. One way to save money is to figure out how long savings and other income sources can carry you before you would need benefits to begin. The first check won't arrive until a month after the elimination period ends.

Benefit period. This is the length of time the policy will pay disability benefits; the longer the period, the higher the premiums. For instance, one company's plan that pays to age 65 costs 40% more than its policy that promises payments for only five years.

Cost-of-living rider. Under this policy addition, both benefits and earning levels can be indexed to keep abreast of inflation. It takes effect after you start receiving benefits and may raise your premium some 20 to 25 percent.

Incontestable clause. An optional provision, this clause states that the insurance company may not contest the validity of the contract after it has been in force for two or three years. This can be important if you have a preexisting medical condition. If you disclose the condition on your application and the company does not disclaim it at that time or within the two- or three-year period, the company must honor subsequent claims.

If you are unaware of a medical problem or don't consider it serious, you may fail to disclose it on your insurance application. Yet your condition could later cause serious illness. Some insurance companies may consider it to be an illness beginning before you had coverage; if you don't have the incontestable clause in your contract, you won't get paid.

Coordination of benefits. This provision integrates disability income with various other insurance sources so that you can't collect more than 100% of the allowable benefits.

Waiver of premium. If the policy includes this feature, you won't have to pay any premiums while you're disabled. Such a provision lasts for the duration of the contract. It is well worth having.

Disability coverage is usually subject to a couple of important limitations. If your company provides coverage under a group plan, you may not be able to buy a personal policy. Many employers pay all or most of the cost of group policies. But you can't take the coverage with you when you leave the company—unlike group term life insurance, which can usually be converted into an individual cash-value policy.

Social security provides long-term disability protection, but it lays down what are probably the toughest qualifying standards in the field:

• Unless you become disabled before age 22, you must have worked in a covered job for five of the last ten years.

• There must be a physical or mental condition that prevents you from doing any gainful work.

• The disability must last at least 12 months or entail a condition expected to result in death.

• You must wait a minimum of five months before receiving any benefits.

The law leaves the job of determining an individual's eligibility under those and other federal guidelines to state officials. A national review is conducted occasionally to check the uniformity of state decisions.

LONG-TERM CARE POLICIES

Most older Americans have no insurance to cover the incredibly expensive long-term care that is often necessary when chronic illness or disability strikes late in life. Nursing home costs alone average about $25,000 a year. At the most expensive centers the bill can go as high as $50,000 or more.

Medicare and traditional medicare supplement insurance will pick up very little of the tab. In fact, the two combined paid less than three percent of total nursing home costs in 1986. What's more, they cover only nursing home skilled care, not the lesser levels of intermediate and custodial care that most people actually require. Most people pay most of the costs out of their own pockets.

The rest of the cost of long-term care is borne by medicaid, the medical assistance program financed jointly by the federal and state governments. But before a person can become eligible, his or her assets, including life savings, must be pared down to a minimum. That has left many beneficiaries virtually impoverished.

For those who think far enough ahead, private insurance is available to ease the burden. More than 70 insurance companies offer policies designed to cover a large chunk of the costs of long-term care. For an annual premium that can range from around $100 to as much as $2,500, depending on the level of care you insure and your age when you buy the policy, you can cover a specified stay in a long-term-care facility and, in an increasing number of instances, be reimbursed for certain home health services. Nursing home coverage can be for as little as two years or as long as a lifetime, with a cap on benefits that can range from $12,000 to $200,000.

These are essentially indemnity policies. That means insurers pay a fixed amount (from $10 to $200 a day) rather than a percentage of the fees, as with comprehensive insurance. An indemnity policy tends to become outdated almost as soon as you sign the agreement. If it has no index for inflation, it's up to you to peer down the road and try to gauge the amount of protection you would need to make a dent in future bills.

Insurance for long-term care is also relatively expensive because policies are sold only on an individual basis, although some trials with groups are under way.

Premiums start out at relatively modest levels for those in their 50s and rise steeply with advancing years, making the insurance costly or even prohibitive. For instance, a policy being sold in the late 1980s cost about $340 a year for a $50 daily benefit if you were 50 years old; the annual premium for the same policy for a 65-year-old was about $1,300—nearly four times as much. Buying at a younger age locks in the lower rate if the policy provides for a level premium and guarantees your insurability before a disqualifying condition or disease has had a chance to develop.

How do the policies pay? To be covered, care must almost always be defined as medically necessary or be preceded by a medical event. Then, depending on the beneficiary's condition and the terms of the policy, care proceeds through several stages.

Skilled care. This is medically necessary care provided by licensed, skilled medical professionals—nurses and therapists, for example—working under the supervision of a doctor. Restoring the patient to a condition approximating the state of health before the illness or accident is the goal.

Intermediate care. This also requires supervision by a physician and skilled nursing care but is needed only intermittently, rather than continuously over a prescribed period.

Custodial care. Even if they escape disabling illness and injury, many elderly people reach a stage when performing such simple tasks as bathing, dressing and eating is difficult. Supervised custodial care, which is the nursing home service in greatest demand, can help. Benefits cover mainly room and board plus payments for assistance with daily living.

Home health care. Depending on the policy, benefits for home health care may range from homemaking and chore services to occupational therapy and laboratory services.

Comparing policies. Like any competing products, long-term policies have contingencies and options that may fit the needs of one person but not another. Whether you want to consider such coverage for yourself or help an aging family member decide, it's essential to have the facts. The more closely a policy can be tailored to the beneficiary's needs, the more sense it will make in the long run. But not so obvious is that a plan without all levels of care—including custodial—is of very limited value. Options to look for: a waiver of premiums once benefits start or three to six months later; language guaranteeing renewal of the policy (renewal at the company's option is more likely to protect the seller than you). Here are other points to compare.

Where will care be delivered? A so-called facilities policy pays for only those services provided in a skilled nursing facility, even if the care given is intermediate or custodial. A care policy will cover levels of care given in less intensive surroundings if it otherwise complies with standard definitions. Language in the policy may require that care be provided in a skilled nursing facility or licensed nursing home. The proportion of such institutions varies from state to state, with more than 90% of California's facilities classified as skilled, for example, compared with only about 5% in Oklahoma. Ask local officials from agencies on health or aging for the makeup of various long-term-care facilities to help you evaluate competing policies.

Is there a health screen? The insurer will want to know the state of the beneficiary's health; stretching the truth could later invalidate the policy. It is safe to assume that applicants with a recent record of illness or institutionalization will not be acceptable candidates for insurance, although this is not usually stated directly in the policies.

When do benefits begin and end? Even the best policies have restrictions that define when care can begin and under what circumstances. Restrictions typically require a stay in a hospital or skilled nursing facility before you can claim other benefits. Even then, between discharge and entry into a nursing home there is usually a delay called a waiting, or elimination, period of up to 20 or even 100 days. This period serves as a sort of deductible in days, with the beneficiary picking up the interim tab. The policy should clarify this, and you should be told what levels of care are covered and for how long.

Does the policy exclude any medical problems? Like conventional health insurance, long-term-care policies carry exclusions for preexisting conditions, which usually won't be covered for six months or a year after a policy is in force. Nearly half of all nursing home patients are confined because of Alzheimer's disease or other organically related mental disorders. Pass up any policy that excludes "mental disorders" unless the seller satisfies you that organically based mental disease is covered.

A booklet, *Before You Buy: A Guide to Long-Term Care Insurance*, by the American Association of Retired Persons, contains useful information for anyone considering these complex policies. For a free copy, write to Fulfillment Section, AARP, 1909 K St., N.W., Washington, D.C. 20049.

SPECIAL KINDS OF HEALTH INSURANCE

Stop-gap policies. Most group plans include a grace period that extends your coverage for a month or so after you leave a job that provided employer-sponsored health insurance. Check with your employer to find out when your coverage will lapse if you find yourself in such a situation. Also ask whether you can convert from a group plan to an individual policy with the same company, picking up the premium payments yourself. An individual policy won't offer as much protection as the group plan.

Your employer may be required under federal law to let you continue group coverage for up to 18 months. Although you must pay the entire premium plus an administrative fee of 2%, the benefit of group rates could save you as much as $100 a month. And you don't have to qualify medically. If you plan to retire soon, find out whether you can remain in your employer's group health plan. Some employers pay all or part of the premium for retirees.

Several companies offer interim insurance plans for people who don't qualify for group coverage but expect to in the near future. Such policies are offered for 60, 90 or 180 days. Contact insurance agents to see what's available. The premium will vary according to the coverage, where you live and the size of your family. It could easily amount to $100 or more per month.

Dread disease insurance. These policies cover only specified ailments, such as cancer or multiple sclerosis. Often, dread disease policies merely duplicate coverage already being paid for in comprehensive health insurance policies. In no case should such policies be purchased as anything other than a supplement to a broad health insurance package, and then only after careful review and cost comparisons with excess major medical policies. Individual cancer policies have been banned from sale in several states on the grounds that they provide minimal economic benefits.

Dental insurance. More and more Americans are able to handle some dental care costs through a dental insurance or prepayment plan. The number covered is over 100 million.

Keep in mind that dental insurance is different in principle from medical insurance. When you buy coverage for medical bills, you're paying for protection against an unknowable future event, a medical problem that could even mean bankruptcy. Basic dental policies cover the recurrent and predictable, such as exams, cleanings and cavities that nearly all of us have at one time or another. So dental insurance is more a way of preventing small problems from becoming large ones than it is of guarding against the unexpected.

Virtually all dental policies are sold to groups, such as company employees, members of unions and associations and school groups. In every group some participants are bound to need little dental care, some a lot. Sharing the risk in this way helps control the costs. If the choice of whether to sign up were left to individuals, those with known problems would more likely be customers than those with sound teeth.

Can you buy individual coverage? Not easily. Most insurers believe individual coverage is a bad deal for them, because there is no spreading of the risk and patients with individual policies tend to use the benefits heavily. So about the only way you can get individual protection is to buy it in the form of an expensive rider on another health policy.

Dental coverage is becoming available in some HMOs, but don't assume all dental work is free after the premium is paid. Like regular dental insurance, HMO coverage stresses improvement in oral health. That means that preventive measures, such as examinations, cleaning and fluoride treatments, are usually covered in full to encourage their use. More extensive work—fillings, caps and the like—often require you to shell out a deductible before benefits start. Orthodontic benefits have lifetime limits; in one big HMO this is $500. Plans also have annual limits for all types of dental care.

Medigap insurance. Despite recent enhancements in medicare coverage (see Chapter 24) many people 65 and over still buy supplementary health policies as a safeguard against big bills. An estimated two-thirds of those under medicare buy medicare supplement, or "medigap" policies.

Here are some tips on choosing such a policy.

• The policy should supplement parts A and B of medicare.

• It should be written in easy-to-understand language.

• It should not exclude coverage of a preexisting health condition for more than six months.

• It should permit cancellation within 30 days without financial loss.

• It should offer reasonable economic benefit in relation to the premium charged.

You can get some help from the Medicare/Private Insurance

Checklist, available from the U.S. Department of Health and Human Services. This four-page worksheet shows the limits of medicare coverage and gives you space to chart the terms and benefits of supplemental policies you are considering. You can get copies of the checklist free from the office that handles your medicare.

If you continue working after age 65, you should know that federal antidiscrimination law now requires employers of 20 or more persons to offer employees age 65 through 69 the same coverage they provide younger employees. Affected workers must designate either their employer's plan or medicare as their primary insurer, that is, the first to be billed for claims.

Previously, medicare was primary. Employer-provided insurance paid only when the government coverage fell short or was used up. Also, employers could excise from their group plans the coverage provided by medicare, or they could simply provide elderly workers with medicare supplement, or medigap, insurance. Medigap can no longer be offered by employers, but insurance for certain items not covered by medicare is permissible.

You can get information about medicare from any social security office. Ask for a copy of *Your Medicare Handbook; Employed Medicare Beneficiaries Age 65 Through 69*; and *Recent Changes in Medicare*. All are free.

INSURANCE ON YOUR CAR

A car insurance policy is not what you would call interesting reading. But if you want to know what you are entitled to for your insurance premiums, your policy constitutes the best single source of information.

The following explanations of the major parts of the typical policy should help you pick your way through the legal thickets so common to insurance contracts.

LIABILITY PROTECTION

This part of the policy provides help when you (or another person driving your car with your permission) injure or kill someone or damage property. To see how liability insurance works, assume an accident for which you are clearly responsible: You run through a red light, strike another car and injure the driver.

Your liability coverage obliges the company to defend you—in court, if necessary—and pay claims to the other driver for car damage and bodily injuries, including medical and hospital costs, rehabilitation, nursing care and possibly lost income and money for "pain and suffering." The liability section of your policy does not compensate you for damage to your own car or any injuries to you. They are covered by other parts of the policy.

Assume now that you are involved in an intersection collision and there are no witnesses or evidence to pin the blame on either driver. Here, too, under your liability coverage, your insurance company agrees to defend you against most proceedings the other driver may take against you.

The company limits its liability payments to the policy limits, or the amount of coverage you select. You can be held personally accountable for any excess.

Liability coverage is mandatory in nearly three-quarters of the states (the others have financial-responsibility laws that are usually met by this coverage). But state requirements are modest—typically up to $25,000 for bodily injury suffered by one person, up to $50,000 for all people hurt in the same accident, and up to $10,000 for property damage resulting from that accident (expressed as 25/50/10 in a split-limit policy). If you bought only enough liability insurance to satisfy your state's minimum but had an accident in a state with a higher minimum, your company may exceed the limit.

Alternatively, the company may use a single-limit policy with one liability limit that applies to total payments arising from the same accident, regardless of the number of people injured or the amount of property damaged.

The company's expenses for defending you against liability actions don't count toward the liability limits. You're also entitled to extra money for bail bonds (up to $250) and earnings lost (up to $50 a day) to attend hearings and trials at the company's request. However, many policies free the company from any obligation to continue your legal defense for sums above the amount it has to pay.

How much liability protection should you carry? You should carry as much as you can comfortably afford, because damage claims today are sometimes settled for millions.

Given the recent surge in medical and repair costs and the likelihood of further increases, it's apparent that the state minimums don't come close to covering the cost of a serious accident. Authorities inside and outside of the insurance industry recommend a minimum of $100,000 per person, $300,000 per accident and $25,000 for property damage, or a minimum of

$300,000 on a single-limit policy. Raising your limits isn't expensive: $300,000 in coverage costs 20% more than $100,000, on average. The rule of thumb: The more coverage you buy, the less you have to pay in premiums per $1,000 of coverage. Ask your agent for precise figures. You may even want to investigate raising your liability coverage further through an umbrella policy (see Chapter 9).

COLLISION PROTECTION

Just as someone who thinks you're responsible for an accident can sue you, you can claim damages from others you believe are to blame. Why, then, protect your car with collision insurance? Collision is optional (although it may be necessary to qualify for a new-car loan); it's expensive; and it may be subject to deductibles ranging from $50 to $1,000. Here are the more obvious reasons you need it.

• Despite the most careful driving, you may cause an accident, or at least be held responsible for one. In that case you can't collect for damage to your car by taking action against the other driver. Collision coverage will pay for the damage, even if an accident is your fault.

• It may take a long time to collect if the other driver's insurer contests your claim. With collision coverage you can have your company repair the car and take over your claim against the other driver (a procedure known as subrogation). Your company is ethically, but not legally, bound to fight for enough money to pay you back part or all of the deductible.

• You could get into an accident in which the other driver is at fault but has no liability insurance. Suing could very well enmesh you in a protracted, fruitless legal tangle. As you will see later, the uninsured (or underinsured) motorist coverage of the auto policy does not necessarily protect your car in these situations. Collision will.

• When your car strikes a tree or a lamppost or runs through a barrier or overturns, there is no one to take action against. Only collision will pay for the damage to your car.

The amount of collision coverage your policy provides depends on the type of car and its age. You can vary the total only by buying a policy with a smaller or larger deductible. Premiums are usually much higher for vehicles that are expensive, accident-prone, easily damaged, frequently stolen or hard to repair. Those that score well for safety and durability often cost much less to insure. How much you will be paid for an accident depends on the nature and extent of the damage, whether new or refurbished parts are used, and so on. However, you should be aware of one special restriction: The company is obligated to pay only up to the car's cash value. That means the market value of the car before the accident, minus the salvage value of the damaged vehicle.

For example, say the car was worth $4,000 before the accident and $500 for salvage afterward. The company does not have to pay more than $3,500 in repairs. If the repairs would exceed the amount, the company can take the damaged car and give you the $4,000. If your car was in the kind of condition that would make it worth more than others of its kind, you've got a fight on your hands to get what you think it's worth.

However, there is an exception for new or recent-vintage cars. For an extra premium, some insurers will offer replacement cost coverage for such cars under the collision (and/or comprehensive) part of a policy. This coverage provides for the full cost of replacing a new or similar car—not just its cash value before the accident—as long as the insurer considers the car not repairable.

Many companies will also extend collision coverage, less your deductible, to cars you rent occasionally for personal use. If you are covered, you can turn down the costly collision damage waiver car rental agents sell when you sign up for a rental car. Check with your insurance agent to find out whether your policy covers rental cars. If not and you're a member of an auto club like the AAA, you can get collision protection covering damage to rental cars above a certain amount. Some credit cards provide similar coverage when you charge a rental to them.

MEDICAL PAYMENTS

You, family members, and perhaps other occupants who live with you, qualify for reimbursement of medical costs resulting from auto accidents while in your car, someone else's car, walking or, in many cases, bicycling, regardless of who is at fault. Guests also qualify if they are injured in your car.

Medical payments coverage is available for $1,000 to $100,000 for each person protected by your policy, but people generally carry $5,000 to $10,000. It costs relatively little to raise the coverage.

The company will reimburse a wide range of expenses, from eyeglasses to funeral costs, subject to varying conditions. One policy may pay medical expenses only for the first year after an accident, another for the first three years afterwards, and still another might extend payments to five years, provided you buy more than a stipulated amount of protection. Payments can be reduced to the extent you receive or are entitled to receive compensation from other parts of the policy or from other sources. In certain situations the company may pay only expenses that exceed the compensation obtainable from other insurance. Before you consider additional medical coverage, check to see if you are duplicating coverage already provided under other medical policies, especially comprehensive, high-limit health insurance.

Medical payments insurance is no longer sold in some states because of the introduction of no-fault systems that also allow you to collect medical expenses, as well as other benefits, directly from your own insurer.

UNINSURED AND UNDERINSURED MOTORISTS

There are a lot of people driving without any—or enough—liability insurance. The uninsured/underinsured motorist section of your policy will provide some financial relief if you or family members who live with you are hurt by one of those drivers while you're in your car, walking or, in some policies, bicycling. Guests qualify if they are hurt while in your car. This coverage also applies when you are struck and injured by a hit-and-run driver and, in some cases, by a driver insured by a company that becomes insolvent.

The other driver must be declared legally responsible for the accident. In most states, when who's to blame is in doubt or the amount payable is contested, you and your insurer have to submit your differences to arbitration. This kind of insurance usually covers only costs arising from bodily injuries. In states in which property damages are included, claims may be reduced by a deductible.

Generally, companies are obligated to pay claims up to the same minimum amount fixed by your state for liability insurance. But often you can purchase higher limits for an additional premium. Most states require insurance companies to offer uninsured or underinsured coverage; some companies combine them. Where they are offered separately, it's a good idea to get both—and at the same limits.

Before you buy it consider whether this coverage duplicates your health or collision insurance. If so, and if it's optional in your state, you may not need it. However, it does provide damages for pain and suffering while the others may not.

COMPREHENSIVE COVERAGE

A combination of liability, collision, medical payments and uninsured/underinsured motorist insurance would seem to take care of all conceivable risks. Yet none of that insurance would necessarily cover losses to your vehicle from these hazards: theft of the car or some of its contents, collision with an animal, glass breakage, falling objects, fire, explosion, earthquake, windstorm, hail, water, flood, malicious mischief, vandalism or riots. Comprehensive insurance, which is optional, will handle those losses, usually up to the car's cash value, either in full or subject to a deductible.

In some areas, if you keep your car in a garage or off-street parking area or install a good antitheft device—for instance, one that prevents the car from being started—you will qualify for a reduction in your comprehensive coverage premium.

You are also entitled to some compensation for renting a car if yours is stolen. Check your policy to see what the daily rate is and how long it lasts; major carriers provide varying allowances, subject to state requirements. A typical example is $10 a day starting 48 hours after you report the theft to the company, up to a maximum of $300.

NO-FAULT INSURANCE

As indicated earlier, liability insurance constitutes your main financial defense against catastrophic accidents you cause that result in long hospital stays, permanent physical impairments or extensive property destruction affecting others. However, the crucial drawback to liability coverage is its requirement that one person must be blamed for an accident in order for another person to qualify for compensation. And proving fault, which is not always possible, can lead to payment delays and expensive legal action.

No-fault insurance is an effort to take the fault out of liability. The idea is to have medical expenses incurred by accident victims paid by their own insurance companies, regardless of who is to blame for the accident, thereby eliminating the costs and delays in legal actions.

Plans that reduce the fault element in some way have been enacted in a number of states, including Colorado, Connecticut, Florida, Georgia, Hawaii, Kansas, Kentucky, Massachusetts, Michigan, Minnesota, New Jersey, New York, North Dakota and Utah. Other states—Arkansas, Delaware, Maryland, New Hampshire, Oregon, Pennsylvania, South Carolina, South Dakota, Texas, Virginia, Wisconsin and Washington, as well as the District of Columbia, have adopted "add on" plans that increase the benefits you can obtain from your own insurance company but do not restrict your rights to pursue a liability claim. No-fault laws vary greatly, but they follow a general pattern.

• Your insurance company has to pay you and others covered by your policy for medical bills, wage losses, the cost of hiring people to do household tasks you are unable to perform as a result of injuries, and funeral expenses up to specified limits.

• Property damage is excluded from the no-fault insurance drivers must buy. (Property losses remain covered by other parts of the policy.)

• No-fault benefits do not include compensation for pain and suffering claims. For those, you have to depend on a liability action.

• You usually can't take action against others on a liability basis until expenses of the type covered by the no-fault insurance exceed a certain amount. And conversely, you are immune to suits by others until their costs exceed that limit. To protect themselves against fault-based suits permitted under no-fault regulations, drivers in some states where the limits are especially high must continue to buy traditional liability insurance. But liability payments may be reduced by compensation received under the no-fault provisions. The add-on plans generally provide benefits similar to, but less generous than, the no-fault programs.

HOW YOUR RATE IS SET

The amount you pay for auto insurance is the product of a complex process that begins when you first apply for a policy. At that point you are screened by a company underwriter who decides whether the company wants to insure you and if so, in what general category to fit you.

One large company, for example, separates drivers into three underwriting categories: preferred, standard and non-standard. Its rates for preferred applicants generally run 15% lower than standard rates. Nonstandard policyholders are charged anywhere from 35% to 75% more than standard rates, depending on the number of accidents they've been involved in and, in many cases, the number of traffic violations.

If you're considered a high-risk driver, you might be rejected and eventually forced into a state assigned-risk plan that requires a regular insurance company to give you protection— at a price that may be at least 50% more than other drivers are charged. Alternatively, one of the regular companies might shunt you into a subsidiary company that specializes in high-risk drivers. Those "substandard" insurers, as they are known in the business, also charge higher premiums.

Once you are accepted for insurance, whatever the plan or premium level, the company has to determine precisely how much you will pay relative to other policyholders for the same amount and type of insurance. To see how that's done, you have to back up a bit in the premium-making process.

Each company periodically computes the premium income it needs in each state in which it operates. It wants enough money to pay for claims and expenses and a margin for profits and contingencies. The total state premium is then allocated among the various territories into which the state is divided for rating purposes. The boundaries are supposed to demarcate areas with significantly different loss records.

The exact relationships vary from one state to another, but according to one study, people in central neighborhoods of small metropolitan areas (100,000 to 400,000 population) generally pay less than the state average; their counterparts in big cities (over one million) pay substantially more. Small-city suburbanites are charged less than the state average; big-city suburbanites are charged somewhat more.

The company establishes in each territory a set of base premiums for the individual coverages that make up auto insurance. Those base rates customarily pertain to a particular stereotype: an adult male with a standard car used only for pleasure. Everyone else pays more or less, depending on the company's evaluation of his or her relative risk potential.

In effect, you are assigned to a group defined according to characteristics that are believed to predict the group's chances of creating insurance losses. Although classification plans differ, the companies employ for the most part these basic criteria: age, sex, marital status, accidents and traffic violations, whether the young driver has taken a driver education course, whether he or she is entitled to a good-student discount, the number of cars, the models, use of the cars (pleasure, commuting, business, farm) and the mileage. Although there have been moves to eliminate ratings based on sex, only two states, Massachusetts and Montana, have done so.

Each characteristic is assigned a numerical weight based on its tendency to increase or reduce the probability of loss. All the factors that apply to you are combined to fix your position on the company's premium scale. A 100 ranking indicates that you pay 100% of the base premium. With a 90 ranking you pay 90% of the base—which means you are getting a 10% discount. If you're pegged at 225, you are charged 225% of the base.

Many companies follow a plan developed by the Insurance Services Office that applies the same weight factors to all parts of the auto policy—bodily injury liability, property damage liability, and so forth.

Despite a few attempts at simplification, risk classification systems have tended to become more complex over the years. Michigan's insurance bureau once estimated that the possible combinations of rating factors in some plans exceeded the number of people insured.

FINDING THE BEST DEAL

As auto insurance rates continue to surge upward, reaching big-ticket purchase status, it pays to search out opportunities to keep your premiums down and still have enough protection. Here are strategies you may not have been using as extensively as you could.

Learn the ins and outs. Posing as ordinary buyers, investigators of the Pennsylvania Insurance Department visited 186 insurance agencies in three cities. Of the 92 Philadelphia agents contacted, fewer than 30% volunteered information on discounts and deductibles that could have reduced premiums 20% to 40%.

If that experience in any way indicates conditions generally, it's best to arm yourself with as much information as you can before approaching agents. You'll find that some kinds of information are easier to get than others. A recent Federal Trade Commission study discovered that it was fairly easy to solicit cost, policy coverage and deductible information from auto insurers; much more difficult was finding out their financial stability and service record—something you'd be interested in knowing if, for example, you get a good cost quote from a company you're not familiar with. You can check out stability from *Best's Insurance Reports: Property-Casualty* at your local library; insurers with an A+ or A rating are considered excellent. (You can also ask an agent how Best's rates his or her company.) For policy service and claims-handling information, check your friends and neighbors for their experiences.

Also contact your state insurance office; many of them keep track of consumer complaints and will share the results if they're asked. Finally, read through your policy carefully so that you're sure of the kind and amount of protection you have.

Contact several companies. The potential savings can be substantial. Every fresh survey confirms that auto insurance companies often charge greatly different premiums for the same coverage. In New York City and elsewhere, premiums of the 20 largest selling companies have been shown to vary sometimes by more than 100%. In a recent survey, *Washington Consumers' Checkbook*, a consumer information magazine published in Washington, D.C., asked 32 insurers for rates on a policy covering a husband, wife and 17-year-old son—all with flawless driving records—living in nearby College Park, Md. The highest premium was $1,409 and the lowest was $563. The average difference between the high and low quotes received was $668.

Rates may not vary as wildly in your area, but the odds are you will discover substantial differences if you take the time to get premium quotations from a number of companies. Begin pricing the insurance you need at a market leader, such as State Farm or Allstate. Then use that quotation as a measure against which to judge identical coverage at other companies. At least 20 state insurance offices distribute auto insurance pricing guides, but the categories they give may not be particularly helpful. Your best bet is to use such a guide to identify your state's most cost-effective insurers. Then get price quotes from a handful and you'll have a truly comparative guide.

Manage your youngsters' driving. Young drivers pay much more than most others because, as a group, they are more accident-prone. Rates will drop several notches when they reach age 25 or if they marry. But meanwhile, if possible, avoid allowing them to become the principal driver of a car. That pushes up the premium even more. Seven of ten leading insurers polled by the Insurance Information Institute give driver-education or good-student discounts to young drivers: commonly 25% off for a consistent B average (good students are statistically superior drivers, hence the break); 10% off for an approved driver-training course; and 10% off for students who spend part of the year at a school more than 100 or 150 miles away from home. A good student away at school who has taken driver's education can actually get a 45% discount from some insurers.

Manage your own driving. Discounts are also common for safe driving records: some companies give 5% off for drivers with three years of a clear record, raising the discount to 10% for drivers with six or more accident- and violation-free years. Depending on who insures you and where you live, you may get discounts if you're a nonsmoker, a woman who is a household's only driver, a senior citizen, or a member of certain professions (such as doctors and lawyers) that are statistically less accident-prone. All ten of the leading insurers polled by the Insurance Information Institute offer a 15% to 20% discount to commuters sharing driving responsibilities in car pools, meaning they don't drive their cars to work every day.

With discounts and merit ratings abounding in the competitive marketplace, heed this caveat: Consider them but don't fixate on them. A discount may very well be offset by a higher premium to begin with.

Check your car's rating. Insurers continue to place surcharges on "muscle" cars, in keeping with their practice of gearing rates to specific makes and models. Some will offer discounts on collision and comprehensive coverage for certain models that score well for safety and durability, but add surcharges for others. The Insurance Services Office provides a rating service used by hundreds of insurance companies.

Before you buy your next car, it might pay to check on such differentials with the insurance company. The companies base their rates on collision-loss experience—the amounts they pay in claims for various vehicles. You can get free loss data on nearly 200 makes and models by requesting the Highway Loss Data Institute Composite chart from the Insurance Institute for Highway Safety, Publications Dept., Watergate 600, Suite 300, Washington, D.C. 20037. Loss data do not necessarily translate into discounts, but they do show which vehicles are most likely to qualify.

Incidentally, a surcharge does not constitute a judgment of a car's quality. The rate variations reflect repair costs, accident frequency, theft losses and other factors.

Consider larger deductibles. A 40-year-old Chicago man who drives his 1987 Chevy Beretta four to nine miles to work every day might be able to cut his collision premiums by about 45% by raising his $100 deductible to $500. He can lower his premium bill for comprehensive by 30% if he increases the deductible for comprehensive coverage from $50 to $250.

With that kind of incentive, it may make sense to choose the highest deductible you can afford to pay without seriously disrupting your finances. With big-ticket awards for liability suits not uncommon, some experts are recommending raising collision deductibles to $500, and even $1,000, while taking on additional liability coverage. The idea is to pay for affordable damage yourself and let insurance kick in for bigger losses. Whatever your situation, you can save something by accepting a larger deductible and thus transferring part of the risk from the company to yourself. It's not an ideal solution, but it's one of the few cost-cutting opportunities that are readily available.

Cut the coverage on an old car. Dropping comprehensive and collision coverage on an old car are a couple of fast ways to reduce your insurance costs. Either course exposes you to additional risk, but remember that the insurance company won't pay more to fix a car than it's worth. Each year's depreciation therefore diminishes the maximum claim you can make against your collision coverage. If your car is five or more years old, you may be better off dropping both collision and comprehensive coverage and banking the savings.

Use the same company for all cars. You are not charged the full rate for the second and successive cars covered by the same policy, so it's usually more economical to put all your cars on one policy. Similarly, consider using the same company for other policies. Some insurers offer discounts of up to 10% if you cover car and home with them.

Avoid installment payments. The company tacks an extra amount onto your premium when you pay in monthly or quarterly installments.

MAKING THE INSURANCE COMPANY PAY

Just about every driver knows how exasperating it can be to

try to collect on an auto insurance claim. The adjuster who does not return telephone calls, the misplaced records, the company that disclaims responsibility, the body shop that argues the job can't be done right at the company's estimate—all these and other annoyances can make the aftermath of a minor accident as upsetting as the accident itself.

There are millions of accidents every year. Maybe 90% of them are covered by insurance. Some of those never reach an insurance company because the policy deductible wipes out the claim or the person at fault elects to pay the damage to avoid the nonrenewal of the policy or an increase in premiums.

When claims are filed, the companies usually settle them reasonably well. Still, a survey commissioned by the American Insurance Association, a large trade group, found that about 25% of the licensed drivers contacted were lukewarm to negative about their companies' claim performance. That finding is supported by the steady stream of complaints to state insurance departments and the fact that many states have adopted rules on unfair claims practices.

The proper strategy for you to follow depends on the issue in dispute, the circumstances of the accident, and so on. Here are several pointers that may prove useful.

Know your rights. If you're dealing with your own company, look for support for your position in the policy, which constitutes a legal agreement between you and the company and spells out its obligations to you. When you're seeking compensation from another company, your agent and friends with experience in similar situations may have an idea of what you can reasonably demand.

Take names. Companies range from the large to the colossal. The largest cover millions of cars and employ thousands of claims workers. To avoid getting lost among the thousands of claims the company is processing each day, record the names and telephone numbers of people you've contacted, take notes on important conversations (don't forget the dates) and make copies of letters and other material affecting your claim.

Don't let them rattle you. Rarely does a government agency offer such sage counsel as in this excerpt from the automobile insurance guide of the Washington State Insurance Department: "Unfortunately, no one can ever be fully compensated for all the trouble and expense that an accident causes. A certain amount of running around is often unavoidable, and petty frustrations sometimes result. Accepting these difficulties is sometimes the only solution, and knowing this in advance may help make a bad situation bearable."

Those words should not be taken as a suggestion to submit gladly to unfair treatment. Anticipating an accident's inevitable inconveniences helps channel your anger into purposeful action. **Be assertive.**   Quietly tell the company representative how you feel and what you need, without derogatory terms that will only harden his or her opposition. If you want a new bumper and the adjuster insists on a rechromed one, state—don't argue—your position: "My bumper was in good condition before the accident. I feel I'm entitled to a new one. I need my car. How can we settle this matter?"

The adjuster is hardly likely to concede immediately. Continue asserting your position calmly and firmly and throw the burden of finding a solution on the adjuster. If he or she won't budge, ask to speak to the supervisor and resume presenting your interests. It may be a transparent tactic, but assertive behavior can work where blustering and name-calling won't.

Don't rush to subrogate.   Subrogation is the process by which your company pays the claim and then goes after the other driver involved in the accident for reimbursement. It's a convenient alternative when the company insuring the driver you believe caused the accident balks at settling. But there are potential drawbacks.

• Your company reduces its payment by your collision deductible. If it succeeds in settling the case with the other insurer, you may be refunded only part of that amount, depending on the sum recovered and the expenses incurred.

• If your company loses its case, you might be judged liable for the accident and become subject to a premium surcharge.

• You may not be entitled to car rental expenses when the claim is covered by your company, as you might be when you take action against the other company.

Check out those possibilities with the agent before you turn over the claim to your company. If you have a strong case against the other driver, it may be better to push the claim with his or her company before you try subrogation.

Complain to the state. Very few states have complete authority to order an insurance company to pay a disputed claim or increase the settlement. Still, state insurance regulators do have influence. A General Accounting Office report a few years ago found that nearly all state insurance departments respond to complaints and often contact the insurance company about them. Moreover, a majority of states have adopted a model law that specifically prohibits several unfair claims practices, including these:

• Failing to acknowledge and act promptly on communications relating to insured claims.

• Failing to provide a reasonable explanation of policy conditions or laws under which a claim is denied or a compromise offer is made.

• Delaying settlement of one part of a claim in order to influence settlement of another. (This would apply, for instance, if the company resists paying car damages to pressure you into settling on bodily injury costs.)

• Not attempting to make prompt, fair and equitable settlements in cases in which liability has become clear.

• Forcing people to start legal action by making unreasonably low settlement offers.

Your state insurance department may have someone designated to handle consumer complaints. If not, write to the insurance commissioner. Keep a copy of the letter and any important material you enclose.

Consider hiring an attorney. If you're injured in an accident, you might want to hire an attorney, even if only for guidance. The decision depends on the extent of the injury and the type of claim.

Attorneys usually charge a percentage of the recovered amount in personal-injury cases. The standard fee is about a third, but you might also have to pay court costs if the case goes to trial. Relatively few go that far.

Look for an attorney with experience in injury claims. If you can't find someone through personal contacts, call the legal referral service in your area. It may be listed in the Yellow Pages.

The available evidence indicates that attorneys obtain larger settlements for their clients than claimants get on their own. However, a study made by insurance companies suggests that the net payment after fees may be less in some cases than unrepresented claimants receive. The standard contingency fee is about 30% to 40%.

Consider paying for the damage yourself. This seems to defeat the purpose for which you bought insurance. But by facing facts as they are, not as they should be, you may find that it costs less in the long run to cover a small loss yourself.

Most insurance companies use demerit rating plans that raise premiums when you violate certain traffic laws or cause an accident that results in physical injuries or damage over a certain amount, say $400. When you take out a policy with some companies, you are assessed penalty points for each incident during the preceding three years, and further points are imposed for accidents and perhaps violations occurring while the policy is in force. All the drivers who regularly drive your car are covered, so you will be surcharged when your spouse or youngster is responsible. Generally, each point sticks on your record for three years.

The premium increase varies with the policy's base premium and the company's surcharge schedule. Just one point might be enough for a 30% hike in the base premium for the collision and liability coverages in your policy. Two points could lead to a doubling of the premium.

Surcharge amounts and practices differ significantly among insurers, so ask about them when you shop for a policy. You'll probably have to ask an agent for the information because it's rarely included in the policy. Find out whether the company has a written explanation of its surcharge and cancellation practices.

Let's say that you scrape the side of the car against a post in a parking lot and the repairs come to $325. If you have a $100 deductible, the company will pay you $225. But if you have already received payment for other small claims, you can be charged with a point that will jump the premium for the next three years by considerably more than $225. You might be better off paying the $225 yourself and saving your points for a big claim.

You're on shakier ground, though, when the accident involves another car or person and you could be considered responsible. Realizing that lawsuits are becoming ever more common, your better bet would be to tell your company promptly about the accident, even if damages are minor and you have no plans to file a claim. The other person might accept your check but come back several weeks or months later with a claim for hidden damages or personal injuries. You would then be forced to refer the case to the insurance company, which, although obliged to pay justified claims against you and defend against unjustified ones, might be reluctant to accept liability. It could argue that you failed to observe the policy clause requiring prompt reporting of accidents. Whether it would actually refuse the case would depend on company policy, state law and the circumstances. Conceivably, it might take a tough position if the delay resulted in the loss of key evidence. Thus, you might add to your problems by paying a claim.

In a survey conducted by the American Insurance Association, about a fourth of the drivers contacted said they had been in accidents in which they or the other person had not filed an insurance claim out of fear their policies would be cancelled or their premiums increased.

Ask your agent for a copy of the company's merit rating provisions. If the figures suggest that it may be advantageous to pay for small losses yourself, you might also consider raising the deductible on your collision policy. That way you will at least save something on the premium.

INSURANCE ON YOUR HOME

THREE COSTLY ERRORS

Insuring your home year after year becomes so routine that you have to be particularly careful to avoid three potentially costly errors:

Assuming that all homeowners policies are alike. Actually, policies come in several varieties, and company versions of those varieties differ.

Taking it for granted that your insurance company charges about the same premium as others. Prices, in fact, sometimes differ by astonishingly large margins.

Failing to update your coverage periodically. Even if your policy protects against inflation, the value of your home may far outpace it; and as you accumulate more possessions, you may find yourself dangerously underinsured.

To make sure you buy the right protection for your property, review the basic aspects of homeowners policies described in this chapter. They're important to know for another reason, too. Homeowners coverage extends over so many fields, some of which seem so unrelated to house insurance, that you may have been neglecting to submit claims for insured losses.

The basic characteristics of the major types of homeowners

policies are summarized on the table on pages 224–226. The descriptions are based on standard forms used by insurance companies and the most common amounts of coverage. Each policy type is identified in the table by number (HO-1, and so on) and, in parentheses, by the name often used in the insurance business. One or the other designation should appear somewhere on your policy, and details may differ. In most states insurance companies have raised the limits on many coverages, and some have added new coverage for debit and fund transfer cards.

Homeowners policies combine two kinds of insurance.

Property protection. These policy clauses pay you for losses to the house and other property. Included is reimbursement for credit card, forgery and electronic fund transfer losses, and for additional living expenses or loss of rental income incurred when someone renting part of your house has to move temporarily because of damage to the living quarters.

The standard amounts payable on losses other than the house itself are generally figured as a percentage of the insurance bought on the house. For instance, with HO-1, 2 and 3, your personal property is automatically insured for 50% of the house amount. (More coverage is available on many policies—see the discussion of "replacement cost" for household contents on page 230.) That 50% is in addition to the insurance on the structure, not part of it. With renter and condominium policies the loss limits are geared to the amount of personal property insurance you buy.

You can increase some coverages without raising the building amount by paying an additional premium. The special limits of liability that are listed in the table represent the maximum paid for those specific items. Usually, jewelry, furs, boats and other items subject to special limits have to be insured separately if you want more coverage. You can also get additional insurance for a number of items or situations that get limited coverage in a standard policy: off-premises theft; coins, stamps, silverware and guns; business losses and household help.

Liability protection. These parts of the policy—the comprehensive personal liability, damage to property of others and medical payments—pay others for injuries or damage caused by you or by an accident around your home. The first obliges the company to pay claims when you are considered legally liable for the injury and to provide a legal defense if necessary. You would be covered, for instance, if a visitor fell into an inadequately safeguarded hole in your walkway or if you struck someone accidentally with a ball on the golf course. To get coverage for medical payments, you aren't required to be legally responsible for the injury.

Liability coverage typically extends to the policyholder and to family members who live in the house.

HOW POLICIES DIFFER

At first sight the house policies (the HO-1, 2 and 3) appear to offer similar protection. And they do on most points. The crucial difference lies in the number of perils your home and property are insured against. A homeowners policy will compensate you for building and personal property losses only if the damage is caused by a peril named in the policy.

Other parts of the policies may not apply unless an insured peril produces the loss. For example, the policies pay for emergency repairs to protect the house after an accident, but on the condition that the damage to the house resulted from an insured peril.

Not all the policies that insure against a particular peril necessarily provide the same degree of protection. The HO-1 payments for broken windows are limited to $100. The HO-1 won't pay for damage to the garage by a car driven by you or someone who lives with you. The HO-2 will pay you in that situation for damage to the garage but not for damage to a fence, driveway or walk. The HO-3 will pay in both cases.

The difference in price between an HO-1 and an HO-3 policy can range from a few dollars to 30% or more. Despite restrictions here and there, the HO-1 gives you good, basic protection. But more cautious owners will undoubtedly feel more secure with the HO-2, which generally costs only 5% to 10% more and covers household breakdowns such as bursting pipes. The HO-3's all-risk coverage on the structure may also

continued on page 227

A GUIDE TO HOMEOWNERS POLICIES

These are the principal features of standard homeowners policies. The policies of some companies differ in a few respects. Policy conditions may also vary according to state requirements.

You can usually increase coverage for some items by paying an additional premium. The special limits of liability refer to the maximum amounts the policy will pay for the types of property listed. Usually, jewelry, furs, boats and other items subject to special limits have to be insured separately if you want greater coverage.

	HO-1 (Basic Form)	HO-2 (Broad Form)	HO-3 (Special Form)	HO-4 (Renters' Contents Broad Form)	HO-6 (Units or Condominiums)	HO-8 (Older Homes)
PERILS COVERED (see key, page 226)	1-11	1-17	1-17 on personal property except glass breakage; all risks, except those specifically excluded, on buildings	1-17	1-17	1-11
STANDARD AMOUNT OF INSURANCE ON house and attached structures	based on structure's replacement value	based on structure's replacement value	based on structure's replacement value	10% of personal insurance on additions and alterations to unit	$1,000 on owner's additions and alterations to unit	based on structure's market value
detached structures	10% of insurance on house	10% of insurance on house	10% of insurance on house	no coverage	no coverage	10% of insurance on house

	HO-1 (Basic Form)	HO-2 (Broad Form)	HO-3 (Special Form)	HO-4 (Renters' Contents Broad Form)	HO-6 (Units or Condominiums)	HO-8 (Older Homes)
trees, shrubs, plants	5% of insurance on house; $500 maximum per item	5% of insurance on house; $500 maximum per item	5% of insurance on house; $500 maximum per item	10% of amount of personal property insurance, $500 maximum per item	10% of amount of personal property insurance, $500 maximum per item	5% of insurance on house, $250 maximum per item
personal property	50% of insurance on house; 5% for property normally kept at another residence or $1,000, whichever is greater	50% of insurance on house; 5% for property normally kept at another residence or $1,000, whichever is greater	50% of insurance on house; 5% for property normally kept at another residence or $1,000, whichever is greater	based on value of property; 10% of that amount for property normally kept at another residence or $1,000, whichever is greater	based on value of property; 10% of that amount for property normally kept at another residence or $1,000, whichever is greater	50% of insurance on house; 5% for property normally kept at another residence or $1,000, whichever is greater
loss of use, additional living expense; loss of rent if rental unit uninhabitable	10% of insurance on house	20% of insurance on house	20% of insurance on house	20% of personal property insurance	40% of personal property insurance	10% of insurance on house
SPECIAL LIMITS OF LIABILITY	money, bank notes, bullion, gold other than goldware, silver other than silverware, platinum, coins and medals—$200; securities, accounts, deeds, manuscripts, passports, ticket stamps, etc.—$1,000; watercraft, including their trailers, furnishings, equipment and outboard motors—$1,000; trailer not used with watercraft—$1,000; grave markers—$1,000; theft of jewelry, watches, furs, precious and semiprecious stones—$1,000; theft of silverware, silver-plated ware, goldware, gold-plated ware and pewterware—$2,500; theft of guns—$2,000				theft on premises limited to $1,000; no coverage for theft of items (named at left) off premises	

continued

	HO-1 (Basic Form)	HO-2 (Broad Form)	HO-3 (Special Form)	HO-4 (Renters' Contents Broad Form)	HO-6 Units or Condominiums)	HO-8 (Older Homes)
CREDIT CARD, FORGERY, COUNTERFEIT MONEY, ELECTRONIC FUND TRANSFER	$500	$500	$500	$500	$500	$500
COMPREHENSIVE PERSONAL LIABILITY	$100,000	$100,000	$100,000	$100,000	$100,000	$100,000
DAMAGE TO PROPERTY OF OTHERS	$500	$500	$500	$500	$500	$500
MEDICAL PAYMENTS	$1,000 per person	$1,000 per person	$1,000 per person	$1,000 per person	$1,000 per person	$1,000 per person

KEY TO PERILS COVERED

1. fire, lightning 2. windstorm, hail 3. explosion 4. riots or civil commotion 5. damage by aircraft 6. damage by vehicles not owned or operated by people covered by policy 7. damage from smoke 8. vandalism, malicious mischief 9. theft 10. glass breakage 11. volcanic eruption 12. falling objects 13. weight of ice, snow, sleet 14. leakage or overflow of water or steam from a plumbing, heating or air-conditioning system 15. bursting, cracking, burning or bulging of a steam- or hot-water heating system or of appliances for heating water 16. freezing of plumbing, heating and air-conditioning systems and domestic appliances 17. injury to electrical appliances, devices, fixtures and wiring (excluding tubes, transistors and similar electronic components) from short circuits or other accidentally generated currents.

include items inside the home; features like wall-to-wall carpet and a built-in dishwasher add value to the house and are often considered part of the structure instead of personal property.

If you're considering the HO-3, check whether the risks you are concerned about are covered. The standard HO-3, for instance, omits damage caused by flood or settling, problems that often concern homeowners. It also excludes damage from such perils as earthquakes, war and nuclear contamination. Strongly consider earthquake insurance if you live in a high-risk area, especially if yours is an older, masonry home or you have much equity invested in it. For this coverage, you have to buy a special add-on, called an endorsement.

When you're looking for a policy to cover items such as pictures, antiques, furs and musical instruments, consider that you might do better by buying additional insurance in the form of riders than by purchasing a homeowners form with more blanket coverage. The so-called upscale policies now offered by many companies may provide more coverage than you need.

Compensation methods. The insurance companies compute payments for homeowners' policy losses in two ways. One, called replacement cost, covers what it would cost to rebuild your home if it were totally destroyed. The other, called actual cash value, takes depreciation into account.

To get the full repair or replacement cost for damages to your home's structure, you must insure it for at least 80% of its full replacement value. That may be higher or lower than the market value, which takes into account such factors as location, land costs, and the foundation and underground piping, not usually damaged by fire. If your insurance falls below the 80% mark, you'll receive either the actual cash value (the replacement cost less depreciation) or a percentage of the replacement cost based on the coverage you do have, whichever is more. The proportion is based on the relationship between the actual amount of insurance and the sum needed to meet the 80% criterion. Thus, if you have $80,000 worth of insurance but need $120,000 to come up to 80%, the company will pay two-thirds of the loss. You would receive only $8,000 for a $12,000 loss, $12,000 for a $18,000 loss, and so on.

Even if you insured your home for 100% replacement value a few years ago, you may need to brush the cobwebs off your policy. Residential construction costs have skyrocketed over the last few years.

Insurance agents have access to cost-index figures you can use to help update the replacement value. Many companies have instituted plans for periodically increasing the amount in line with inflation. When you compute the required amount of insurance, remember to eliminate the value of the land, excavations, foundation, underground pipes and similar building components not likely to be damaged.

Most accidents involve only parts of the house, so you may be entitled to the full replacement cost even if you insure for only 80%. But what if the house is destroyed? Then the company will pay only up to the face amount of insurance, leaving you to foot the other 20%. That's why you should consider insuring for 100%; several companies now require that your house be insured for 100% of its replacement cost.

Premium rates. Take time to get price quotes from several insurers. You may discover some surprising variations in rates. Differences of 100% for comparable coverage aren't unheard of. You can't survey all the companies selling insurance in your area, but contacting just a few might produce enough savings to convince you to switch companies.

There's enough uniformity among the companies' policies that you can use their standard forms to compare premiums. Companies sometimes modify the standard provisions, but it's not always easy to tell whether the changes broaden or narrow your protection, so compare carefully.

You're usually entitled to a lower rate for a brick home than for a frame structure. Also, you might qualify for a discount if your house is new or only a few years old, or if you have installed smoke alarms or antitheft devices. Be sure to take advantage of deductibles. The base deductible moved up in recent years, from $100 to $250. Consider raising yours further still; many companies will reduce premiums in return for not covering the small losses. However, discount plans are not as common for homeowners insurance as they are for auto policies.

If the insurance agent computes the replacement cost of the house on the basis of its square footage, be sure to check the figures before you agree to the resulting premium.

Replacement cost guarantee. Most major insurers offer a replacement cost endorsement that will cover all costs of rebuilding or replacing your home in case of a total loss, even if the expense exceeds the amount of coverage you currently carry. This is a feature worth considering if yours is an area where residential construction costs have outpaced inflation in recent years. A typical replacement guarantee comes as part of a 100% coverage policy and requires you to accept an inflation-adjusted clause each year and notify the insurer of any additions that might alter the value by more than $5,000.

Insurance for older homes. Good as it may be for ordinary homes, the replacement cost system presents problems for old houses that might cost more to restore to their original condition than to replace using modern materials. If you insure a house with a market value of $100,000 for 80% of its $160,000 replacement cost, or $128,000, the house is overinsured.

That's why insurers have developed a special policy for older homes that may be entitled to lower insurance limits based on their market value. Some companies sell them subject to different conditions, and some don't sell them at all. The plans take three forms:

1. A homeowners policy that pays for repairs with less costly and more pedestrian modern materials instead of those orig-inally employed (a parquet floor, for instance, replaced by carpeting over a plywood base). These repair-cost policies generally cost less than other homeowners policies because they cover less.

2. A policy that pays the actual cash value of the loss. This amount might be interpreted by the company as the current market value of the structure, or its replacement cost minus depreciation.

3. An endorsement—policy addition—that allows you to insure for less than 80% of the replacement cost of your

structure without giving up your right to replacement cost for partial losses.

For furniture, appliances, awnings, outdoor equipment, clothing and other personal property, the company usually need not pay more than the cash value. If your couch goes up in flames, the claim is adjusted for wear and tear.

Replacement cost coverage for contents. Many home insurance companies sell an endorsement that extends replacement cost coverage to personal property. For an additional premium, some companies will increase the total for personal property from 50% of the insurance on the house to 75%. Endorsements typically exclude fine arts, antiques and other items that are expected to appreciate. It also limits payments for other items to a maximum of four times the cash value. Other insurers also offer replacement cost endorsements to their homeowners policies.

KEEP AN INVENTORY

If damage is done, you'll want to be in a position to assess your losses. It's easy if you make a good inventory of your home and belongings. The best method is by videotaping them; use close-ups to highlight items of particular value, making a slow sweep of each room, closet and storage area. Keep the videotape and receipts for high-ticket items in a safe deposit box away from home; also enclose a list of each item with either its actual cash value or the current replacement value, depending on your type of policy.

Tips on Homeowners Insurance, a booklet describing types of coverage and how much you need, also tells how to make an inventory. It is available for $1 from the Council of Better Business Bureaus, Suite 300, 1515 Wilson Blvd., Arlington, Va. 22209. Enclose a self-addressed stamped envelope.

MAKING A CLAIM

Covering yourself with the right insurance can turn out to be pointless if you file a claim incorrectly. Notify your agent or broker of damages as soon as possible. If your losses are covered, he or she will probably arrange to have the adjuster inspect the damages and estimate the repair cost.

If damage from a fire, windstorm or other natural disaster is extensive, you may want to have a public adjuster represent you in filing your claim.

Do not make any permanent repairs before the insurance adjuster arrives. The company can legally refuse to reimburse you for repairs made prior to inspection, although usually it won't refuse.

You don't necessarily have to defer to the insurance company if your claim is refused; policies often allow for varying interpretations. One insurance company adjuster might consider your request for expenses to have someone thaw out frozen pipes an uninsured maintenance cost; another would consider it an insurable peril. Persistence pays.

Don't sign a final settlement agreement if you're dissatisfied with the terms. Accept partial payment to make necessary repairs, as long as the insurer formally acknowledges that it is only a partial payment. If you can't negotiate a settlement, file a written complaint with the company. If that yields no results, you could either enter into arbitration with the company or contact your state's insurance department, which often acts as a referee in such disputes. Only after you've exhausted those avenues should you consider filing a suit against the company.

TITLE INSURANCE

When you buy a house, the mortgage lender will require you to purchase insurance on the title that protects the lender's lien on the property against a defect in the title or a lien or some other encumbrance that you didn't know about when you bought the place. If you want to protect yourself as well, you'll have to purchase an owner's title insurance policy.

There is an important difference between the lender's policy and yours. The lender is protected to the extent of the mortgage, which declines as time goes by. You want protection for the price of the house, which includes your downpayment. If you suffer a loss, then your title insurance company is on the hook, not you. Most title insurance policies follow the same general format. You are protected against loss or damage from forgery, misrepresentations of identity, age or other matters that could affect the legality of the ownership documents, as well as from liens recorded in the public records that may come to light after the deal is closed.

Some title insurance companies offer special reissue rates on policies for homes changing owners. If you're buying, find out whether the current owner has title insurance and whether the company offers a reissue rate.

Part Four

INVESTMENTS
FOR TODAY
AND TOMORROW

INVESTING IN TIMES LIKE THESE

T here's nothing like a quick drop of 508 points in the Dow Jones industrial average to strike fear into the hearts of small investors. It's been quite a while now since "Black Monday," but somehow the memory stays fresh. Could it happen again? Those who have studied the events of that day very closely tend to agree on the answer: Yes.

All of which greatly complicates the question of what you should be doing with the money you're setting aside for the future—for the down payment on a home, the kids' education, your retirement years.

If you have even a modest amount at stake, there's a dazzling array of possibilities to choose from—so many, in fact, that some, immobilized by the choices and mindful of the lessons of recent stock market history, decide to stick with safety: savings accounts and certificates of deposit because they are federally insured and provide quick access to the cash; money-market funds because they let you hook on to the interest-rate markets and have a virtually unblemished safety record; maybe bonds for reliable income.

That's not such a bad idea, really. It has served millions of people well. The problem is it rules out opportunities to improve your results beyond the ordinary. The interplay of inflation, interest rates, corporate profitability, and consumer and investor expectations affects the prospects of different kinds of investments in different ways at different times. And brokerage firms, banks, insurance companies and others who cater to the needs and wishes of those with money to invest are pretty good at devising new ways to take advantage of such changes. Alert investors keep track of these opportunities to make their money grow.

The next chapters describe a number of them: some new, some old. They range from ultraconservative, supersafe investments to frankly speculative ones. Some you wouldn't want to touch with a ten-foot pole. Fine. Stick to what feels comfortable.

SOUND PRINCIPLES OF INVESTING

There are three principles on which most investment advisers would surely agree: 1) No one kind of investment works best all the time; 2) diversification of your invested funds offers the best chance for finding profitable opportunities and avoiding major reversals; and 3) liquidity—the ability to change a substantial portion of your asset mix quickly—is the key to survival in an uncertain investment climate.

Black Monday was an expensive testimonial to the wisdom of diversification. Diversification does not mean dividing your money equally among stocks, bonds, real estate and so forth. You have to find investments that are by their nature suited to your objectives and then mix them in combinations that are suited to market conditions. There are investments suited to practically every purpose, and deciding on your purpose is the first step in developing an investment approach that will serve you well in good times and bad and allow you to sleep at night. Here's how to do just that.

Adopt a clear-cut strategy. You don't have to read very many brokerage-house reports or financial publications before you realize how contradictory their advice can be. The same factors used to explain today's drop in stocks may be cited as the reason for tomorrow's rise. While one financial expert urges buying utility stocks and selling steel, another may be advising his clients to sell utilities and buy steel. It's the unpredictability of the future, not a deliberate attempt to confuse the public, that creates such absurd contradictions.

In fact, security analysts, brokerage firms and the financial press produce a lot of useful information. But don't depend on them to create an investment program for you. You have to formulate your own strategy. It needn't be very elaborate, but it should be specific. For example, three different investors might devise strategies like the following, based on their own tolerance for risk and expectations about the future.

• *Investor number one:* "Common stocks scare me, but I can read the charts and I recognize that they offer good returns over the long run. Therefore, I'll bite off just a little, limiting my stock investments, even during rising markets, to 15% of my total invested assets. The rest I'll keep in places I'm more comfortable with: CDs, rental property and bonds."

• *Investor number two:* "I think that real estate, despite its occasional setbacks, offers the best chance of long-term gain. I will try to keep 50% of my assets in real estate and diversify the rest, putting some in the money market for liquidity and some in major growth-company stocks to balance the risks in real estate."

• *Investor number three:* "I can't possibly keep up with what's going on in the investment markets, so I'll be a passive investor, spreading my funds across a wide range of investments in the hope that gains in some categories will offset losses in others. I will try to invest 20% in growth-company stocks, 30% in bonds, 10% in convertible bonds, 30% in money-market funds and certificates of deposit, and 10% in shares of a real estate investment trust."

Take regular note of where you stand. At regular intervals— say, once a year—sit down and add up the value of your investments, including the equity in your home. (The forms in Chapter 1 will help you do this.) To get a picture of your asset distribution, compute each type of investment—stocks, bonds, real estate, gold and so forth—as a percentage of the total. If you haven't achieved a suitable asset mix, this exercise will show you which parts have to be increased, which cut back. As the years go by the percentage mix of your investments will change without your lifting a finger, as some parts of your portfolio rise in value and others fall. This is what makes a periodic review so important.

Stay in your risk zone. How much risk you are prepared to assume should influence the kinds of investments you have and the return you can expect. You can get by nicely most of the time by observing two commonsense rules:

First, don't invest in anything that still leaves you uneasy after you have investigated its strengths and weaknesses.

Second, don't buy anything you don't know how to sell. Some investments, such as collectibles and gemstones, are very easy to buy but may take specialized assistance to sell because there are no organized resale markets.

Be prepared to change. Just as you have to adjust your investments from time to time to stay within the limits you've set for yourself, you may occasionally want to revise your strategy as your situation changes. Retirement, for instance, may suggest a switch from growth-oriented investments such as stocks to income-oriented investments such as bonds.

You can change your asset mix gradually by allocating new investment money from savings, dividends and interest to the category you want to increase. But sometimes you'll get caught off-guard and whipsawed by the market: A stock drops, you sell and switch to bonds, the stock recovers and the bonds decline.

Only clairvoyance will unfailingly tell you the correct moment to sell or buy, so resign yourself to making mistakes. Institutional investors aren't necessarily any better at timing portfolio revisions than you are, despite all their expert help.

Some investors try to avoid the problem by selling on the basis of fixed gain-and-loss limits. They sell when the price increases or declines by predetermined amounts. Such techniques are described in the next chapter.

You can diversify your investments more easily with mutual funds than you can with individual stocks or bonds. A mutual fund gives you a stake in a diversified portfolio of similar securities. You can usually move from one no-load (no commission) fund to another without incurring any commission costs. And many of the load-fund groups permit you to exchange shares in one fund for another in the same group without paying an additional sales charge. See Chapter 17 for more on this.

Keep your expectations realistic. The profits you can expect will depend not only on the investments you select, but also on when you buy and sell them. Potential gains are easy to exaggerate by fixating on an investment's most favorable period—the stock market from the summer of 1982 to the summer of 1987, for instance, or the real estate markets in the high-inflation years of the late 1970s and early '80s.

In fact, back in the 1970s, you would have done splendidly by holding gold, silver and collectibles. The decade's top performers, as measured by Salomon Brothers investment firm in terms of compound annual rate of return, were oil, gold, silver and U.S. coins. But throughout most of the 1980s, financial assets— stocks, bonds and Treasury bills—led the way.

Whatever the ups and downs of the various investment markets, it's important to keep in mind the trade-off between risk and reward. As a conservative investor, you sacrifice potential gain to limit potential losses. An aggressive investor sacrifices safety to raise the potential gain.

INVESTMENT OPPORTUNITIES IN THE YEARS AHEAD

Although no one can predict the future in much detail, there are always trends in motion that create investment opportunities. The trick is being able to spot them.

Shifting population patterns are a key indicator of the changes that lie ahead. The census of 1990 is expected to find a U.S. population of about 250 million. By the year 2000, the country's population will be approaching 270 million. That means about 20 million more people will be creating demand for additional goods and services.

Which goods and services? Well, look at the population mix. The single largest adult age group right now are the 25- to 34-year-olds. They constitute a prime market for homes and the things that go in them. Sellers of such products should do a brisk business as the decade proceeds.

The next oldest group, the 35- to 44-year-olds, will account for one household in five in 1990, and the number of two-income households in that age group with incomes of $50,000 or more will have more than doubled since 1980.

Meanwhile, the number of new 18- to 24-year-olds is shrinking, easing pressures on the job market to create entry-level positions for new workers but creating stiffer competition for experienced, middle-management positions.

All these changes suggest shifting tastes in the things people buy. We've already seen the retail markets change their chief focus from young baby boomers to the middle-aged. Older adults, further along in their working lives, have more money to spend than those just starting out. They represent a potential boon to businesses that serve them.

As a nation, we're getting older. The median age of the country's population in 1985 was about 31. By 1990 it will be 33. By 2000 it will be 36.

In 1990 there will be some seven million fewer 15- to 24-year-olds than there were in 1980, though there will be 35 million of them. There will be 12 million more 35- to 44-year-olds, 2.5 million more 45- to 54-year-olds. Numbers like that create major markets for business and translate into promising investment opportunities.

Stocks. Difficult as it is to select individual companies that stand to benefit most from developments in the rest of the century, it is possible to anticipate what industries seem most likely to gain. Some, like high technology, offer the glamour and excitement of new discoveries. But there's very little excitement in many of the sectors that stand to benefit from the economic climate of good growth and modest inflation that many forecasters see for the decade of the 1990s.

For instance, well-managed banks should benefit from the spread between low borrowing costs and higher lending rates. Food-processing companies stand to gain from generally low commodity prices.

Choosing individual companies can be especially tricky on the high-tech side, where failures outnumber successes, promises often outrun reality and brilliant technical innovators have a way of turning out to be lousy managers. Look for companies that already have products on the market and a reasonable prospect for earnings growth. And keep in mind that many of the leaders in high technology are small divisions of huge, diversified companies where a technological breakthrough or two probably won't have a great impact on the price of the stock. Areas to watch: computers, office automation, robotics, consumer electronics, genetic engineering, telecommunications, superconductivity.

Other promising areas for investment include the stocks of companies that manufacture furniture, appliances, carpets and rugs and the materials that go into them. They should find good markets for their products as homebuilding continues to respond to a growing population. The demand for so-called starter homes will probably decline as baby boomers get older and fewer new households are formed. But the demand for remodeling projects, move-up houses, vacation homes and upscale retirement communities should take up the slack. The home entertainment industry looks strong, as do the travel and leisure industries. Financial service companies should do well as a group.

None of these areas can be expected to enjoy an uninterrupted boom. The economic markets simply don't work that way. All will have their ups and downs and should be viewed as long-term investments. You'll find stocks discussed in detail in the next chapter.

Real estate.   A large supply of empty buildings and a dwindling supply of tax breaks: That's the situation confronting real estate investors as we approach the final decade of the 20th century. In Sunbelt cities like Tampa, Oil Patch centers like Houston and Rocky Mountain meccas like Denver, recent vacancy rates for office and apartment buildings could sometimes be confused with football scores.

With so many cities overbuilt for so long, surely there must be bargains to be had at fire-sale prices. There are, but only for experienced investors with knowledge of local markets, cash to minimize borrowing and patience to wait for those buildings to fill up and rents to rise. You can hire such expertise through real estate investment trusts and limited partnerships, which are covered in Chapter 18.

Meanwhile, the problems experienced by real estate investors in the last few years has created what the Real Estate Research Corporation, a national consulting group, calls a new realism among real estate developers and investors. They're going back to basics, which means putting less emphasis on the leverage and tax shelter aspects of real estate and more on properties that can pay for themselves through rents, starting from the first day of ownership. As you consider investment real estate that will pay off in the 1990s, keep that in mind.

Tangible assets. The outlook for precious metals, gems, antiques and other so-called hard assets depends less on market demand than do financial instruments such as stocks and bonds and the ultimate hard asset, real estate. Long-term forecasts for price movements of gold, silver and other tangibles are easy to find but are often based more on political prognostications than economic ones. You'll find these investments discussed in some detail in Chapter 20.

HOW NOT TO GET RIPPED OFF

There's hardly a legitimate investment that isn't considered fair game by crooks. They sell gold, silver, platinum, rare coins, commodity contracts, diamonds, real estate—you name it and someone will find a way to make a scam out of it.

Investment rackets often originate in telephone boiler rooms, where squads of high-pressure salespeople canvass the nation with get-rich-quick schemes. Sometimes the approach is low-key, sometimes it's so pressure-packed that usually sensible people get rattled into parting with their money. Whatever the approach, the message is the same: You can make a lot of money or save a lot in taxes by taking advantage of the rare opportunity you're being offered, and you'd better move fast.

A few of these scams are so comical that it's hard to believe anyone would fall for them. But people have been sold shares in companies purporting to be in the business of developing underwater homesites, pelts from giant rabbits, electronic asparagus cutters. We all like to think we'd never fall for anything as laughable as that, and we probably wouldn't. But the crooks are usually more clever, talking jargon and spinning out scenarios so fast that their victims aren't sure what's happening to them. To guard against becoming one of their victims, approach any unfamiliar investment with the following rules firmly in mind.

Deal only with established businesses. Hard as it may be to believe, a poultry-stand operator in Baltimore allegedly bilked customers out of $4 million by selling them diamonds, second mortgages and other "investments" he never owned. A parking lot attendant in Pennsylvania was charged with swindling police officers, luring them into phony deals with promises of 40% to 50% returns.

Moral: Confine your dealings to well-established local or national firms whose reputations you trust. If there truly are fantastic deals to be had, you can bet they'll be aware of them.

Don't fall for inflated promises. The surest tipoff to ripoff is the promise of big profits, real fast, with little or no risk. If the pitch sounds too good to be true, watch out.

Don't buy what you don't understand. Penny stocks, oil and gas deals, commodity contracts, art prints, rare coins—these are all specialized areas of knowledge in which the experts make money sometimes and the amateurs almost always lose. If you don't understand what you're dealing with, seek the advice of someone who does—an accountant, lawyer or tax adviser. Meanwhile, don't be pressured into a purchase.

Check out the seller. Contact the appropriate organization to see if complaints have been filed against the firm you're dealing with.

Stockbrokers and mutual funds: Securities and Exchange Commission, 450 Fifth St., N.W., Washington, D.C. 20549.

Business opportunities: Federal Trade Commission, Sixth St. and Pennsylvania Ave., N.W., Room 130, Washington, D.C. 20580.

Interstate land sales: Office of Interstate Land Sales, U.S. Dept. of Housing and Urban Development, 451 Seventh St., S.W., Room 6266, Washington, D.C. 20410.

Commodities contracts: Commodity Futures Trading Commission, Office of Communications and Education Services, 2033 K St., N.W., Washington, D.C. 20581, or the National Futures Association, which has a toll-free number: 800-621-3570 (in Illinois, call 800-572-9400).

Anything that comes in the mail: U.S. Postal Service, Postal Inspector in Charge, P.O. Box 96096, Washington, D.C. 20066, or contact the postal inspector in your area.

If you get suspicious, get out fast. Stop payment on your check. Demand your money back. Threaten to go to the authorities. This sort of fuss works more often than you might think. A crook doesn't want some disgruntled victim making a lot of noise and attracting the attention of the authorities. So if you think you're being ripped off, holler.

HIRING HELP: HOW TO PICK A FINANCIAL PLANNER

Investment markets change fast and it's hard to keep up. In addition, it's not always easy to take a dispassionate view of your own financial situation and decide on the proper mix of insurance, investments and the like. If you'd like someone to make specific recommendations based on your specific needs, you may be in the market for a personal financial planner.

Candidates aren't hard to find; just look in the Yellow Pages of your local phone book. You can also get names of planners in your area from the profession's major membership organizations.

• The International Association for Financial Planning, Two Concourse Parkway, Suite 800, Atlanta, Ga. 30328.

• The Institute of Certified Financial Planners, Two Denver Highlands, 10065 E. Harvard Ave., Suite 320, Denver, Colo. 80231.

• The International Association of Registered Financial Planners, 4127 W. Cypress St., Tampa, Fla. 33607

• The American Society of CLU & ChFC (Chartered Life Underwriter and Chartered Financial Consultant), 270 Bryn Mawr Ave., Bryn Mawr, Pa. 19010.

• The National Association of Personal Financial Advisors, 1130 Lake Cook Rd., Suite 105, Buffalo Grove, Ill. 60089. (Members are fee-only planners.)

• American Association of Personal Financial Planners, 21031

Ventura Blvd., Suite 903, Woodland Hills, Cal. 91364. (Members are fee-only planners who are also certified public accountants.)

After you have the names, select at least three candidates. Visit his or her office and ask each for a detailed statement of fees and services, a résumé and references. Your purpose is to compare them on the following points.

Experience.   Personal financial planning is still a young business, and many of the people in it do not fulfill the popular image of the sage, seasoned counselor. Nevertheless, your planner should have, at the very minimum, a few years of experience in planning or allied fields, such as accountancy, securities analysis or trading, or law.

Credentials.   Many practitioners are trying to pull themselves above the growing crowd calling themselves planners by taking courses and passing examinations that lead to a professional designation.

Certified Financial Planner (CFP) is probably the best-known credential. Graduates must take a series of courses, pass a six-part exam and complete three years of work experience to earn the CFP designation. In addition, the planner must take 30 hours of continuing education each year to keep the credential. The coursework usually takes a couple of years to complete and covers virtually all aspects of financial planning for individuals.

Chartered Financial Consultants have earned the designation from the American College in Bryn Mawr, Pa., which also grants an insurance business certification, Chartered Life Underwriter. The ChFC has successfully completed a ten-course sequence over a period of two to four years and passed two-hour exams on each.

The *Master of Sciences in Financial Services* (MSFS) is also conferred by the American College, after 40 credits of coursework and a two-week residency requirement.

Registered Financial Planners have met the requirements of the International Association of Registered Financial Planners, which confers the designation on planners who meet certain academic and work-experience guidelines.

These titles should not be confused with college degrees. But they do provide the assurance that the planner took the trouble to take the courses to raise his or her skill and knowledge level in the field.

Access to experts. No one person, however well trained, has the encyclopedic knowledge to deal in depth with all the problems that can affect an individual's financial affairs. That would demand knowing as much about, say, divorce settlements as commodity futures. A planner should be able to demonstrate that he or she consults regularly with experts in a variety of fields.

Fees and commissions. There is no standard fee system or scale in the planning business. At one end of the spectrum are the planners who work on a fee basis only. At the other end are the firms that operate entirely or almost entirely on commissions. In between are the larger number who depend on a combination of fees and commissions. In some cases the planner might partly credit commissions against the fee to encourage the client to buy insurance or other financial products through the planner's company.

A planner who feels confident of being able to sell a high-commissioned product might gamble on a low fee. Assume, for instance, you're charged $1,000 for a complete plan plus a certain number of hours of interviews and consultation time. If you also invest $20,000 in a partnership in which your planner is selling shares, he can make another $1,600 in commission. On a $20,000 investment in a load mutual fund with an 8½% sales charge, your planner could make as much as $1,700.

Unless you're dealing with a fee-only firm, you can expect to get suggestions that you purchase an investment or insurance product that the planner happens to offer. There's nothing wrong with that, provided the product is suitable for someone in your financial situation and compares favorably with the scores of others you might buy elsewhere.

If the product is insurance, for example, and the policy is right for you and competitively priced, you might as well buy it from the planner. But your attitude should be different about mutual funds and securities. Why buy a load fund when there are so many no-load funds available? Why buy the stocks recommended by the planner at standard commission rates when you can use a discount broker? The decision is all yours.

INS AND OUTS OF
COMMON STOCKS

WHY INVEST IN STOCKS?

There's really only one reason to take on the risks that go with investing in the stock market: the hope of a higher return on your money than you could get elsewhere. And that's not an unreasonable hope. There are plenty of charts and graphs showing that stocks have far outperformed other kinds of investments over the long run. That's no promise that the market will beat, say, bonds or real estate in any particular time period. The stock market was a lousy place to be for most of the 1970s, for instance. Along with most other so-called financial assets, stocks went virtually nowhere while "hard assets"—real estate, gold and even diamonds—seemed to be making a lot of people rich.

So why even consider stocks? Because they have shown they are capable of generating spectacular returns in some periods and steady returns over the long haul (even allowing for the market crash in October 1987, stocks were the best place to be in the '80s); because they offer a chance to share in the economic growth of the country by owning a piece of the companies that are making it happen; and because they have an important role to play in diversifying your investment assets and thus spreading your risk.

As an individual investor your main concern isn't merely the general direction of the market. What you have to do is pick the right stocks—the ones that will repay your faith with solid profits. That's the subject of this chapter.

HOW TO PICK THE RIGHT STOCKS

A lot of the information and advice you need to pick stocks is available free. Maybe that's the problem. In any given week brokers and analysts will recommend hundreds of stocks; you can buy only a few. But by knowing how to use the basic tools that analysts themselves use to separate the good stocks from the bad, you should be able to find the ones most likely to meet your special needs. Take a look at the principal methods professional money managers use to measure security values.

Earnings per share. EPS constitutes that bottom line you hear so much about because it distills all the company's financial experience into a neat, easily understood figure.

Simply defined, earnings per share is the company's net income (after taxes and after funds are set aside for preferred stock dividends) divided by the average number of common stock shares outstanding. EPS figures are sometimes refined to differentiate between income produced by regular operations and income resulting from unusual transactions, say the sale of a subsidiary. When a company is described as growing at a certain rate, it's usually the EPS that's being used as the measure.

Price-to-earnings ratio. Divide the current price of a stock by its EPS for the last 12-month period and you have the price-earnings ratio—or the price-earnings multiple, as it is often called. The P/E is probably the single most widely used analytical tool. What makes it so important is that it mirrors investors' opinions of a particular stock compared with the stock market as a whole. Actually, there are two ways to express a P/E ratio. Using the previous year's earnings is the most common way, and the number is called a trailing P/E. Sometimes analysts use their earnings forecasts to calculate a potential P/E for the company under study, in which case it is called an anticipated P/E or something similar.

The fact that investors are willing to pay 12 times earnings for stock A and only seven times for stock B tells you instantly that A is more highly regarded than B. Presumably, investors feel more confident that company A will be able to increase its earnings, increase them faster, or pay higher dividends. Dividends are an especially significant consideration during bear markets, when they can help cushion declines in stock prices.

A company's P/E doesn't provide an investment clue until it's compared with P/E values of the same company over past years, the P/Es of other companies in the same business, and the P/E of stock indexes representing the market as a whole. A stock selling for $2 a share with earnings of two cents a share may seem cheap. But its P/E of 100 actually makes it vastly more expensive than a $50 stock with earnings of $2.50 a share (a P/E of 20). A stock with a very high P/E may be the victim of unrealistic expectations on the part of the market. So much future earnings are built into that price that even a slight stumble may send the price tumbling. (The same is true of the P/E multiple of the market as a whole. When the October 1987 crash occurred, the P/Es of the Dow Jones Industrial Average, the Standard & Poor's 500 Stock Index and the NASDAQ index of over-the-counter stocks were all at or near all-time highs.)

The idea is to buy your stock at the lowest possible P/E. As other investors begin to recognize the stock's potential, they may bid up the multiple, thereby giving the stock additional price momentum as the company's earnings per share rise. That is your hope, but reality doesn't always oblige. In depressed markets a rise in earnings per share may actually be accompanied by a drop in the multiple.

Book value. Stripped of technicalities, book value—or stockholders' equity, as it is also called—is based on the difference between a company's assets and its liabilities. Dividing book value by the number of outstanding shares gives you the book value per share, another useful reference point for a stock.

Theoretically, book value represents the amount stockholders would receive for each share they own if the company were to sell all its assets, pay all its debts, and go out of business. Few companies whose shares are widely traded ever do shut their doors. Still, stocks are often recommended as cheap because they are selling below book value or very little above. Sometimes stocks selling below book value become take-over candidates, attracting the attention of so-called corporate raiders who see a chance to buy up the company on the cheap—an effort that can drive up the price of the shares and thus reward investors who spotted the bargain sooner.

Such possibilities could be significant, but you should have more information to go on before you start buying. It's possible, for instance, that a company's stock is selling below book value because that company or its industry is experiencing bad times that make it a risky investment.

Return on book value. A company's total annual net income, expressed as a percentage of total book value, measures how much the company earns on the stockholders' stake in the enterprise. Return on book value, also called return on equity, varies greatly among companies and fluctuates with economic conditions.

Total return. Stockholders tend to think of gains and losses in terms of price changes. Bond owners may focus on interest yields and be less concerned with price changes (but see Chapter 16).

Compartmentalizing price changes and income often makes sense. If your objective is to maximize current income, you're interested primarily in dividend and interest yields. On the other hand, you may prefer a stock with a low dividend but a lot of price potential.

Nevertheless, both price changes and income you receive from a stock should be taken into account to evaluate investment performance. Together, they show your total return, which makes it possible to compare stocks with bonds, preferred stocks, Treasury bills and other alternative investments.

Volatility. Some stocks' prices move slowly and within a relatively narrow band; others bounce around a lot. The volatile stocks naturally involve more risk because when they go down, they may go way down. Analysts have developed a measure of price volatility called beta, which tells you how much a stock characteristically moves in relation to a change in the S&P 500 stock index. A 1.00 beta stock moves in step with the index. A 1.10 beta stock historically rises or falls 10% more than the index. A 0.98 beta stock is less volatile than the index—it would be expected to go up 9.8% if the market rises 10% or down by 9.8% if the index falls 10%.

Your broker can probably get you some betas for the stocks you're considering. Or you can estimate a stock's volatility for a given period on your own by using this shortcut formula:

$$\frac{\text{high price} - \text{low price}}{\text{average of high} + \text{low price}} \times 100 = \text{volatility \%}$$

This gives you a rough guide you can use to compare different stocks, but it isn't a beta figure. The volatility percentage you calculate this way for any stock has to be measured against similarly computed figures, not the actual betas for other stocks you are considering.

Technical analysis. The concepts described so far—P/E ratios, book value and the like—are derived from the fundamental financial strengths and weaknesses of a company, and using them as tools for spotting stock values is called fundamental analysis. From time to time you may come across buy or sell recommendations that reflect what is known as technical analysis. Technicians examine the whole market or individual issues and try to forecast price movements by examining previous price changes, shifts in margin debt, the ratio of advancing to declining stocks, the volume of short sales, and a wide and sometimes bewildering range of other statistical material. To technicians these factors, often plotted on charts, reveal the basic forces that they believe raise or lower prices.

Technicians speak their own language, particularly when referring to chart patterns they feel have special significance: heads and shoulders, channels, saucers, wedges, pennants, double bottoms. Although critics may scoff at such apparent mumbo jumbo, technical analysis commands respect among many in the investment business. And committed adherents of fundamental analysis often check a stock's technical position before acting.

DEVISING A STRATEGY

By yourself you can't possibly sort through the thousands of stock issues traded on the various exchanges and over the counter for the relatively few stocks you intend to buy. Once in a while you may come across an interesting company through business or personal contacts. For the most part, though, you have to look for investment prospects among the recommendations of the brokerage firms and financial publications. Sifting through their leads will be much easier if you first take the time to decide on an overall investment strategy.

The buy-and-hold approach. Investors in this category prefer to hold their stocks a long time—three, five, ten years or more. They are prepared to ride out market declines in the hope that the inherent strength of their companies will ultimately reward them with higher earnings, dividends and prices.

Buy-and-hold investors generally stick with high quality, large capitalization stocks with a long history of dividend increases, such as IBM and Procter & Gamble.

If you're essentially a conservative buy-and-hold type, ask your broker to suggest a few favorably priced big companies with consistently high earnings and a record of increasing dividends. Among brokers they are often referred to as the quality companies or blue chips.

Moving with the economic tides. If you're paying close attention, you should be able to improve your returns by anticipating or at least moving with the ups and downs in the economy. If you anticipate boom times, it would be logical to concentrate on industries that should benefit most: retail stores, entertainment companies, machinery producers, autos and so on. Then you sell them as the economy starts to top off and shift into issues that tend to resist recessions: household-supply manufacturers, retail food chains, life insurers and others, referred to as defensive issues.

Betting on one industry. Individual industries are always pushing to the forefront of the investment field as a result of economic or social changes, technological developments and marketing innovations, and sometimes for obscure reasons that seem no more weighty than market fads. New marketing concepts can create whole new businesses—emergency medical centers and off-price retailers, for example. Technological advances continue to spawn a host of new products and services.

Your hope to capitalize on such trends lies in picking stocks in the industry before the boom starts or while it is in its early stages. For maximum effect, look for what the analysts call pure play companies, those that specialize in the field and so stand to gain most. Many big corporations are so highly diversified that gains in any one product may not substantially increase total profits.

In most cases you should plan to sell a stock when its price appears to be reaching a plateau. In the best of circumstances, you might find a company that turns into a growth leader that you can hold for the long pull.

Executives may be better placed than outsiders to spot opportunities in their own industries, so look first in your own field. Trade journals sometimes provide good clues, and many professional analysts read them religiously.

Going for broke. When you're speculating, the long-term qualities of the stock aren't as important as the near-term potential. You're looking for issues that will jump rather than crawl: companies selling stock to the public for the first time, corporations likely to be bought out by another company or to buy out another company, "concept" companies promoting some new product or service, or turnaround stocks that have been severely depressed and are expected to snap back.

You can speculate with any stock by the way you trade it. Buying on margin (financing part of the purchase with a loan from the broker) and selling short (selling borrowed shares in the hope of replacing them later with shares bought at a lower price) increase the risk and the potential return. Options and futures are favorite tools of speculators (see Chapter 19).

Another speculative approach involves betting on relatively short-term swings in the market. When the market appears ready for a rise, you buy high-volatility stocks, the ones with high betas, because they should go up more than the market as a whole. When prices are topping off, you cash in everything and put the money into a more neutral investment—perhaps a money-market fund—to wait for the next upswing.

Doggedly diversified. Committing all your funds to one or two of even the most conservative issues could expose you to greater losses than owning a basket full of riskier stocks.

J. Russell Holmes, who delved into stock returns produced over a 107-year period, concluded that one of the three keys to succeeding in the market was to think in terms of portfolios, not individual issues. (The other two, according to Holmes, are taking time to select issues with growth potential and holding stock for the long term—ten- to 15-year periods.)

How many stocks it takes to diversify enough depends on several factors. One study indicates that you need a minimum of ten separate issues if you're dealing with high-quality companies. Another way to spread the risk would be to buy just a few individual issues and buffer them with shares in mutual funds, or to stick with mutual funds exclusively because their portfolios usually hold no fewer than several dozen issues. Mutual funds are the subject of Chapter 17.

HOW TO PICK THE RIGHT BROKER

For many investors, their broker is the single most valuable source of help in making good decisions. On the other side of the coin, an inept or unresponsive broker can make your life miserable, as well as cost you money.

The best place to begin a search for a broker is with your friends and relatives who are investors. You can get some valuable insights based on their first-hand experience. Another source: investment seminars sponsored by local brokerage firms and advertised in the newspapers. These seminars are designed to draw in potential customers, but they can be educational and provide you with a chance to size up the broker making the presentation, as well as the firm he or she represents.

Brokers can differ in several ways. There are full-service and discount firms; there are national, regional and local firms. All sell more than just stocks: They sell municipal bonds, units trusts, tax shelters, annuities. But when you get right down to it, the chief distinction is between the full-service and the discount firms.

Full-service brokers. Whether regional outfits known mostly in their own area of the country—such as Nashville-based J.C. Bradford and Minneapolis-based Piper, Jaffray & Hopwood—or national giants such as Merrill Lynch or Shearson Lehman Hutton, these companies are the place to go if you want access to a small army of research analysts who study firms and industries in search of good investments and pass along their recommendations to you through your broker, who gets paid a commission when you buy or sell. Brokers may be called account executives, financial counselors or some other title. Rarely are they officially referred to as brokers.

Full-service firms offer a wide range of customer services, including research reports, individual attention, asset-management accounts (see Chapter 4), consolidated account statements and seminars on retirement planning, tax shelters and other investment-related topics. You pay for all this through the firms' commission rates.

Discount brokers. Here you get execution of your order—no research, no hand-holding, no advice (although some firms do make helpful literature available). Salespeople are paid a salary, not commissions. Once thought of as "pipe rack" brokers because of their no-frills approach to the business, discounters have long since polished up their image. Today the offices of the major discount firms, such as Charles Schwab and Fidelity Brokerage Services, are virtually indistinguishable from the offices of their full-service brethren, complete with stock tickers, plush chairs and computer terminals for checking on the value of your holdings.

CUTTING THE COSTS OF BUYING AND SELLING

Ordinarily the last thing you worry about when you choose a stock is the commission you'll have to pay to buy and sell it. But commission costs can't be easily ignored, and shopping around for the best rates can pay off.

Unfortunately, commission rates can be difficult to compare among the full-service brokerages. A businessman with more than $100,000 in the stock market once complained to the *New York Times* that when he tried to get commission schedules from several large brokerage firms, his requests were mostly ignored. One firm claimed to have no published schedule. Another said he could get the rates from a broker executive if he were preparing to place an order. Among the schedules he did receive, some were so complicated that they were practically indecipherable.

If you have a good working relationship with a broker, and if he or she provides valuable help in making your investment decisions, then commissions aren't much of a concern. Most people select a brokerage firm for reasons that have nothing to do with commissions, anyway—perhaps its office is conveniently located, its research reports are useful, or the account executive is helpful. Factors such as these can easily compensate for the commissions, especially for relatively modest investors.

However, if you don't want or don't need such services, or if you make a sizable number of trades during the course of a year, then the easiest way to save is to use a discount broker or go through a bank or savings and loan that offers discount services. The commission rates of discounters are much easier to compare; most advertise them freely in their effort to attract your business.

Some discounters are members of the New York Stock Exchange and have offices in several cities around the country. A few provide research reports, but most are set up only to execute buy and sell orders for investors who make their own decisions. Most have toll-free telephone numbers for distant clients or will accept collect calls. Discounts, depending on the size of the transaction, can amount to as much as 80% of what you'd pay a full-service broker, although 20% to 30% is a more representative saving. You can commonly save about 50% on transactions in the $5,000 range.

It is simple enough to open an account with any broker by walking into the office or by calling or writing for an application. Some discounters operate through banks and savings and loan associations. The larger firms have walk-in offices in major cities. But before you sign on, find out if there is a minimum commission charge. Some firms set a $25 or $30 minimum fee regardless of the size of the trade. On small trades, that could wipe out the savings you might be anticipating.

Also ask about annual service charges. Some firms, wishing to limit their business to well-heeled investors, levy an annual fee to keep the small ones away. It's important to shop around. A trade of one size may be cheaper at, say, Fidelity Brokerage Services than at Muriel Siebert & Co., whereas another transaction will cost less at Siebert than at Fidelity.

One rule of thumb you can use in comparing fee schedules at either type of brokerage is that a firm whose commission depends on the number of shares traded rather than the price of the shares should be cheaper for trading big blocks of higher-priced stocks.

Here is a listing of the major discount brokers. All are members of the Securities Investor Protection Corporation, meaning customers' accounts are protected up to $500,000 against the possibility of the firm's failure. Some of the firms have offices in more than one city. For them, the location of the headquarters office is given. Toll-free numbers are for out-of-state calls. If the firm has a toll-free number for long-distance calls within its state, that is listed second. The last number given is for collect calls.

C.D. Anderson & Co., Inc.
San Francisco
800-822-2222
415-433-2120

Brown & Co. Securities Corp.
Boston
800-225-6707
800-225-6707 (Mass.)

Burke, Christensen & Lewis Securities, Inc.
Chicago
800-621-0392
800-972-1633 (Ill.)

W.T. Cabe & Co., Inc.
New York
800-223-6555
212-541-6690

Columbine Securities, Inc.
Denver
303-534-3344

Fidelity Brokerage Services, Inc.
Boston
800-225-1799
800-225-1799 (Mass.)

Icahn & Co., Inc.
New York
800-223-2188
212-957-6318 (N.Y.)

Kashner Davidson Securities Corp.
Sarasota, Fla.
800-678-2626
813-951-2626 (Fla.)

Norstar Brokerage Corp.
New York
800-221-8210
212-806-2888 (N.Y.)

Odd Lots Securities, Ltd.
New York
800-221-2095
800-442-5929 (N.Y. state)
212-661-6755

Ovest Securities, Inc.
New York
800-344-4141
212-747-1111

Andrew Peck Associates, Inc.
New York
800-221-5873
212-363-3770

Quick & Reilly, Inc.
New York
800-221-5220
800-522-8712 (N.Y. state)
212-943-8686

ReCom Securities, Inc.
Minneapolis
800-328-8600
800-328-8600 (Minn.)

Rose & Company
Chicago
800-621-3700
312-663-8300

Charles Schwab & Co., Inc.
San Francisco
800-648-5300
800-648-5300 (Cal.)

Security Pacific Brokers
Pasadena, Cal.
800-272-4060
818-578-0606

Muriel Siebert & Co., Inc.
New York
800-872-0444
212-644-2400

Springer Investment & Securities Co., Inc.
Indianapolis
800-433-8049
800-752-5912 (Ind.)
317-255-6673

Stockcross
Boston
800-225-6196
800-392-6104 (Mass.)
617-367-5700

Tradex Brokerage Service, Inc.
New York
800-522-3000
212-233-2000

ZieglerThrift Trading, Inc.
Minneapolis
800-328-4854
612-333-4206

WHAT INVESTMENT CLUBS DO

Serious investing is hard work. It takes careful research, attention to detail, nearly constant alertness to shifting economic tides. Most of the time, not much happens: an excellent investment choice may take from several months to several years to fulfill its potential. Meanwhile, the job can be tedious, discouraging—and lonely. That's why hundreds of thousands of people around the country band together to form investment clubs.

A typical club has about 15 members—friends, neighbors or co-workers, usually—and meets once a month to consider its portfolio decisions. Members are assigned different tasks. One team may track economic conditions; another may report on the investment climate; a third may present charts, graphs and other material to back up specific investment recommendations, which are usually decided by majority vote.

To fund the portfolio, club members pitch in $25 or $30 a

month, although in some clubs the amount may be a little smaller or much larger. With the money, a typical club accumulates a portfolio of about 15 stocks, ownership of which the members share in proportion to their contributions to the investment kitty.

For most members, the club is not the only place they invest. In fact, they tend to have individual portfolios that are much larger than what they have tied up in the club. This makes investment clubs popular with brokers, who like the thought of serving all those individual members' portfolios.

How well do clubs do? A few years ago the National Association of Investors Corp. (which used to be called the National Association of Investment Clubs) surveyed members and estimated that their holdings rose in value by an average of 28% compounded annually over a nine-year period. Another study found an annual growth rate of better than 10% for older clubs. That covers good years and bad.

The mortality rate for new investment clubs is discouraging: About half of them break up within 18 months, usually over differences of opinion on investment philosophy or individual portfolio selections. That statistic underlines the importance of forming a compatible group, the members of which share the same general investment goals.

You can get guidance in starting and running an investment club from the National Association of Investors Corp., 1515 E. Eleven Mile Road, Royal Oak, Mich. 48067.

STANDING UP FOR YOUR RIGHTS

When stock prices plunged on Black Monday, October 19, 1987, the breathtaking speed of the fall revealed more than the weakness of some investors' stock selections. The breakdown in the market also affected many of the communications links that make possible the matching of buy and sell orders on the floors of the various exchanges. The first link in that chain is your phone call to the broker to say "buy" or "sell." When that link broke down, many investors felt abandoned by their brokers. Unable to get their orders through, they watched helplessly as the prices of their shares sank.

Many got mad and complained. More than a few set out to sue, only to discover that they couldn't. Why not? Because the vast majority of broker-investor agreements, which you sign when you open your account, contain a clause that says you can't. Instead, you must submit your complaint to binding arbitration. (Older broker-investor agreements may not contain the clause.)

Luckily, most complaints against brokers can be settled with a letter or a phone call. Serious complaints—churning (a lot of buying and selling for the purpose of generating commissions) of your account, high-pressure tactics that result in your choosing an unsuitable investment—might require more serious steps. In most cases that will be arbitration, so you should know something about it. Any member of a securities exchange or of the National Association of Securities Dealers (NASD) is subject to a uniform binding arbitration procedure, whether the squabble is over a few hundred dollars or several thousand, and even if the dispute isn't over money at all but over a matter of procedures or ethics.

The National Association of Securities Dealers, the Municipal Securities Rulemaking Board and each of the stock exchanges are known as self-regulatory organizations (SROs) and are overseen by the Securities and Exchange Commission in Washington. The SEC doesn't arbitrate disputes but refers them to the arbitration program run by the SRO involved in the dispute.

Before it comes to that, the SEC, the NASD and most of the SROs will try to mediate. They'll send your complaint to the brokerage firm, ask for a written explanation and try to get both sides to agree to a settlement. If that doesn't work, it's up to you to decide whether to seek arbitration. If you do, the process will be conducted by the appropriate SRO.

Your initial cost for filing a claim ranges from $15 for claims of $1,000 or less to a maximum of $750 for disagreements in excess of $100,000. Fees may be returned to you at the discretion of the arbitrators, and you can get all but $25 back if you settle the dispute before arbitration actually begins. Cases take several months to complete.

You can hire an attorney to plead your case, but with or

without a lawyer, you forfeit the right to sue later should the arbitrator or panel of arbitrators rule to your dissatisfaction.

To file a claim, first you must get the forms from the director of arbitration of the proper securities exchange. Just about any exchange could have jurisdiction because most securities firms are members of all major exchanges, some or all of the regional boards and the NASD.

A firm cannot refuse to cooperate with the process, but it can file a counterclaim if it believes your contentions are frivolous. You won't get anywhere, for example, if you merely lost money on a recommended stock, unless you can show that the broker promised you its price wouldn't fall or held back information of a negative nature.

If your case involves less than $5,000, the exchange will put it through a simplified arbitration procedure. The one arbitrator assigned will rule from evidence but is unlikely to call a hearing.

The procedure becomes more like a trial if your claim is for more than $5,000. The exchange will schedule a hearing in a nearby large city at a convenient date and appoint a panel of arbitrators. You and your attorney, as well as the respondent, can call witnesses. The arbitrators and either side's counsel can subpoena persons and documents. The proceeding is under oath and all documents are kept confidential.

The arbitrators will not rule on the spot but will mail their decision to you and the responding firm within 30 days if at all possible. You may or may not get an explanation with the ruling, which can include a monetary award. The decision is final.

For more information, contact the director of arbitration at NASD (Two World Trade Center, 98th Floor, New York, N.Y. 10048), the NYSE (20 Broad St., Fifth Floor, New York, N.Y. 10005) or any other exchange.

EIGHT INVESTMENT MISTAKES YOU DON'T HAVE TO MAKE

It has been said that the winners of tennis matches, football games, even battles, are those who make the fewest mistakes. Or, to put it another way, the winners are those who manage not to lose. The same could be said for the stock market. One major requirement for successful investing is to keep mistakes to a minimum.

What are the most common ways investors go wrong? *Changing Times* magazine has examined this question over the years and has discovered eight mistakes that recur with unnecessary frequency. Forewarned is forearmed.

1. *Not having an investment plan or philosophy.* This error takes various forms. Without the guidance of a long-range objective, you fail to decide in advance what type of company you want to own stocks in—long-term growth companies, cyclical or speculative ones. You don't decide whether you want current income or capital gains. You shoot from the hip. If by chance you do have a plan, you abandon it when the market is bursting with optimism or sulking with pessimism.

2. *Not taking the trouble and time to be informed.* Failing to get information about a company before investing in it is the most common form of this mistake. Some investors actually buy stock in a company without knowing what the company makes and what the future might be for that kind of product.

3. *Not checking on the quality of your advice.* Many investors don't check on a broker or adviser before doing business. They don't investigate, for example, his or her educational background, how long the person has been in business or been handling other people's money, or how well he has done. They don't ask to see sample accounts. In the words of the manager of a large mutual fund complex, "Following the advice of a mediocre broker is known as a 'cut flower' program. The broker keeps picking flowers and selling them to you. When one bunch withers, he sells you another."

4. *Investing money that should be set aside for another use.* Too often people tie up money that should be available for emergencies or for purchase of a new car or some other predictable expense. If you invest what should be emergency funds in stocks, you may be forced into selling stocks at a time not of your own choosing. Fate often decrees that this will be a period of low prices when you must take a loss.

5. *Being optimistic at the top and pessimistic at the bottom.* Optimism and bullishness are infectious, as are pessimism and

bearishness. Thus, even when the market is high by such standards as the ratio of prices to earnings, people go right on buying. They do it because everyone seems to be buying, or because they extrapolate recent trends and assume that what has been happening will continue to happen, or because they mistakenly think there is an exact correlation between the stock market and business conditions. People grow increasingly pessimistic as the market drops and tend to reach the bottom of the pit when stocks are cheapest. This may be when you should be buying, or at least holding on to what you have.

6. *Buying on the basis of tips and rumors.* There's hardly any chance that the average investor will get advance or inside information about any company whose stock is publicly held. And even if you do, it probably won't do you much good. Professional speculators are watching the market news all day long, ready to buy or sell on a minute's notice. There are also specialists who make a market in each stock listed on the various exchanges. At any rumor about a company or any unusual change in the volume of trading, the specialist calls the company's management and gets the facts. So remember, no matter how hot a tip you hear, someone knew it before you did.

7. *Becoming sentimental about a stock or an industry.* Some investors grow as attached to their stocks as they do to their pets. As a result, they hold onto companies long after the potential for growth and profit has passed. A similar mistake is to fail to sell a stock because you hate to admit you were wrong to have bought it in the first place.

8. *Buying low-priced stocks on the theory that they will show the largest percentage gains.* A low-priced stock may be a bargain, but not necessarily because it is low priced. The price of a stock is what the marketplace believes a company to be worth divided by the number of shares outstanding. A stock that sells for peanuts does so because that's what the market thinks it's worth.

BONDS AND OTHER FIXED-INCOME INVESTMENTS

They won't admit it any more, but many investors used to consider bonds a humdrum approach to investing—boring at best and maybe even a little chicken-hearted, suitable mainly for retired folks or those in need of a steady income. But a couple of things happened to change that image, probably for good. First came the hyper-inflationary years of the late 1970s and early 1980s and the tendency of interest rates to stay high even after inflation had subsided. Then came the clincher. When the stock market collapsed at the end of the great bull market of 1982–1987, guess what escaped the carnage: bonds.

Boring they're not, nor are they quite as safe as you might suppose, especially when interest rates are jittery. Consider what happens to your investment in bonds and other fixed-income securities as interest rates bounce around. Say you buy a bond issued to yield 8%. Then interest rates rise. Other investors aren't going to pay full face value for that bond when they could obtain, say, 10% interest somewhere else. Thus, your bond would lose market value. If you sold it, you'd have to sell it at a discount. Your income would remain the same, but your capital would have shrunk.

Now suppose rates fall. If new bonds are offering 7%, then the value of your 8% bond is enhanced. If you sell it, you can get more than face value and make a profit. And indeed, if interest rates fall significantly over the years, then bonds bought when rates are relatively high could pay off handsomely if their owners choose to sell them at a premium or hold onto them and collect the interest.

But investors in search of fixed-income securities aren't limited to the choice of whether or not to buy bonds. The marketplace is wide and diverse, and it contains opportunities to hedge inflation, trim taxes, even secure capital gains that are virtually guaranteed. This chapter will discuss those and other opportunities.

A PRIMER FOR INCOME INVESTORS

Definitions. In their basic form, bonds and other credit instruments, such as notes, bills and commercial paper, are IOUs—basically, receipts for money borrowed from the investor. They bind the issuing organization to pay a fixed amount of interest periodically (usually semiannually) and repay the full face amount on the maturity date, which is set when the instrument is issued.

Corporations and governments regularly finance their operations by issuing such credit instruments. Agency securities are issues of various U.S. government–sponsored organizations, such as the Federal National Mortgage Association. Municipals, also known as tax-exempts, are issued by state and local governments.

Secured bonds are backed by a lien on part of a corporation's plant, equipment or other assets. Unsecured bonds, known as debentures, are backed only by the general credit of the corporation. Zero-coupon bonds are issued at a big discount from face value and pay no interest until maturity.

General obligation municipal bonds are secured by the full taxing power of the issuing organization. Revenue bonds rely on revenues from a specific source, such as bridge or road tolls. Some municipals are secured by revenues from a specific tax.

Corporations also pay a fixed annual amount on preferred stock, when profits permit, but preferred shares represent an ownership stake in the corporation, not a debt. However, because of the fixed return, the price of preferred stocks tends to fluctuate more like bonds, in response to interest rate changes, than like common stocks.

Some bonds, debentures and preferred stocks are convertible into the corporation's common stock at a fixed ratio—a certain number of shares of common stock in exchange for a certain amount of bonds or preferred shares. Convertibles may sell at lower yields than nonconvertibles because of the possibility that the owner can make a profit on the conversion. There's more information about each of these kinds of securities later in the chapter.

Denominations. The standard face value for bonds is $1,000 or $5,000. Some are issued in larger denominations; smaller denominations are less common.

Forms of ownership. Bonds and notes usually must be registered with the issuing organization in the name of the owner, just like common stock. Sometimes ownership is in book entry form, meaning the issuer keeps a record of buyers' names but no securities actually change hands. Treasury bills are issued this way. Bearer bonds, which are no longer issued by anyone, are unregistered and presumed to belong to anyone who holds them, like money. You clip and mail in coupons to get the interest.

Schedule of interest payments. Most bonds pay interest semiannually. Many mutual funds and unit trusts invested in bonds pay dividends monthly as a convenience to shareholders. Discount securities, such as U.S. Treasury bills and savings bonds, pay interest by deducting it from the sales price, or face value at the time of issue, then paying full face value at maturity.

Terms of maturity. Short term refers to securities maturing in two years or less; intermediate term means maturities of up to ten years; and long term means securities maturing in ten or more years. Many bonds are issued with 25- to 30-year maturities. Notes usually run about seven years. The lines separating the categories aren't hard and fast, however, so it's important to check the actual number of years to maturity for any security you're considering.

Call rights. Issuers often retain the right to call, meaning redeem, a bond at a specified date before the scheduled maturity. An issuer may call in its bonds if, for instance, interest rates fall to a point where it can issue new bonds at a lower rate. It has been customary to pay owners of called bonds a small premium over the face value.

Sinking funds. Some bond issues are retired gradually in installments under a sinking-fund plan. The bonds to be redeemed early are selected by lottery or bought on the open market.

Tax considerations. Interest and capital gains on corporate credit instruments are normally subject to federal, state and local income taxes. Income from Treasury and agency securities is subject to federal income taxes, but all Treasury and some agency securities are exempt from state and local income taxes. Interest on most municipal bonds is exempt from federal income taxes. Most state and local governments exempt interest on their own bonds but tax income on securities issued by other states. Because of their tax advantage, municipals pay a lower interest rate than taxable bonds.

Yields. The coupon rate is the fixed annual interest payment expressed as a percentage of the face value. A 10% coupon bond, for instance, pays $100 a year interest on each $1,000 of face value. The rate is set when the bond is issued and does not change as the bond's price fluctuates. There are also other kinds of yields a bond investor should be familiar with.

Current yield is the annual interest payment expressed as a percentage of the bond's current market price. Thus, a 10% coupon bond selling for $900 has a current yield of 11.1% ($100 interest divided by the $900 price × 100).

Yield to maturity takes into account the current yield and the eventual gain or loss it is assumed the owner will receive by holding to maturity a bond selling at a discount or a premium. If you pay $900 for a 10% coupon bond with a face value of $1,000 maturing five years from the date of purchase, you will earn not only $100 a year interest but also an additional $100 five years later when the bond is redeemed for $1,000 by its issuer. By the same token, if you buy that bond for $1,100, representing a $100 premium, you will lose $100 at maturity. The loss, however, could be more than offset by the extra interest earned on a premium-priced bond because its coupon rate presumably exceeds the current yield available on comparable securities. Tax considerations could also make the capital loss worth taking. For bonds selling at a discount, the yield to maturity probably provides the best estimate of total return.

Yield to call is computed the same way as yield to maturity, except that it is assumed the bond will be redeemed at the first call date for the face value plus the call premium.

The effect of interest rate changes. Because the amount of interest paid on a bond or note commonly remains fixed for the life of the issue, the bond adjusts to interest rate movements by changes in price.

To see how that works, consider a newly issued $1,000 bond with a coupon interest rate of 10%—$100 a year. If interest rates rise to 11% after the bond is issued, you can sell your 10% bond only by offering it at a price that will deliver an 11% current yield to the buyer. So the price becomes whatever $100 represents 11% of, which is $909. Thus, you lose $91 if you sell. By the same token, if interest rates decline to 9% while you're holding your 10% bond, you can sell it for whatever $100 represents 9% of, which is $1,111. That's a $111 capital gain.

These examples oversimplify the relationship, since in the actual marketplace prices are also strongly influenced by the time remaining to the bond's maturity or possible call. But the underlying principle is the same: As interest rates rise, bond prices fall; as interest rates fall, bond prices rise. (More on this in the discussion of discount bonds later in the chapter.)

How prices are listed. If you look them up in the financial pages of a newspaper, you'll find bond prices identified by the abbreviated name of the issuer, the coupon rate and the maturity date. The more common price lists give only the current yield, but your broker can get the yields to maturity and call for you. Prices are reported as a percentage of $100. To get the actual price, multiply the decimal equivalent of the percentage by 1,000. Thus, a Commonwealth Edison Company 8% bond maturing in 2003 might be reported as CmwE 8s03 85¾, meaning the issue is selling at the time of the listing for $850.75 per $1,000 face value, a fairly hefty discount.

HOW TO USE THE BOND RATINGS

When you set out to buy bonds, it is tempting to look for the highest available yields. But yield figures can be misleading unless you also take into account the quality of the bond itself. If there is any doubt about the ability of the bond issuer to pay off on time, high yield could be poor compensation for the risk. In general, small investors should stick to high-quality bonds. But what is high quality? And how high is high enough?

The safety scale. At the top of the safety scale stand all those issues for which the U.S. government has a direct obligation to meet interest and principal payments. The government, after all, is the only borrower on the market that can print money to pay its debts, if necessary.

Below that lofty level lies a vast array of securities issued by U.S. agencies, corporations and local government units— states, counties, cities. There you will find bonds ranging from those that are as solid as U.S. government issues to those close to or already in default.

Bonds, like people, have credit ratings. The difference is that bond ratings are made public and can quickly be checked by anyone. Most widely traded bonds are rated by at least one of the major agencies in the field—Moody's Investors Service and Standard & Poor's Corporation. Their judgments can be valuable provided you know what they mean and how they affect market prices. The rating categories they use are shown in the table on the opposite page.

Standard and Poor's AA, A, BBB, BB and B ratings are sometimes supplemented with a plus (+) or a minus (−) sign to raise or lower a bond's position within the group. Moody's may add the numeral 1 for tax-exempt issues in the A and Baa groups with somewhat stronger standings.

	S&P	MOODY'S
INVESTMENT GRADES	AAA	Aaa
	AA	Aa
	A	A
	BBB	Baa
	BB	Ba
SPECULATIVE GRADES	BB	Ba
	B	B
	CCC	Caa
	CC	Ca
	C	C
	D	

Ratings modified by P, for provisional, or Con., for conditional, indicate that some condition has to be fulfilled before a final judgment can be made. For example, the bond may be backed by revenues from a project not yet completed.

The investment grades include the bonds that individual and institutional investors seeking stable income and safety ordinarily buy. BBB/Baa is the lowest rating that qualifies for commercial bank investments, but it's a borderline group for which, in Standard & Poor's words, adverse economic conditions or changing circumstances are more likely to lead to a weakened capacity to pay interest and repay principal than for bonds in higher-rated categories.

Below BBB/Baa you're in speculative territory. Because of their higher risk of default, such bonds must pay higher yields. They are often gathered together into the portfolios of so-called high-yield bond mutual funds. Bonds in the C and D ranks are in or near default and are often referred to as junk bonds.

Moody's and Standard & Poor's don't always agree on a bond's rank. It's not unusual for them to rate an issue one grade apart.

The price of quality. Credit ratings play a big role in determining the relative levels of bond prices. Normally you pay a higher price (and thus receive a lower yield) with each notch you move up the quality scale. A triple-A usually costs more than a double-A with comparable characteristics, a double-A costs more than an A, and so on. The higher the quality, generally, the lower the yield.

Few investment-grade issues have ever defaulted. But there have been enough cases to reinforce the attraction of the highest ratings.

Many institutional investors, such as pension plans and mutual funds, limit themselves to A or higher-rated issues either by choice or for legal reasons. Some institutional investors have developed their own rating program or hired special services to grade issues with greater precision than the broad categories used by Moody's and Standard & Poor's.

The rating agencies are supposed to track the financial condition of issuers and update their ratings if necessary. In fact, many issues are either upgraded or downgraded each year, so you have to check current ratings when buying bonds that have been on the market for some time.

THE LURE OF HIGH-YIELD BONDS

A discount bond sells for less than its face value, which is the price the issuing company or governmental agency will ultimately pay when it redeems the bond from the owner at maturity. A deep-discount bond is one selling at a large discount.

Sometimes bonds are issued at a discount. But the big discounts develop mainly as a result of changes in the general level of interest rates. As an illustration of how that happens, start with a 20-year corporate bond issued ten years ago at par—$1,000 or multiples of that amount—with a 6% coupon interest rate.

You wouldn't give the owner $1,000 for that bond today for obvious reasons. It still pays $60 a year interest because the coupon rate was permanently fixed when the bond was issued. Interest rates have risen since then and you expect to earn a lot more than $60 for each $1,000 you invest in bonds now.

At what price would that 6% bond become a good buy? To judge discount bonds properly, you employ the three yield measures discussed earlier in this chapter.

Current yield.   This is the annual interest payment divided by the present price. Let's assume that the bond is selling for $720. The current yield, therefore, comes to 8.3% ($60÷$720 × 100).

Yield to maturity.   As you scan bond price lists, you will see current yields of only 6% among bonds issued by corporations as reputable as those issuing bonds paying 9% at the same time. The reason for that seemingly illogical difference probably lies in the nature of the income the bonds produce for the investor.

The 6% bond used in our example will give you $60 a year, no matter what you pay for the bond. In addition, the company that issued the bond will redeem it in ten years at its par value of $1,000, which is $280 more than the current price. You won't realize the $280 for ten years, but for mathematical convenience let's say you receive the discount as equal installments of $28 for each of the ten years. The percentage figure that tells you how much you are earning from interest and the amortized discount is the yield to maturity. But don't simply add and then divide. It's more complicated than that. Bond dealers use bond tables and programmed calculators to compute yields, and some hand-held financial calculators can do it. But you can approximate the yield to maturity with the following shortcut formula:

$$\frac{\text{annual interest payment} + }{\text{Average of Par Value}} \times 100$$
$$\frac{\text{annually accumulated discount}}{\text{and Current Price}}$$

For the bond in the example:

$$\frac{60 + 28}{860} = \frac{88}{860} \times 100 = 10.2\%$$

The same formula can be used for bonds for which you pay a premium. In those cases you would subtract the annually accumulated premium from the annual interest payment.

Yield after tax.   Deep discount bonds attract many investors because of the tax advantage of the built-in capital gain if the bond was issued before mid 1984 and acquired before October 22, 1986. (The bonds also appeal to speculators betting on a drop in interest rates.) The tax rules are complex in this area; in some cases you can choose to report a proportional share of the gain in each year leading up to maturity or resale of the bond, and in other cases you have no choice but to do so.

You can roughly approximate the after-tax yield by adapting the shortcut formula used earlier. Subtract the income tax you would pay on the annual interest payment and the tax due on the annually accumulated discount and then proceed as before.

Deep-discount bonds should be compared with state and local tax-exempt issues as well as regular bonds. However, keep this fact in mind when evaluating tax-exempt yields: Although all the interest from a tax-exempt bond escapes federal and possibly state and local income taxes, any capital gains from discounts are taxable.

When you compare taxable bonds, take into consideration one feature that makes deep-discount bonds a particularly good vehicle for speculation. Deep-discount bonds carry low coupon interest rates, and low-coupon bonds fluctuate more widely than high-coupon issues. The added volatility works to your advantage if interest rates fall after you buy the bond because its price should rise more than that of a higher coupon issue. It works against you if rates rise.

BUYING TIPS ON BONDS

Your broker may not follow the bond markets, but the firm's research department should be able to suggest a number of worthwhile issues. Here are a few general buying tips that will make it easier to select good bonds.

Update the credit rating.   A bond's quality rating may be revised after it is issued because of a change in the issuer's financial position. Many bonds have been on the market a long time, so it's important to check current ratings.

Be sure you can bail out.   Although you may buy a bond firmly intending to hold it to maturity, it usually doesn't make sense to freeze yourself into an investment. Ordinary investors should restrict themselves to investment-grade bonds that can be priced and sold easily.

Time the maturities.   Often you can select bonds that will mature exactly when you need large sums—say, for college expenses or, at retirement, for reinvestment in bonds with high current yields to supplement your pension income.

ZERO-COUPON BONDS

With a conventional bond you can typically expect to receive an interest payment every six months. "Zeros," on the other hand, don't pay any interest until maturity. You buy the bond at a substantial discount from its face value, then collect the full value years later. Zeroes usually come in denominations as low as $1,000 and are sold at discounts from face value of 50% to 75%, depending on the maturity.

There's one big hitch. Even though you receive no annual interest, the IRS requires that you report it as if you had. The difference between what you paid for the bond and what you'll receive when it matures is taxable annually on a prorated basis. This makes zeroes attractive chiefly to people with individual retirement accounts, on which they needn't pay tax until they take the money out (see Chapter 24). You can buy a zero-coupon bond, sock it away in an IRA and forget about taxes until you actually withdraw the money. Zeroes are also an attractive way to give financial gifts to minors, who may be taxed at a lower rate than their parents (see Chapter 5 for some cautions about this idea). Zeroes are also available as municipal bonds, which spare you the annual reporting chore, and Treasury issues.

Zeroes entail the usual market risks for investors, with this added kicker: The company that issues it could conceivably default without ever having paid you a penny of interest.

U.S. GOVERNMENT SECURITIES

Because they can't be matched for safety, securities issued by the U.S. government and its agencies are the choice of many conservative investors concerned with preservation of their capital. The U.S. Treasury has been in the credit markets in such volume for the past decade or so that its debt instruments have found their way into other investors' portfolios as well. There are dozens of government issues to choose from—some, such as Treasury bills, readily salable in the open marketplace; others, such as U.S. savings bonds, less liquid. Yields on government issues usually run a little lower than on high-grade corporate issues because of the safety factor. Here's a rundown of the most widely held government debt instruments.

Treasury bills. These are short-term issues, usually carrying three- or six-month maturities, which are auctioned off to investors weekly. Minimum purchase is $10,000. Some bills run for a year and are auctioned less often. T-bills are sold on a discount basis, then redeemed at maturity for the full face amount. This means they pay the interest up front. If the rate is 6%, for instance, you pay $9,400 for a $10,000 bill, then collect $10,000 when it matures. This "auction," or "discount," rate actually understates the yield when compared with other securities, which are usually described in terms of their bond equivalent yield. To find the bond equivalent yield for a T-bill, calculate the relationship between the amount of interest paid and the cash you actually had to lay out to get it. In the example above, you're laying out only $9,400 in order to collect $600 in interest. Thus, assuming this is a one-year bill, your bond equivalent yield would be 6.38%.

In addition to their safety, T-bills, along with other Treasury securities, are exempt from state and local income taxes. They are issued in book-entry form, meaning you don't actually receive any certificates, just a notification that you own them.

If you live near a Federal Reserve bank or branch, you can stop by and pick up the forms for purchasing T-bills. Otherwise, you must write to a Federal Reserve bank or branch for instructions and an application form, return it with payment for the amount of purchase, and wait for notification that a bill has been purchased in your name. For information on how to proceed and addresses of Federal Reserve banks and branches, write to the Bureau of the Public Debt, Dept. F, Washington, D.C. 20239-0001. Commercial banks and brokers will make the purchase for you, but their fee, usually around $25, cuts into the yield.

Treasury notes. Notes run for one to ten years. They are coupon issues in much the same way as corporate bonds. As with T-bills, you can purchase them directly through a Federal Reserve bank or branch, or you can have a broker or a commercial bank do it for you. Interest is paid semi-annually, the notes are not callable prior to maturity, and the minimum purchase is $5,000 for maturities of less than four years, $1,000 for longer-term issues.

Treasury bonds. T-bonds generally carry maturity dates more than ten years after issue. Most cannot be called in early by the Treasury. Minimum purchase is $1,000.

U.S. agency securities. A number of U.S. government agencies and federally sponsored enterprises issue debt securities. They usually do not carry the full faith and credit of the government, but this difference is really quibbling because it is doubtful that the government would allow one of its agencies to default on an obligation. Nevertheless, the difference is usually reflected in the relative yields of agency vs. Treasury debt instruments. Agency issues, being the "inferior" risk, pay a bit more, despite the additional fact that some agency securities— but not all—are exempt from state and local income taxes, just as Treasury issues.

A description of the various securities available would amount to a description of the functions of the issuing agencies. Each has its own financing needs, each goes to the markets to fulfill them, and each pays the going rates. Some, such as the Federal Farm Credit System and the Federal Home Loan Bank System, often issue short- as well as long-term debt instruments. Most float mainly intermediate-term issues. Minimum purchase requirements vary greatly, ranging from $1,000 to $10,000 or more. Purchases must usually be made through brokers, who can supply a listing of the securities available.

Among the most popular of agency securities are those backed by the Government National Mortgage Association, or Ginnie Mae, whose job it is to help create a secondary market for home mortgages. Actually, Ginnie Mae doesn't issue securities. It insures pools of FHA and VA mortgages assembled by mortgage bankers and other lenders. Ginnie Mae insurance has no loopholes: If a borrower on a mortgage in the pool fails to make a monthly payment of principal and interest, the agency will make good if the issuer of the security doesn't. Because the FHA and VA mortgages in the pool are also backed by the federal government, your investment should be doubly secure against default.

Ginnie Mae securities are called pass-through certificates, and they come in minimum denominations of $25,000. But for as little as $1,000 you can buy into a Ginnie Mae mutual fund or unit trust sponsored by a number of fund managers and brokerage firms. Some pass along only the interest payments and use the principal to invest in more mortgages. Others pass along both interest and principal to investors.

Freddie Mac participation certificates (issued by the Federal Home Loan Mortgage Corp.) and Fannie Mae securities (issued by the Federal National Mortgage Association) round out the market for mortgage backed securities from quasi-government agencies. Denominations start at $25,000. Fannie Maes are not an obligation of the federal government but carry the guarantee of the agency.

Mortgage-backed securities can be a solid addition to an investment portfolio, but many investors don't seem to understand the risks. Like bonds, their market value declines as interest rates rise. But Ginnies, Fannies and Freddies carry another risk: As mortgage rates go down (an event you would expect to enhance the value of securities bought at higher rates), homeowners tend to refinance to take advantage of the situation. And when they refinance, their mortgages get paid off and drop out of the pool. Investors get the principal back, but their 12% return goes up in smoke. This has the perverse effect of driving the price of Ginnie Maes and similar issues down at the very time that the price of bonds is going up.

The action of homeowners refinancing mortgages held in a Ginnie Mae or Freddie Mac pool is comparable to a corporation calling its bonds in that you get your principal back earlier than you expected but because you're at the mercy of thousands of homeowners making independent decisions about when to refinance, the principal comes back in unpredictable chunks. Your cash flow is erratic, and so is your yield. To compensate for this uncertainty, mortgage pools have generally had to pay a percentage point or two more than Treasury bonds, which are much more predictable.

Collateralized mortgage obligations (CMOs) are a relatively new investment idea designed to take some of the uncertainty out of the situation by building in some protection against early prepayments. Backed by Ginnie Maes, they pay interest quarterly or semiannually, instead of monthly. A typical CMO is divided into several different maturities—short, intermediate and long term, with finer divisions in between. As prepayments are received, they're used first to pay off the short-term investors, then the intermediate-term investors and so forth until the entire issue is retired. The minimum investment in a CMO is usually $1,000. A variation on the CMO idea, the real estate mortgage investment conduit, or REMIC, may contain mortgages that are not backed by government agencies.

U.S. SAVINGS BONDS

Savings bonds come in two varieties.

EE bonds mature in eight to 12 years, depending on when they were issued. If held for at least five years, they pay interest equal to 85% of the average yield on five-year Treasury securities or a minimum rate, whichever is more. The minimum rate is 6% for bonds issued after November 1, 1986, and 7.5% for bonds issued November 1, 1982, through October 1986. The variable rate is adjusted every six months, in May and November. (You can get current rate information by calling 800-US-BONDS, or USA-8888 in the Washington, D.C., area.) EE bonds are sold at a 50% discount from face value in denominations of $50, $75, $100, $200, $500, $1,000, $2,500, $5,000 and $10,000. EE bonds replaced the old E bonds some years ago, but most E bonds continue to earn interest.

Bonds bought before November 1982 and held for five years after that date qualify for the variable rates. The exceptions are E bonds issued more than 40 years ago, which have already reached final maturity and are no longer earning interest. If you cash in a bond dated November 1982 or later before five years have passed, you will receive a graduated scale of interest, starting at 4.16% and rising to a rate that depends on how long you held the bond.

EE bonds are sold at banks and other financial institutions or through payroll-deduction plans. There is no sales charge or commission.

HH bonds are the other type. The only way to acquire HH bonds is to trade a minimum of $500 worth of E or EE bonds or reinvest a Series H bond that has reached its final maturity.

If you have $600 in E or EE bonds (meaning not face amount but redemption value, which depends on how much interest you have earned), you can exchange them for one $500 HH bond and take the other $100 in cash or add $400 and take a $1,000 HH bond. You cannot buy HHs just for cash.

HHs mature in ten years. Bonds issued since November 1, 1986, pay 6% interest in semiannual installments via check or electronic funds transfer to the holder's bank account. Like EE bonds, their maturity can be extended. Some early H bonds have reached final maturity.

HH bonds come in $500, $1,000, $5,000 and $10,000 denominations. There is no limit on the amount of E or EE bonds you can exchange for HH bonds in a year, but EEs must be six months old before they can be exchanged.

You must trade for HH bonds at a Federal Reserve Bank or the Bureau of the Public Debt, a division of the Treasury. The bureau's address (you can make a trade by mail) is simply Washington, D.C. 20226. Ask for Form PD 3253. Most banks and other agencies that issue EE bonds will have the forms you will need to fill out to exchange Es and EEs for HH bonds.

Reasons to buy savings bonds The yields on EE bonds have been improved considerably since 1982, making them attractive as investments. But most bond buyers are probably motivated by other considerations as well: safety, convenience and, in many cases, substantial tax advantages.

Safety. There's no safer place to put your money. Savings bonds of both types are backed by the full faith and credit of the

U.S. government. Payment of the interest and principal is guaranteed. Lost, stolen, damaged or destroyed bonds can be replaced free. (For information about that, write to the Bureau of the Public Debt, Parkersburg, W. Va. 26106-1328.)

Savings bonds are not transferable. You can cash them in, but you can't sell them. Their market price doesn't rise when interest rates fall or fall when rates rise. A savings bond will never have to be cashed in for less than you pay for it.

Convenience. Payroll savings plans sponsored by employers make it easy to accumulate EE bonds. This convenience is attractive to savers who need an incentive to put something aside on a regular basis. EE bonds can also be easily purchased at banks and other financial institutions. You can even order them over the phone and charge them to your credit card (800-US-BONDS).

Tax advantages. Were it not for this feature, savings bonds would probably be much less widely held. To begin with, the interest on EEs and HHs is exempt from all state and local income taxes. And although the exemption doesn't extend to federal taxes, your options for paying the federal tab on EE bonds create opportunities to increase your effective return considerably.

You can (1) pay the tax each year as the interest accrues, or (2) postpone the day of reckoning until you cash in the bond or dispose of it (by giving it away, for instance) or until it reaches final maturity. You also have the option of exchanging your EE bonds (and the older E series as well) for HH bonds and thereby continuing to put off paying tax on the accumulated E or EE bond interest until you cash in or dispose of the HHs or until they reach final maturity. Here's how investors in certain circumstances can profit from these options.

Investors with young children. If you'd like to start, say, a college fund for a child, you can take advantage of the option to report the interest on EE bonds as it accrues. You simply purchase bonds in the child's name (list yourself as beneficiary in case something happens to the child, but don't make yourself co-owner). This will make the child liable for the tax. And since it will probably be several years before the child has enough income to incur any tax liability, the income from the bonds will accumulate, for practical purposes, tax-free. (But see the discussion on the limitations of this technique in Chapter 5.)

You set this up by filing a federal income tax return in the child's name when you first start the program and stating on the return that your child will be reporting the interest yearly. Report all the interest earned up to then. This establishes your intent. No further returns are necessary until the child's bond interest plus other income reaches the level at which a return would be required by law. At that time the child need report only that year's interest. Previously accrued interest escapes tax.

Workers with an eye on retirement. In this case taxpayers with high incomes can take advantage of the option that allows postponing the federal income tax on E or EE bond interest until the bonds are cashed. You will almost certainly drop into a lower tax bracket after retirement, and the difference can boost your effective return substantially.

Take another example. Say you belong to a pension fund financed in part by your own contributions. When you retire, the taxable portion of your pension benefits may be reduced until you've recovered your contributions. Cashing in your bonds during that period may permit you to escape some of the tax on their interest because your taxable income will be comparatively low.

There's yet another choice: You could exchange your E or EE bonds for HH bonds, further postponing taxes on the accumulated interest until you cash in the HHs. In return you'd get semiannual checks for the interest on the HH bonds. You'd have to pay taxes on that interest, but you will have effectively beaten the tax on the E or EE bonds for as long as you hold onto the HHs.

TAX-FREE MUNICIPAL BONDS

Relatively high rates of return and the progressive federal income tax tables have made these bonds popular with middle-income investors who once thought of them chiefly as havens for the rich. They are described in detail in Chapter 22.

TAXABLE MUNICIPAL BONDS

Municipal bonds that pay taxable interest are by-products of the Tax Reform Act of 1986, which put limits on the tax-free status of bonds issued for "nonessential" purposes. Nonessential bonds include those issued by states or municipalities to finance home mortgages, student loans and small industrial-development projects.

Taxable munis, which generally are scheduled to mature in seven to ten years, have a number of attractive features. Like Treasury bonds, their interest is usually exempt from state and local taxes, and their yields can be a percentage point or two higher than Treasuries of the same maturity. An important potential drawback is the relatively small size of the taxable muni market. That has tended to keep big investors such as mutual funds away and could make it difficult for individual investors to find a buyer if they want to sell their bonds.

Most taxable municipal issues are backed by the revenues of a project rather than the taxing power of the municipality itself. To make such bonds attractive, most are also backed by some kind of insurance that pledges to pay off investors if the issuer defaults. The insurance has boosted the ratings of most issues to AAA, regardless of the creditworthiness of the issuer. But all insurance is not equally trustworthy, so the prices and yields of taxable munis depend a lot on how the market perceives the strength of the company backing the issue.

If you can afford the $100,000 stake that's often required to invest in this market as an individual, look before you leap. Compare the yields available from tax-exempt munis against the after-tax yields being offered by taxable issues. Because the yields are relatively high but the market is relatively illiquid, taxable munis are probably best suited for IRAs, Keoghs and other tax-sheltered pension plans.

CERTIFICATES OF DEPOSIT

There are several kinds of savings and investment vehicles commonly referred to as CDs. They range from so-called time-deposit savings certificates, available in modest denominations at banks, savings and loan associations, and credit unions, to negotiable certificates requiring minimum deposits of $100,000.

Most restrictions on these kinds of accounts have been lifted by federal regulators, so financial institutions are generally free to set their own maturities, interest rates and other terms. (Some examples are discussed in Chapter 4.)

One thing that sets CDs apart from most other fixed-income investments is the possibility of having to pay a penalty if you need to withdraw your money before the certificate has matured. Penalties vary from institution to institution and thus are impossible to generalize. Be sure to get a clear explanation of what you'll have to pay if you redeem a CD early.

Another thing to be aware of when using a certificate of deposit is the rollover provision. In some cases the certificate will be automatically rolled over (that is, another certificate purchased for you) if you don't notify the institution within a specified number of days before the certificate's maturity.

MAKE YOUR MONEY GROW 17

MUTUAL FUNDS AND OTHER INVESTMENT POOLS

$\mathbf{T}$he enormous popularity of mutual funds and other investment pools isn't hard to understand. Hardly any of us have the time or ability to do a competent job of sorting through thousands of stocks, bonds and other investment possibilities in search of the few that fit our own portfolios.

Investment pools simplify the task. Instead of picking individual stocks or bonds, we can pick a pool with investment goals that match our own. We can pick a manager with the kind of experience we wish we had ourselves. In most cases we can even monitor performance on a daily basis if we're so inclined. What's more, each kind of investment pool has specific advantages that can make it especially attractive to investors with particular goals in mind.

MUTUAL FUNDS

Whether you're investing a little or a lot, mutual funds offer a combination of advantages that simply aren't available anywhere else.

Small minimum investment. Initial requirements of $500 or

$1,000 are common, but some funds will accept as little as $25 or $50. A few have no minimums. And regardless of their initial purchase requirements, most funds will take smaller amounts once you become a shareholder.

Instant diversification. Buying a share of a mutual fund gives you partial ownership of a professionally selected portfolio of dozens of stocks, bonds or other securities. Diversification doesn't insulate you against market movements, but it does help dampen the impact of wide price swings that may affect individual securities.

Easy liquidity. Mutual funds are by definition "open-ended." That means they are constantly issuing new shares and re-deeming old ones. When you want to sell your shares, the fund is required to buy them back. Transactions can be accomplished through the mail or, in many cases, by telephone or wire.

Automatic reinvestment of earnings. Virtually all funds will automatically reinvest dividends and capital gains earned by your account as a result of the fund's buying and selling of investments for its portfolio.

Automatic payment plans. Most funds will arrange automatic withdrawal of earnings or principal or both for shareholders who want regular income.

How they operate. Mutual funds use the money from their shareholders to buy their portfolios. Most funds offer shares to the public continuously, either directly through advertisements or through stockbrokers and other dealers. Occasionally a fund will close its doors to new investors but continue to operate for the benefit of existing shareholders.

Professional management. Mutual funds are run by management companies that administer their day-to-day operations, provide their staffs, and guide their investments. The management company may also sell the fund's shares through an affiliate. Many funds are managed by stock brokerage firms or investment counselors who serve other clients. Some management companies administer two or more funds, a collection referred to as a "family" of funds. You can usually exchange shares in one fund for shares in another in the same family by paying a small service charge.

Fees. The management company is paid an annual fee, commonly one-half to three-fourths of 1% of the fund's average assets. The rate is often stepped down as the fund's assets increase—the larger the fund gets, the smaller the percentage. Some funds use an incentive system, periodically adjusting the fee according to the fund's performance compared with the stock market as a whole: the better the performance, the higher the fee.

Investment objectives. The majority of funds invest in common stocks or bonds or both, but some buy gold or other kinds of assets. Some concentrate on only one industry or on particular types of securities, such as bonds and preferred stocks. Portfolios are assembled to meet specific objectives: safety of capital, high income, moderate capital appreciation, or fast growth, for example. The most speculative funds may employ such techniques as short selling, buying on margin, or investing in "letter" stocks (securities that have not yet been registered for general sale).

Investment policies, as well as other details of a fund's operations, are spelled out in its prospectus, which is available on request and must be given to each prospective buyer.

Pricing of shares. The value of a fund share is expressed in terms of its net asset value, which is the fund's total net assets (the value of its portfolio minus any money the fund owes) divided by the number of shares outstanding. Because net asset value rises and falls with the market prices of a fund's holdings, the funds calculate the figure each day. A few specialized funds value their shares hourly. The price at which you buy fund shares or sell them back to the fund is based on the next calculated net asset value following receipt of your order. When you invest by dollar amounts, your purchase will probably include a fractional share. For instance, $1,000 will buy 61.728 shares of a no-load fund with a $16.20 asset value.

Fund income. A fund makes money from dividends and interest on the securities it owns and from capital gains made on the sales of those securities or other investments. If its portfolio selections are bad or the market turns sour, the fund may lose money. Virtually all income left after payment of management fees and other expenses is distributed to share-holders.

What you pay. Some mutual funds impose a sales charge, which is almost always figured on a sliding scale. Although these sales loads, as they're called, vary a great deal, a schedule might start at 8.5% for investments up to $10,000 and then go to 7.5% for $10,000 to $25,000, 6% for $25,000, and so on down to 1% for extremely large purchases. It's important to realize that this load is calculated on the gross amount of your investment. If you give an 8.5% fund $1,000, $85 will be deducted as a sales charge and $915 will be invested in the fund's shares. An 8.5% sales charge thus works out to about 9.3% of your net investment in such a case.

Hundreds of funds, including virtually all money-market funds, charge no up-front sales fee and are known as no-load funds. They have no salesmen, so you have to get in touch with them through the mail or by telephone. In other respects, they operate like the load funds.

Some former no-load funds now have a sales load of less than 8.5% but still more than zero. The load may be only 2% or 3%, but the irony is that low loads may be charged by companies that sell shares directly by mail or telephone—companies that don't need loads to pay outside commissions.

Mutual fund prices published in newspapers and other periodicals show two quotations: the net asset value, or "bid," price at which you can sell a share, and the "offering," or "asked," price at which you can buy a share. The offering price includes the maximum sales charge. With no-load funds the bid price is identical to the asked, or offering, price.

There are a number of other possible charges you'll have to check before you'll know how much it will cost you to own a particular fund.

Contingent deferred sales charges. These fees are deducted from your account if you redeem shares before a specified period elapses from the date you bought the shares. The amount of the charge and any conditions under which you may be exempt should be explained in the prospectus, but the descriptive language may be confusing. A key point to check is whether your entire interest in the fund or just the amount you originally invested for shares is liable to a deferred charge. If increases in net asset value, capital gains distributions or dividends are exempt, you know going in the maximum charge you face and that your profits are shielded.

Redemption fees. Slightly different from contingent deferred sales charges, redemption fees are more worrisome if you are investing for capital gains rather than dividend or interest income. A redemption fee is levied against the net asset value when you sell, so it nips profits as well as the amount you invested.

Marketing fees. Many funds take a special deduction from assets for advertising, marketing and other expenses that may amount to more than the management fee. These are called 12b-1 funds.

HOW TO PICK A WINNER

Although a mutual fund saves you the trouble of having to select the individual investments in a portfolio, it doesn't eliminate the risks. If you choose a fund that performs poorly, you take the loss just as surely as if you had chosen its portfolio yourself.

It is important, therefore, to know what you are getting into. Mutual funds are not all alike. Some, as mentioned earlier, take a conservative approach; others are decidedly risky; many fall somewhere in between. When setting out to select a fund, your first task is to formulate your own investment objectives. Then you can look closely at the funds that seem to match them.

You can get lists of funds and information about their investment objectives and performance from a number of sources. Several magazines, including *Changing Times, Money* and *Sylvia Porter's Personal Finance*, publish monthly rankings of top-performing funds. Those publications, plus *Forbes* and *Business Week*, also issue annual roundups of fund performance. Weisenberger Financial Services publishes an exhaustive compilation of information on investment companies and updates it annually. The book, called *Investment Companies*, is expensive, but brokerage offices and libraries have copies. The

American Association of Individual Investors, 612 N. Michigan Ave., Chicago, Ill. 60611, publishes a useful guide titled *The Individual Investor's Guide to No-Load Mutual Funds*, which costs $19.95. You can get a listing of key facts on some 400 no-load and low-load funds in *The Investor's Guide and Mutual Fund Directory* from the No-Load Mutual Fund Association, P.O. Box 20004, Dept. PG, JAF Building, New York, N.Y. 10116. The cost is $5. A listing of load and no-load funds, called *Guide to Mutual Funds*, is available for $2.50 from the Investment Company Institute, 1600 M St., N.W., Washington, D.C. 20036.

Once you have compiled a list of funds that seem to meet your investment objectives, write for their prospectuses and annual reports and compare the funds on past performance in good markets and bad. See which are members of families of funds, meaning you would have the flexibility of switching your money among different types of funds as market conditions changed.

The following major groupings offer more options than you'll probably ever use.

Aggressive growth funds. These strive for big profits, generally by investing in small companies and developing industries or by concentrating on volatile issues. Some use speculative techniques, such as trading with borrowed money and short selling. The greater the drive for high profits, the greater the risk. Here are a few funds that try for maximum capital gains and have compiled good long-term results, along with the toll-free number you can use to request a prospectus: Fidelity Magellan Fund (800-544-6666); Putnam OTC Emerging Growth (800-225-1581); Lehman Opportunity Fund (800-221-5350); Twentieth Century Growth Investors (800-345-2021).

Growth funds. These look for long-range capital gains by buying the stocks of companies that supposedly have unique characteristics that will enable them to grow faster than inflation. Growth and income funds, which form another group, have much the same objective, but they put greater emphasis on capital preservation and try to produce more current dividend income. Examples: Phoenix Growth (800-243-1574);

Fidelity Fund (800-544-6666); IDS Growth Fund (800-328-8300); Mutual Shares Corp. (800-457-0211).

Income funds. Designed to return a higher level of dividends than others, these funds invest in bonds, preferred stocks and high-yielding common stocks. Examples: Vanguard High-Yield Stock (800–662-7447); United Income (800-821-5664); Oppenheimer Equity-Income (800-525-7048); Decatur I Series (800-523-4640); Financial Industrial Income Fund (800-525-8085).

Balanced funds. Assets in these funds, too, are generally distributed among common stocks, preferreds and bonds, but their purpose is to minimize risk. Most keep 20% to 40% of assets in bonds or preferreds at all times and the rest in well-capitalized major companies. Examples: Phoenix Balanced Fund (800-243-1574); Loomis-Sayles Mutual (800-343-7104); Strong Investment Fund (800-368-3863); IDS Mutual (800-328-8300); Vanguard Wellington (800-662-7447).

Specialized, or sector, funds. A number of funds concentrate their investments in one or two fields or industries. They may invest largely in stocks of utility companies, U.S. government securities, bank shares, or stocks of gold mines. Examples: Fidelity Select Health (800-544-6666); Fidelity Select Financial Services (800-544-6666); Lexington Gold Fund (800-526-0056); Prudential Utility Fund (800-872-7787); Alliance Technology (800-221-5672).

International and global funds. International funds are U.S.-based but invest in securities of companies traded on foreign exchanges. Global funds reserve the right to mix in some U.S. issues as well. Either are good places to be when the value of the dollar is falling because their holding may be denominated in foreign currencies, and investors profit from the favorable exchange rates on those currencies. Examples: Merrill Lynch Pacific Fund (available through brokers); Alliance International (800-221-5672); Putnam International Equities (800-225-1581); T. Rowe Price International (800-638-5660).

Bond funds. They divide into four categories: taxable, non-taxable, high quality and high yield. High-yield funds specialize in lower-rated bonds that must pay more interest to attract investor interest. High-quality funds stick to top-rated corporate or municipal issues. Examples: United Bond Fund (high-quality corporate, 800-821-5664); Kemper High Yield (corporate, 800-621-1048); Stein Roe Managed Municipal Bonds (high quality, 800-621-0320); IDS High-Yield Tax Exempt Fund (800-328-8300).

Total return funds. These look for a combination of dividends and capital gains as the route to riches and are suitable for long-range investors. Examples: Strong Total Return (800-368-3863); FPA Paramount (800-421-4374); Merrill Lynch Capital (available through brokers); Evergreen Total Return (800-325-0064).

Money-market funds. They invest in U.S. Treasury bills, commercial paper (essentially the IOUs of corporations), certificates of deposit, and other more esoteric short-term debt instruments. They usually credit interest to your account daily; most allow you to draw checks on the balance in your fund. These funds are discussed in detail later in this chapter.

Tax-free funds. For investors interested in tax-free income, there are funds that invest in municipal bonds and pass along the interest. There are also funds known as tax-free money-market funds because they invest in short-term tax-exempt obligations. There's more on each of these kinds of funds in Chapter 22.

HOW TO TELL HOW YOUR FUND IS DOING

The mutual fund tables in the newspapers list daily net asset values (NAV). The price of your shares is a key concern, of course, but you need more information than that to be able to judge how your fund has been performing. Suppose, for example, that the NAV shows virtually no change for some extended period, say a year. That does not necessarily mean that the fund's value to you didn't change. The fund might have distributed income dividends and capital gains during that period. In fact, a capital gains payment acts to depress the NAV because the fund is actually distributing money that previously was included in its portfolio.

You can't get the true measure of a fund's performance, therefore, unless you take dividends and capital gains payments into account along with changes in the net asset value. What you really need to know is the fund's total return. Essentially, that's what the funds promote when they issue their periodic reports to shareholders. The fund states the total return for a shareholder who reinvested all payouts and compares this with the results if the shareholder took all payments in cash.

On your own, you can compute your fund's performance in several different ways and get several different answers. For an idea of how a return varies with the approach you use, consider this simplified illustration: The XYZ Fund, a fictional no-load growth fund, starts the year with a net asset value of $10 a share.

After six months, a market rally pushes XYZ's value to $15 a share. The fund sells assets and distributes $5 a share in capital gains. This returns its NAV to $10. The shareholders have a choice of taking the $5 in cash or reinvesting it in the fund.

In the second half of the year, XYZ's investments continue to do well. It ends the year with an NAV of $20. Because XYZ is a growth-oriented fund, assume it pays no cash dividends. If you ignore the capital gain distribution, the fund jumped 100%—from $10 to $20 a share.

A better approach is to include the $5 in the return even if you took the money in cash. The $5 plus the $10 increase in the ultimate price of a share means the $10 at the start of the year is worth $25 at the end. That's a 150% increase.

Another way to figure total return, and probably the most accurate, is to assume that the $5 distribution is reinvested in XYZ shares. The $5 goes back into the fund when shares have a $10 NAV, so you now have 1½ shares instead of one. Each share is worth $20 at the end of the year, for a total of $30—a 200% return on the original $10.

The key to understanding the total-return concept is to think about the total wealth generated from your initial purchase, not just the market price of one share at the end of the measurement period.

CLOSED-END FUNDS

Closed-end funds also pool shareholders' capital for investment, but they don't issue new shares and they don't redeem old ones when investors want to sell. You buy the shares on a stock exchange or in the over-the-counter market and sell them the same way, paying a commission to a broker.

Because the market, not the value of the underlying assets, determines the price of a closed-end fund, their shares often sell at discounts from their net asset values. A few go at premiums from time to time. No one seems to have a completely satisfactory explanation for either phenomenon. The discounts don't automatically make the shares a bargain, since you usually have to accept a discounted price when you sell them. You could profit if for some reason the discount narrows, but you could lose if the discount widens. Closed-end funds, like mutuals (which are open-ended), invest in diversified or specialized groups of securities.

Over the years, several closed-end funds have converted, either voluntarily or under pressure from dissident investors, to mutual funds. Because mutual fund shares are priced at NAV and closed-ends often sell at a discount, open-ending can hike the worth of a closed-end fund investment 10%, 15% or more overnight.

In recent years there has been an explosion in closed-end offerings, although the market crash of October 1987 slowed it down considerably. Fueling the boom has been a desire on the part of investors to enlist the expertise of certain high-profile money managers who were starting such funds and to cash in on foreign stock markets that were flying even higher than the U.S. markets.

For instance, funds operated by Martin Zweig and Charles Allmon provide small investors access to the perceived investment prowess of those men, who ordinarily require minimum portfolios of $175,000 or more for individual management. Closed-end funds operating in Korea, Taiwan, Japan, Australia, France, Italy and other countries provide access to those markets.

In considering a closed-end fund, the safe route is to stick with funds that have been around long enough to establish a track record of consistent performance. It's probably not a good idea to buy a fund as a means of playing short-term market swings because the discounts and premiums serve to exacerbate the effect of price changes. On the other hand, well-managed closed-end funds can be a sensible place to look for dividends. Consider this: If a fund with a net asset value of $10 sells at a 10% discount, you can get $10 worth of assets earning dividends for you for only $9. That kind of leverage isn't available everywhere.

MONEY-MARKET FUNDS

Money-market mutual funds were originally designed as a place to park money temporarily between more permanent investments. But occasional sharp rises in short-term interest rates and the continuing volatility of the investment markets in general has made them a permanent fixture in many portfolios. They pay more interest than most savings accounts, there's no price volatility, and you can become an investor for as little as $250, although a more typical minimum initial investment is $1,000.

What they are. Money-market funds invest in securities known as money-market instruments. The money market isn't a place but the collective name given to deals by which the government, banks, big corporations, securities dealers and others borrow and lend money for short periods. The deals may be for overnight or a few days, but never more than a year or they're not part of the money market.

A fund's prospectus describes the types of instruments and investment techniques it may use, and its quarterly financial statements report current holdings. You can't judge a fund sensibly until you get the hang of what those instruments are. The makeup of the portfolio determines the yield and safety of your investment. These are the principal instruments you're likely to find in a fund portfolio.

Treasury bills and notes. Bills are issued with three-month, six-month and one-year maturities. Notes run longer, but they, like bills, are widely traded and can be bought when they are closer to maturity. Treasury issues constitute direct obligations of the federal government, so they rate tops in safety.

Agency securities. The funds may also buy short-term securities issued by individual government agencies or government-sponsored organizations. Some are backed by the full faith and credit of the federal government; others are guaranteed only by the agencies, but they rank just below Treasuries in safety because it's assumed that the government would not permit an agency to default.

Commercial paper. Essentially, these are IOUs issued by corporations to raise funds for limited periods, usually 60 days or less. Paper is rated for quality by credit-analysis firms according to the issuing company's financial strength. Standard & Poor's top rating is A-1; Moody's is Prime-1.

Banker's acceptances. These loans originate largely in import and export transactions in which the buyer gives the seller a note payable by the buyer within a fixed period of time. If the bank financing the transaction accepts the note, thus guaranteeing payment at maturity and thereby making the draft salable in the open market, it becomes a banker's acceptance. A money-market fund can buy the acceptance at a discount and get paid the full amount at maturity.

Certificates of deposit. The money market deals in large-denomination, negotiable certificates, not the relatively small amounts familiar to savers. Domestic CDs are issued by U.S. bank offices here. Yankee CDs are issued by foreign bank branches in the U.S.; Eurodollar CDs are sold by U.S. bank branches in Europe and payable in U.S. dollars. Eurodollar issues are regarded as a shade riskier than the others because of the possibility that redemption of the CDs might be impeded by some unfavorable action, such as the imposition of exchange controls by the foreign government.

Repurchase agreements. Repos, as they are known in the money-market trade, work a couple of different ways. In their most common form, they are created when a bank wishes to borrow money for a short while, maybe only one day. The bank sells Treasury bills it is holding to a money-market fund with a promise to buy them back the next day at a higher price or a specified interest rate. In effect, the repurchase agreement amounts to a loan with Treasury securities as collateral.

In a reverse repurchase agreement the transaction goes the

opposite way: The fund sells its bills to a bank and agrees to buy them back. Here it's the fund that is borrowing money from the bank. A fund may leave itself the option of executing reverse repos as a means of handling heavy shareholder redemptions. The borrowed money can be used to pay shareholders' withdrawals so portfolio securities that the fund wants to retain don't have to be sold.

How safe are they? Money-market funds are quite safe, but they aren't guaranteed. Because most funds hold several kinds of securities, the risk often depends on what those securities happen to be and how large they loom in the portfolio.

For maximum safety, look for a fund with a high proportion of U.S. government securities, CDs from well-known domestic banks, and top-rated commercial paper. Some investors prefer the funds ·that invest chiefly in U.S. and U.S.-guaranteed securities—Capital Preservation Fund, Kemper Government Money Market Fund, Merrill Lynch Government Fund, and several others. Normally you sacrifice a percentage point or two of yield for the safety of U.S. government securities.

You can fine-tune the risk to some extent by diversifying among two or more funds with different portfolios.

How they value their assets. This is one of the trickiest aspects of fund operations. If you follow yields, you will notice that occasionally one or more funds report surprisingly high or low yields compared with most other funds. Much of the difference may result from the fund managers' superior or inferior performance. For instance, if a fund manager thinks interest rates are headed down, he or she can delay the effect on the portfolio by lengthening the average maturity of the holdings, delaying for a time the need to invest in those new, lower-rate securities. If the manager thinks rates are going up, he or she shortens maturities in order to be in the market when it happens. A fund that exercises good timing on upswings and downswings can produce better performance than a fund with poor timing.

But that's not the whole story. Differences in yields can also stem from differences in the way funds compute the value of their portfolios. Funds prefer to maintain a fixed net asset value, usually $1. Interest income and profits from the sale and redemption of securities are paid out in the form of dividends. And the dividends buy additional shares to add to your account.

However, a portfolio's value really fluctuates daily as short-term interest-rate changes raise or lower the market price of the securities in the portfolio. The funds insulate their net asset values from those price changes by using different valuation methods, and the choice can have an effect on their yields, especially over a short measurement period such as a week. Over longer periods, the differences tend to wash out, underlining the futility of chasing yields based on technical factors such as valuation methods. Over the longer haul, superior management will make the important difference.

Fees and services. Variations in services and fees may appear trivial, but they sometimes produce unnecessary costs and annoying delays. Normally you deal with funds directly, although in a few cases you may have to go through the brokerage firm that sponsors the fund and perhaps open an account with the firm. If you buy shares through a bank or a broker other than the sponsoring broker, you might be charged a fee for services.

Management and sales fees. The overwhelming majority of money-market funds do not charge sales fees. Some funds, though, charge account-maintenance fees of a couple of dollars a month. All charge management fees, which average 75 cents per $100 earned. Some charge considerably more, and higher management and office fees come directly out of the pockets of investors. You can check on fees in the prospectus.

Checking privileges. This is one of the most attractive features of a money-market fund. All allow you to write checks on your account balance, usually in minimum denominations of $250 or $500, and most give it to you at no extra cost. By all means, sign up for the check plan when you open an account.

Expedited purchases. The slowest way to buy shares is by sending a check through the mail. To expedite the process, your bank, for a fee, will wire money directly to the fund. Investors in a broker-sponsored fund should be able to make the purchase through the firm's local office. If you buy shares by

TEN BIG MONEY-MARKET FUNDS

FUND NAME	MINIMUM INITIAL INVESTMENT	MINIMUM CHECK SIZE	PHONE
Capital Preservation Fund	$1,000	$100	800-472-3389
Cash Equivalent Fund	1,000	500	800-621-1048
Daily Cash Accumulation	500	250	800-525-7048
Dreyfus Liquid Assets	2,500	500	800-645-6561
Fidelity Cash Reserves	1,000	500	800-544-6666
Kemper Money Market	1,000	500	800-621-1048
Prudential-Bache Moneymart	1,000	500	800-872-7787
Shearson Daily Dividend	2,500	*	212-321-7155
T. Rowe Price Prime Reserve	1,000	500	800-638-5660
Vanguard MMR Prime Portfolio	1,000	250	800-662-7447

*No check writing

Source: *The Donoghue Organization, Inc.*

mail and your check is drawn on a member bank of the Federal Reserve System, funds start paying dividends one or two business days after your check is received. But to guard against nonpayment, most of the funds won't allow you to redeem shares bought until your check has been paid by your bank. The wait may be only a few days, but some funds fix arbitrary waiting periods that run much longer.

Expedited redemptions. You can redeem shares by mail, but money-market funds usually allow telephone and telegram redemptions and send the money directly to your bank. They will also usually wire payments above a certain amount, so you can have access to the money either the same business day or the next one. If you plan to use the telephone and wire services, you must register your bank account with the fund beforehand.

It's impractical to close out a fund account by writing a check against it because the account earns dividends daily and you can never be sure of your exact balance. If you like, you can write a check for most of the total and then redeem the rest by mail, telephone or wire.

The Investment Company Institute will send you a list of money-market funds that belong to it, as will the No-Load Mutual Fund Association (see addresses on page 292). Another good central source of information—names, addresses, services offered, portfolio makeup, recent performance records—is *Donoghue's Money Fund Directory,* available for $24 from Box 540, Holliston, Mass. 01746.

UNIT INVESTMENT TRUSTS

When you buy into a unit trust, you get part ownership, measured in units, of a fixed portfolio of securities. Unit trusts are a popular way to buy tax-exempt bonds and are also used by brokerage firms to package offerings of corporate bonds, utility stocks and pools of government-backed mortgages, known as Ginnie Maes (see Chapter 16).

For investors who want to put money into a particular type of security, unit trusts provide professionally selected, diversified portfolios that can usually be bought in multiples of about $1,000. Because the trusts hold onto their original securities instead of trading them, the investor gets a fixed dollar return that won't change much for a long period. The trusts don't dissolve and return the remaining capital to investors until most of the bonds in the portfolio have been redeemed or called.

The ability to lock in a certain rate is attractive if you want a steady, assured income or think interest rates will decline, thereby increasing bond prices. Of course, if interest rates increase, you'll be stuck with a low-level return that lowers the value of your units, for reasons explained in detail in Chapter 16. Those are the risks faced by anyone who buys fixed-income securities.

Unit trusts are sold so casually that many investors mistakenly assume they are interchangeable pieces of the same product, differing only in yield and type of security. Actually, trusts are far more complex than they seem, as anyone who reads a prospectus quickly learns, and they can differ significantly.

Buying a unit trust. Sponsoring brokerage firms try to sell out unit trusts within a matter of days after they are registered with the Securities and Exchange Commission. As a result, investors often have to place their orders before they receive a prospectus, relying on advance information from their brokers.

Usually, you can't get more than a few sketchy details in advance—the approximate yield, the sales charge, the distribution of the bonds according to quality rankings (AAA, AA, etc.), and a summary description of the issues in the portfolio. But there are a lot of other facts you should know. For instance, if you're trying to lock in a high yield for the long term, you'll want to know the call provisions of the bonds in the portfolio. Bonds with short-term call dates give the issuers greater freedom to call the bonds for redemption if interest rates decline; the high-rate bonds can then be paid off with funds raised by selling new bonds at lower rates.

You have an opportunity to check those and other details when you receive the prospectus with your bill. If the information given to you earlier by the broker turns out to be incorrect, you can ask to have your order canceled. Brokers may comply as a matter of good customer relations even when no mistake has been made. To avoid misunderstandings, make clear when you place the advance order that it's conditional on your being satisfied with the prospectus.

Commissions. Brokers' sales charges on newly issued trusts vary by firm and trust. You can expect to pay about 3% to 4½%. The percentages work out somewhat higher when the fees are computed on the net amount of the investment used to buy the underlying securities instead of the public offering price, which combines the net investment and the sales commission. Here's an illustration:

amount per unit invested in bonds	$970.57
sales charge	$45.73
public offering price per unit	$1,016.30

A quick trip to the calculator reveals that the $45.73 commission represents 4.5% of the $1,016.30 but 4.7% of the $970.57. This small difference becomes more impressive when you consider that some trusts require a $5,000 minimum purchase. Some sponsors graduate fees downward for large purchases.

Getting out. You can dispose of your units either by redeeming them through the trust or by selling them to or through the broker.

Trusts redeem units on the basis of the bid rather than the offering prices of the securities in the portfolio. The spread between bid and offering prices widens and narrows with market conditions. Municipal bond bid prices average 1% to 2% less than offering prices.

Although not obligated to do so, as prospectuses carefully point out, unit trust sponsors maintain a secondary market for their own units and are prepared to buy or sell them as they would other securities. The brokers don't charge a commission when they buy from you.

THE BASICS OF REAL ESTATE INVESTING

WHY REAL ESTATE CAN STILL BE ATTRACTIVE

I t is widely believed that the Tax Reform Act of 1986 effectively killed off real estate as an attractive investment. But it's not true, especially for the individual investor in rental properties. The fact of the matter is that tax reform happened to coincide with a couple of economic cycles that served to make real estate much less attractive than it had been only a few years earlier. For one thing, farming and the oil business hit the skids, leaving cities like Denver and Dallas with blocks and blocks of office and apartment buildings and no tenants. At the same time, inflation, a friend of real estate investors and practically no one else, went into hiding, disappointing investors who were counting on it to push up the price of their holdings fast. Only then did tax reform come along, with its stretched-out depreciation periods, tricky new rules on things like "passive" income and lower tax brackets that made deductions of all kinds a little less rewarding. Although the new tax rules may be guilty of kicking real estate while it was down, it can't really be convicted of killing it.

Besides, real estate isn't dead. While it's in the doldrums in some places, it actually booms in others. And as an investment, although it may not be quite as alluring as it used to be, it's still got quite a lot going for it—a combination of features that should serve to keep it uniquely attractive to patient investors.

The lure of leverage. Leverage is nothing more than using borrowed money to minimize your own up-front outlay. You use leverage when you take out a mortgage to buy a house, an apartment or a commercial building. The bigger the mortgage as a proportion of the property's value (and the smaller your down payment), the greater your leverage. And it's leverage that produces the spectacular returns sometimes available in real estate. Say you purchase an $80,000 condo with no loan and sell it several years later for $100,000. The $20,000 gain represents a 25% return on your $80,000 outlay. Not bad. But assume that you had invested only $20,000 of your own money and borrowed the other $60,000. In that case your result is considerably better: You have made $20,000 on a $20,000 investment. That's a 100% return.

Unfortunately, leverage can also act to magnify losses. For example, if you are forced to sell the $80,000 condo for $70,000, the $10,000 loss wipes out half of your $20,000 investment—a 50% loss even though the value of the property declined by only 13%. That's why leverage is sometimes called a two-edged sword. The keys to avoiding the bad side: well-selected properties and the ability to wait out bad markets.

Tax breaks: Alive and kicking. Few, if any, other investments can match the tax benefits available in real estate. It was true before and it's still true today. Chiefly, the breaks fall into two categories.

Current deductibility of expenses. While you own rental property, your operating costs, mortgage-interest payments, real estate taxes, and other expenses can be deducted from rental income, just as you would offset income with expenses in other businesses. (The portion of your mortgage payment that reduces the principal balance of the mortgage loan can't be deducted, of course, because it is not actually an expense. On the contrary, it increases your equity in the property.)

Compare this with the deductibility of expenses incurred for most other investments. If you own stocks and bonds, for example, you can deduct the cost of professional advice, portfolio management fees and other expenses of generating profits only to the extent that they exceed 2% of your adjusted gross income. For an income of $50,000, that means the first $1,000 comes entirely out of your pocket. In direct ownership of rental property, you can deduct every qualified cent you spend to rent or maintain the place, including mileage for driving over there. The difference, in the eyes of the tax laws, is that your rental property puts you in the real estate business; your stocks and bonds are strictly personal.

Depreciation.   The crowning tax break, the one that distinguishes real estate from such investments as stocks and bonds, is the right to deduct each year a certain amount of depreciation on a building used for business purposes. Depreciation represents a noncash expense. You don't have to spend a cent for repairs or maintenance to claim it. Nor does the property have to be deteriorating physically. The fact that the building's market value is rising does not stop you from claiming a depreciation deduction. If you buy the property from someone who has already depreciated it, you can start the depreciation cycle over again, as can the buyer after you.

Depreciation helps create a tax shelter because the effect is to shield part of your income from the property from taxes. And if your other income is within certain limits described below and you meet other tests, you can use depreciation on rental property to shield up to $25,000 of that income as well. The government eventually recaptures some of the taxes given up through depreciation when you sell the property. At that time, the depreciation must be deducted from the cost of the property, thereby increasing the amount of taxable gain realized on the sale.

Depreciation schedules allowed by the tax law have bounced around so much in recent years that's it's been difficult to keep track. Before the Economic Recovery Tax Act of 1981 (ERTA), a small residential property was ordinarily depreciated over a period of perhaps 25 to 30 years. Property bought after 1980 and before March 16, 1984, can be depreciated over as few as 15 years. The Tax Reform Act of 1984 raised that to 18 years for properties placed in service after March 15, 1984, and before May 9, 1985. The period was then stretched to 19 years, and the Tax Reform Act of 1986 boosted it all the way up to 27.5 years for residential buildings placed in service after 1986. Commercial properties, such as office buildings and stores, must be depreciated over a period of 31.5 years.

Investors who put their properties into service in past years get to keep the depreciation schedules in effect then. The current schedule is the least generous in quite a while, but even it can serve to turn a losing property into a winner, as the following example shows.

Suppose you buy a $100,000 condo as an investment. You take out an $80,000 mortgage at 10%, giving you monthly payments of $703. The condo fee adds another $100 to your monthly outlay, and property taxes, insurance, maintenance and repairs add up to another $100. Total out-of-pocket expense: $903 a month. You rent the place out and discover that you can get only $850 a month. Your simplified annual balance sheet before taxes looks like this:

Expenses:	$903/month × 12 months =	$10,836
Income:	$850/month × 12 months =	$10,200
Cash flow:		(-$ 636)

A negative cash flow, meaning expenses are larger than income, can be the kiss of death for most investments, but not necessarily for real estate. The reason is depreciation, the tax savings for which can convert a pre-tax negative cash flow into after-tax money in your pocket.

Let's apply the 27.5-year depreciation schedule to this greatly simplified example. The property cost $100,000, but the land on which your building sits is not depreciable and must be subtracted from the total before the depreciation allowance is applied. The IRS has no cut-and-dried formula for this, but allowing 20% of the total for land is safe enough. That leaves $80,000 to which to apply depreciation.

You must apply an equal proportion for each of the 27.5 years, which comes to 3.48% in the first year (because you actually get credit for only 11.5 months in the first year of ownership). That's an additional deduction in this case of $2,784. In the 33% tax bracket, that saves you $919 in cash—taxes you don't have to pay. Apply that against your negative cash flow of $636, and you actually squeak through the year with an after-tax positive cash flow of $283—not a princely sum considering you put up $20,000 as a down payment, but a positive return nonetheless. (Actually, your return would be slightly less because you wouldn't be able to deduct the entire mortgage payment. The payback of principal is not deductible because it actually increases your equity in the property. But annual principal repayment is a small amount, especially in the early years of a mortgage.)

Despite the ability of depreciation to turn a loser into a winner, a better property would be one that returned a positive cash flow, or at least broke even, before taxes. A positive cash flow could be offset by the depreciation, thereby giving you cash in your pocket with no tax liability. If you have more depreciation than you need to offset income from the property, you may be able to use it to shelter income from other sources—an activity that used to be a favorite among real estate investors but which has been limited to some degree by tax reforms.

If you "actively manage" the property, the meaning of which the IRS hasn't made entirely clear but probably means that you at least set the rent, approve tenents and decide on capital improvements, then you can deduct up to $25,000 in rental losses against other income, including salaries. You are denied 50 cents of the loss allowance for every dollar your adjusted gross income exceeds $100,000, until it disappears at $150,000 of income, regardless of how actively you manage the property. Actually, these losses are never gone completely because you get to save any disallowed amounts to apply against rental or other "passive" income in future years (see Chapter 22). If you don't get a chance to use them that way, you can add disallowed amounts to the cost basis of the property when you sell it, thus reducing any profit and any tax you'd owe on the profit.

Meanwhile, the disallowance rules covering losses outside the $25,000 limit are being phased in for properties acquired before October 23, 1986, and for properties on which there was a binding contract to acquire in effect on August 16, 1986, or on which construction had begun by that date. In 1988, 40% of such losses will be deductible; 20% will be deductible in 1989; and 10% will be deductible in 1990.

In addition to the depreciation schedules available to all rental property, the law provides special tax breaks for investors who rehabilitate old structures. For rehabilitation costs incurred on qualifying buildings after 1986, you can take an investment tax credit of 10% to 20% of the expenses on top of depreciation, depending on the type and age of the building. The credit is available for the cost of "substantial rehabilitation" of qualifying buildings. There are several tricky angles to claiming this investment tax credit, so don't attempt it without the help of a qualified accountant or tax attorney.

Price appreciation. Real estate prices have generally kept up with or surpassed the rise in consumer prices over the years. Of course, averages do not necessarily reflect the results for individual pieces of property or for all parts of the country. Real estate prices are strongly influenced by local conditions.

Throughout most of the 1970s, real estate prices rose so steadily in so many parts of the country that investors came to depend on capital gains for part of their investment return. Today it would be a mistake to take appreciation for granted. You must take care to select properties carefully.

TIPS ON BUYING RENTAL PROPERTY

Select properties for investment in much the same way you would if you were buying your own home. Pick a property that's typical, not one so special that it will appeal only to tenants with tastes that match your own.

• Compare prices of similar properties to make certain the property you're considering isn't overpriced.
• Compare rents for similar units nearby. Be skeptical of a seller's assurance that you can raise the rent once you take over. If it's so easy, why didn't that owner do it?

• Make sure the agreement you sign requires the seller to turn over tenants' damage deposits when you settle on the property.

• Examine existing leases before closing so you know how long they have to run, who the tenants are and how long they've been there.

• Be wary of investing in property on which maintenance has been put off. The seller's income and expense statements could show a handsome return because the owner hasn't spent enough for repairs.

• Check for local code violations. You don't want to get stuck with the expense of correcting them.

• Keep loan payments affordable so you won't get hurt by occasional vacancies.

REAL ESTATE INVESTMENT TRUSTS

A real estate investment trust is to real estate what a mutual fund is to stocks. A shareowner in a REIT participates in the pooled ownership of income-producing properties, such as apartment houses, shopping centers, office buildings, warehouses or a combination of these, or in the pooled ownership of mortgages on such properties, or in a mixture of buildings and mortgages. Shares are traded on the major stock exchanges or over the counter every day, which makes REITs the most liquid form of real estate investment you can find.

The main distinction you should be familiar with is between equity REITs and mortgage REITs. Equity REITs own income-producing properties. Mortgage REITs provide long-term mortgages and short-term construction loans. REITs in the lending business often demand some piece of the projects they finance and withdraw from the market when conditions are weak. There are also hybrid REITs that have a portion of their investments in mortgages and a portion in equity positions.

Equity trusts use shareholders' money and additional money they borrow to buy or build real estate. They hire a management firm to run the properties. The day-to-day manager is often an affiliate of the REIT, perhaps the real estate unit of the bank that organized the REIT in the first place.

Federal tax laws allow REITs to pay no taxes on income or

gains if they distribute at least 95% of earnings to shareholders and meet a number of other specific conditions. Because they pass on nearly all of their earnings, REITs are attractive to investors seeking relatively high dividends as well as a chance that share prices will rise. Mortgage REITs tend to pay out a little more than equity REITs, but both generally pay high dividends.

Sometimes dividends are paid not from earnings but from shareholders' equity. They are designated as returns of capital and treated as a refund of part of your investment. Instead of paying income taxes, you deduct the payment from the cost basis of the shares when you sell the stock. If your basis falls below zero, further returns of capital become taxable.

The risk in equity trusts is that markets in which they hold properties will turn sour, leaving them with empty buildings, no tenants and thus no rental income to pass along to shareholders. Mortgage trusts can be damaged by upswings in interest rates, which tend to hurt mortgage demand, and by recessions, which may impair mortgage borrowers' ability to repay their loans.

What to look for in a REIT. Study the annual reports of REITs that interest you. Once you've narrowed your choices, get from the companies copies of the 10-K reports that they are required to file with the Securities and Exchange Commission. Check the following.

Dividend history. Check especially on the consistency of payouts, and compare different trusts on this point.

Location and tenant mix. Watch out for inflated predictions of rent increases; overly optimistic outlooks for condominium sales or conversions; heavy investment in old open-air shopping centers in well-to-do areas where merchants can afford to pay higher rents in new malls; aging apartment complexes, which are expensive to maintain; and dependence on a few tenants or on one-industry towns.

On the plus side, look for strong investments in recession-resistant industries; a good geographic mix or a solid position in local markets you can keep an eye on yourself; and relationships with grade-A tenants such as major retailers and the U.S. government.

Appraisals. An annual report may show the properties' current appraisals. Take those figures with some caution. A trust that liquidates properties won't necessarily get top dollar on the open market. On the other hand, impressive differences between the book value of a REIT's holdings and their current market values may make the trust attractive for takeovers by investors looking to buy real estate assets at bargain prices. If that bids up share prices, investors should benefit.

Nonperforming loans. Trusts state the proportion of loans not earning interest or in default. If a trust forgoes too much income or has to keep repossessing property, its loan selection should be questioned.

REAL ESTATE PARTNERSHIPS

In a real estate partnership, money put up by investors is used to buy land, mortgages, apartments, office buildings, shopping centers or other property. Most are set up as limited partnerships. The organizer and manager of the program—a company or individual—assumes the role of general partner and receives fees and commissions for the service, plus a share of any profits. Investors are called limited partners, because their liability for losses is limited to the amount they invest.

Income from rents or other sources is allocated to the limited partners in proportion to their investment. Tax deductions can be claimed by the partners for their share of depreciation, property taxes, interest on loans, and certain expenses, including some fees paid to the general partner. Tax credits can be claimed for some rehabilitation projects. After several years— five to 12 is a common period—syndicates typically dispose of or refinance their assets and distribute the proceeds to the partners.

A few years ago, real estate limited partnerships, or RELPs, were commonly set up as tax shelters. But the limitations put on the deductibility of so-called passive losses, as described earlier, changed the nature of the business. These days RELPs are likely to stress income and capital gains.

On the surface, the considerations for investing in a limited partnership are similar to those for evaluating real estate investment trusts. Both offer professional selection and management of a portfolio of properties. But that's where the similarities end. REITs and RELPs aren't set up the same way and they aren't bought and sold the same way. If you consider a partnership, it's important to know the differences.

Today you can invest in a real estate partnership as easily and quickly as you can buy stocks and bonds. And if you express an interest in doing so, you are likely to be swamped with more information than you ever received about a stock or a bond: a ponderous prospectus or comparable document, a sales brochure, pictures of buildings, and sometimes even a booklet explaining the principles of this kind of investing.

The pictures are usually attractive and the booklets can be informative, but the prospectus, the key document, can be difficult and perplexing reading for those who are not experts. Nevertheless, you should make the effort.

How they are set up. In a typical arrangement the tax shelter syndicator sells interests in a new partnership that will construct or buy apartment houses, shopping centers, theaters, mobile home parks, or other commercial real estate. Buying an interest makes you a limited partner. Customarily, as a limited partner, you would be responsible only for the amount of capital you have contributed. For instance, your salary or other assets couldn't be attached by the partnership's creditors if it couldn't pay its debts.

The business itself is run by a general partner. In certain circumstances limited partners might be able to vote on a general partner, but otherwise you usually can't participate in management.

You can buy partnership interests from several sources. An attorney or accountant might have regular contact with local syndicators who put together private offerings. Securities firms market both public and private offerings, and many RELPs are sold through financial planners.

Size of investment. Public offerings are commonly issued in $1,000 units with a $5,000 minimum purchase, although minimums may be as small as $1,000. You may need considerably more to get into a private offering.

Liquidity.   Each partnership sets a termination date, but the partnership is likely to dispose of its properties well before then—say in five to 12 years—and distribute the proceeds. What if you want out earlier? You'll discover that it's a lot harder to get out than it was to get in. Although the general partner or the securities dealer who originally sold the plan might try to help find a buyer, there is no organized secondary market for partnership interests. Even if there were, the value of your share in the partnership cannot be accurately determined until the properties have been sold. If you sell before that time, you'll almost certainly take a loss. One organization attempting to match partnership sellers with potential buyers is the National Partnership Exchange (NAPEX) in St. Petersburg, Fla. Its toll-free number is 800-356-2739; in Florida call 800-336-2739.

How they pay off. As a limited partner, you share in the income, but you're not exactly entitled to the same tax benefits you would receive if you owned property directly because every penny is subject to the limitations on passive losses. That is why the emphasis shifted from tax shelter to income-producing RELPs after the Tax Reform Act of 1986. Still, you get some benefits.

Cash flow.   A partnership functions as a conduit, passing both income and deductions through to you. You offset the income with your share of the losses and report the net on your tax return. As a member of the partnership you are taxed on your share of its taxable income, if any, even if it is not distributed to you. Any capital gains will be taxed when the partnership sells its properties.

Depreciation.   Each $1 of ordinary depreciation neatly offsets $1 of income from the same partnership.

Mortgage interest.   Mortgage payments consist largely of interest in early years, thereby building up the front-end deductions.

Expenses.   Operating expenses can be offset against rental income.

Role of the general partner. The prospectus will quickly make it clear that the general partner may not be one person or one company but a constellation of affiliated people and companies that run the partnership from start to finish. They put the shelter deal together; they buy, build, or contract for the construction of properties for the partnership; they rent the buildings; they manage the property; they may sell insurance to the partnership; they handle the partnership's relations with limited partners; and they act as agents for refinancing or selling the properties.

The partnership's success depends to a great extent on the general partner's honesty and competence, so carefully check the prospectus material on the general partner's previous projects and the leading officials involved. You want administrators with substantive experience in real estate and with demonstrable records of having performed well for their investors.

All this expertise isn't cheap. Start-up fees of 20% or more used to be common. Distress in many markets, plus the stingier tax rules, have combined to knock those fees down a bit, although you will still have to pay higher fees than for practically any other investment. You'd pay some of those even if you invested on your own—brokers' commissions, management fees. You can guard against paying too much by checking the partnership on the following points.

• How much of your initial contribution will be left for investment? The prospectus should contain detailed figures, but you may need help in interpreting them because of vague or overlapping expense categories.

• Are there percentage or dollar limits on the general partner's fees?

• Does the partnership agreement prohibit dealing with affiliated companies that serve only to increase the general partner's revenues?

For example, are independent appraisals required for properties bought for the partnership from an allied company?

• Is the general partner's insurance brokerage firm required to get competitive bids from a few insurance companies?

• Are you entitled to a prescribed minimum return before the general partner takes part of the cash flow?

• Are some of the fees contingent on successful performance? For instance, will proceeds from the sale of properties first be applied toward repaying your investment before the general partner takes a share?

Partnerships set up to construct buildings after collecting investors' money should be considered high risk. Also, if the syndicate is set up as a blind pool, meaning the partnership has not specified which properties it will invest in, you are dependent solely on the judgment of the general partner. Investments in known properties, or options to buy them, are safer.

MASTER LIMITED PARTNERSHIPS

In an effort to remedy the lack of liquidity in traditional limited partnerships, syndicators devised what's called the master limited partnership, or MLP. Real estate MLPs are very much like RELPs except that their shares are traded publicly, like stocks and bonds. This does make them easier to sell, but it creates a few problems of its own.

For one thing, investors in MLPs have tended to fixate on yield, ignoring the underlying value of the partnership's holdings. That means that share prices behave like bonds, rising when interest rates fall and falling when rates rise.

There's a reason yields are so attractive. Because they are partnerships and not corporations, some MLPs—but not all— have an advantage over corporate issues: Their earnings are taxed only once, at the investor level. A corporation must pay tax on its profits before it distributes dividends to its shareholders, who are also taxed on dividends they receive. This so-called double taxation reduces payouts to corporate investors by diminishing the amount the corporation has to distribute. Investors in exempt MLPs, which includes many of those that concentrate on income-producing real estate, benefit by comparison. For some, the benefit is being phased out. Before you invest in any MLP, make sure your know which kind you're considering.

RAW LAND AND UNDEVELOPED PROPERTY

If you buy undeveloped property, whether as an investment or a place to live, vacation or retire, you may be taking risks you didn't consider. Tens of thousands of buyers in virtually every state have invested thousands of dollars in land that is worth much less than they have spent, and in a number of cases it is worth nothing at all on the resale market. They are stuck with property with no sewer, water or electric lines. It may not support a septic tank and a well, or the expense of those improvements could double the cost of the plot. The land might be subject to periodic flooding. Local ordinances might effectively prohibit building there at all.

There really isn't much to protect you from becoming a victim except your own awareness. Some laws at the federal level and in some states and localities are designed to protect buyers. Overall, however, crackdowns generally come only after buyers have been gulled.

There is a federal statute designed to protect consumers in the market for land. The Interstate Land Sales Full Disclosure Act covers companies offering more than 100 subdivision lots across state lines, with certain exemptions.

Affected companies are required to file with the Office of Interstate Land Sales Registration (OILSR) a statement of record, which is a detailed description of the lots for sale or lease, plus financial and legal information. The company must also file a shorter version, called a property report, which includes information on sewers, water lines, possible flooding conditions, legal problems and so forth. It should be required reading for any prospective buyer, and the law insists that you be given a copy before you sign a sales contract.

If you are seriously considering buying a piece of undeveloped property, take your time and follow this procedure.

• Write for and read three publications. Two of them, *Before Buying Land . . . Get the Facts* and *Buying Lots From Developers*, are available from OILSR, U.S. Department of Housing and Urban Development, Room 6278, 451 Seventh St., S.W., Washington, D.C. 20411. The other is *The Insider's Guide to Owning Land in Subdivisions*, available for $1.50 from a public interest group called INFORM, 381 Park Ave., New York, N.Y. 10016.

• Ask one or more independent brokers in the area whether they would be willing to list the property and what its selling price would be.

• Visit the property. Don't buy anything sight unseen.
• Make sure that any representations about property improvements and the services that will be provided are added to the sales contract and signed by the sales manager. If he or she won't sign it, you shouldn't either.
• Find out whether the land can actually be used as a homesite. Write, phone, or visit the appropriate offices of the local government. Ask what kinds of permits must be obtained before you can build on the property and whether sewer and water hookups are available.
• Determine whether the developer's bonds for improvements—swimming pool, utility lines and the like—are the surety kind, so that if he or she goes bankrupt the money will still be available. Escrow accounts can also be used for this purpose. A corporate bond for further improvements is only as good as the corporation itself.

Finally, take the time to read the property report, the sales contract and all other papers thoroughly. Then take them to an attorney who deals in land transactions for an evaluation before you sign anything.

OPTIONS AND FUTURES

Ladies and gentlemen, place your bets. If you want to shorten the wait for profits from your investments and don't mind stepping up the risks in exchange, then stock options or futures contracts may be to your liking. Options give you a right to buy or sell a certain stock at a specified price within a specified time. Futures contracts commit you to buy or sell a specified amount of a particular commodity ranging from plywood to pork bellies at a specified price within a specified time. Options and futures contracts can also be used to speculate on the direction of interest rates, stock prices and currency values. You can even buy options on futures. These kinds of transactions have attracted growing numbers of investors over the past several years, some of whom are using options to hedge their bets rather than engage in risky speculation.

BUYING AND SELLING STOCK OPTIONS

There are essentially two kinds of stock options. A *call* gives its owner the right to buy a particular stock at a specified price while the option is in force. Whoever sold (or "wrote") the call agrees to complete the transaction if the option is exercised by selling the stock at the specified price. A *put* gives its buyer the right to sell a stock at a specified price within a specified time, and obligates its seller to do the buying. As a rule, calls are bought and puts sold by traders who think the price of the underlying security will rise. Sellers of calls and buyers of puts think the price will fall, or at least remain the same.

How they work. Each exchange specifies a list of stocks against which puts and calls can be sold and bought. For the most part, the stocks represent big, nationally known corporations, such as AT&T, IBM, Sears and others.

The options are standardized contracts covering 100 shares of the particular underlying stock. The exchange opens trading in options to buy a stock at a set price, known as the exercise or striking price, within a certain period. The "strikes" are fixed near the current market price of the stock in $5, $10 or $20 multiples. If the stock is selling for $48 per share, the exchange would place the striking price at $50 per share. If and when the stock's price changes substantially, the exchange launches another option with a new striking price closer to the new market value. Trading in the old option continues for months, so after a while brokers may be dealing in several options for the same stock at different striking prices.

Because of the different striking prices and time periods, it's possible to trade in different options for a single stock not only at several striking prices but also in several time periods. The Chicago Board Options Exchange (CBOE) could list, for example, options for a company's stock at $40, $45 and $50 per share for exercise at the end of April, July and October. In practice, some possible option combinations may not be offered or traded because of lack of interest among buyers and sellers.

Suppose you are the seller, or writer, of an April 35 call. That means you pledge to sell 100 shares of a particular stock at $35 a share by the prescribed date in April if formally requested to do so through the exchange. For that right, you receive whatever price, called a premium, you can get on the exchange at the moment. The buyer is paying you for the right to buy 100 shares at $35 a share before that date, no matter what the price of the stock happens to be at the time he or she chooses to buy.

What you are selling here is not the stock itself. The premium pays only for the option. If a buyer exercises his or her call—that is, wants the stock—he or she has to put up $3,500 for those 100 shares, in addition to the premium previously paid for the option. You as the call seller receive that $3,500, in addition to the premium obtained earlier.

The buyer and seller do not actually negotiate with each other. Once an option is sold, the link between the two is broken by the Options Clearing Corporation, an organization set up by the exchanges. This clearing arrangement makes it possible for buyers and sellers to move in and out of the options market by closing out their original transaction with an offsetting one. For example, if you sell an April 35 call, you can cancel your obligation to deliver 100 shares at $35 a share by buying an April 35 call for the same stock. If you originally bought an option, you'd cancel it by selling one. The great majority of options transactions are consummated this way and not through the delivery of the underlying stock.

Brokers charge different commissions for option transactions than for stock trades. But if an option is exercised, the buyer and the seller each pay regular stock commissions for the sale of the underlying securities.

How you win or lose. Most options contracts are for calls. Premiums for calls rise and fall with the price of the stock, although not necessarily by the same amount. Rising stock prices tend to increase premiums; declining prices depress them.

A call with a striking price under the stock's current price maintains an intrinsic value equal to the difference between the two. For example, when a stock is selling at $55 a share, an option to buy it at $50 a share should sell for at least $5 a share, or $500 for the 100 share option. Normally the option will sell for somewhat more than the difference right up to the expiration date, because there's always a chance of a stock price increase. The option becomes worthless after the exercise deadline. Calls that have an intrinsic value because the striking price is under the stock price are known as in the money options; calls that exceed the stock price are out of the money.

Options with more distant expiration dates should command

a higher premium than those with closer dates, all other things being equal. The longer the period, the longer the option holder can afford to wait for a rewarding rise in the stock's price.

For an idea of how a seller can win or lose trading in options, start with a basic, nonspeculative transaction known as writing a covered call. You buy 100 shares of one of the stocks on the options list at $40 a share, or $4,000 for the lot. (To keep things simple, omit commission costs, although on small amounts they could become an important consideration.) You then sell, or write, an April 40 call on the exchange at a premium of, say, $2 a share, or $200 for the option. That gives you an immediate 5% income on the $4,000 investment. Also, you continue to receive whatever dividends the stock pays.

Furthermore, the option provides a hedge against a drop in the stock's price. For example, assume that the stock falls to $38 some time after you sell the option. You have lost $2 a share, or $200 on the 100 shares originally purchased. But you received $200 for the call, so you remain even. You don't lose, therefore, until the stock falls below $38. In market lingo, the call produced "downside protection to 38."

If the stock remains under $40, it's unlikely that someone will exercise the call and compel you to sell the stock at that price. You could merely wait for the option to expire at the prescribed date in April and keep the $200 premium. If you don't want to risk the possibility that the price will rise to over $40, which would put the April 40 in the money and make the option more likely to be exercised, you could buy an April 40 call to cancel out the April 40 sale.

As you might expect, the April 40 premium would fall as the stock declined to $38. By mid April the option could be selling for as little as ½ (50 cents), or $50 for the 100 shares. By buying the call at that point, you net $150 on the deal ($200 received for the original sale of the call minus $50 paid for the closing call).

What happens, though, if the stock jumps to $42? The 100 shares you own are now worth $4,200. But if the call you sold is exercised, you will have to sell the shares at the $40 striking price, or $4,000. The loss of that $200 gain is offset by the $200 received for the option.

The $42 price represents the upside break-even point. Not until the price rises above that level will the potential gain on the exercise exceed the premium received. If the stock rises to $43 and the option to $3, you will have to pay at least $300 to buy an April 40 option to cancel out the one you sold for $200. If you do, you lose $100. If you don't, the stock could be called at the 40 striking price (which is what you paid for it) and you miss out on the price rise. You still have the $200 for the option you sold, but commissions could cut deeply into that.

The key for buyers: leverage. Given the proper circumstances, a call option seller can obtain immediate income on his or her stock plus some downside protection. But what's in it for the buyer?

What usually attracts buyers is leverage. It makes a little money do the work of a lot. In stock options it operates this way:

Say you are interested in buying a stock now selling at $40 because you think it could soon go up to $45. If you buy 100 shares outright for $4,000 and the stock does hit $45, the investment produces $500, or a 12½% gain.

But suppose that instead of buying the stock, you purchase an April 40 call option at 3 that costs $300 in all. In order for you to make back your premium, the stock must rise to $43. A seller is prepared to write the call because he thinks the stock won't go up, at least not above $43. But if the stock does increase to $45, the April 40 call becomes worth at least $500, or $5 a share, its intrinsic value. You close out the transaction by selling your April 40 call at $500 and make a net of $200. That $200 represents a 66⅔% return on your $300 investment. Actually, you would probably make more than that because the April 40 call probably would rise to more than $5 a share on the possibility of even further gains in the stock.

You come out ahead on your April 40 call any time the stock goes over $43. At $44, for instance, the option should be worth at least its $400 intrinsic value and you can close out with a $100, or 33⅓%, profit. Had you bought the shares, they would have appreciated to $4,400, a 10% return on your $4,000 investment.

However, the leverage that produces those exciting returns can also result in painful losses. If the stock tops out at $42, the intrinsic value of the option would be only $2 a share, or $200. If you close out the transaction at that point by selling the April 40 call, you lose $100 ($300 minus $200), or 33⅓% of the amount put into the option. If you had simply bought the shares at $40 and sold them when the price rose to $42, you would have made a profit of $200, or 5%, before commissions.

The option, though, has one advantage: You can't lose more than the $300 it cost, and that assumes you hang on to it until it expires, worthless. Losses or gains could be much heavier than those shown in the example if, instead of spending $4,000 on stock, you buy not one but several options totaling that amount in order to boost the potential return and reduce commission charges on each option.

You can play this same game in a declining market by trading puts instead of calls. Fewer investors buy and sell puts, however, possibly because they are more difficult to understand.

Puts can be used by conservative investors to protect capital gains on stocks they don't wish to sell. If you fear a drop in the price, you can buy a put and sell it when the price of the underlying stock goes down. That permits you to hedge against the decline without actually selling your stock and incurring tax on any profits.

Obviously, options are not long-term investments. They have to be watched closely and turned over frequently. As with many other investments, the rewards depend on your daring, skill and luck.

Incidentally, stocks aren't the only thing on which you can buy and sell options. They are available on various stock indexes, such as the S&P 100 and the AMEX Major Market Index, on specialized indexes for computer technology, business equipment, and oil and gas issues, and even on foreign currencies. These markets are thinner and probably best left to professional investors.

TRADING IN COMMODITY FUTURES

The futures exchanges make it possible to trade in a

remarkable array of products—from basic farm crops, such as corn, wheat, soybeans and oats, to financial instruments, such as U.S. Treasury bills and foreign currencies.

As a futures trader you won't be bothered with corporate annual reports or voting proxies because you are not investing in companies. Nor will you have to keep track of dividends or interest checks, because there aren't any. Whether you win or lose depends completely on whether the price of your futures contract moves in the direction, up or down, you think it will.

Actually, what you trade in the futures markets is not a product but a standard agreement to buy or sell a product at some later date at the price set when the contract is negotiated for you on the floor of the exchange by open bids and offers.

All the contract terms other than price are fixed by each exchange for each of the products in its jurisdiction. For instance, the live cattle contract of the Chicago Mercantile Exchange specifies that you deal in 40,000 pounds of steer. The CME prescribes the minimum amount of earnest money, or margin, that you must deposit with a broker when you buy or sell the contract.

You can choose a CME live cattle contract that expires in February, April, June, August, October or December. Those trading months, often called the delivery months, vary according to the seasonal or marketing patterns associated with the product and its storability. As one delivery month expires or nears expiration, a corresponding position is added to the end of the roster.

How the markets work. As an illustration of how the futures business operates, suppose you decide to take a flier in pork bellies. The first step is to open an account with a commodities broker. You think prices are likely to rise, so you instruct the broker to buy one July contract calling for delivery of 38,000 pounds of pork bellies at 60 cents a pound before the contract expires on July 21. You give the broker a margin deposit of, say, $2,000 and sit back to wait for the price to go up.

At this point, you may be wondering what you will do with the pork bellies that the seller of the July contract is obligated to deliver. How will you pay the $22,800 for the entire lot? For that matter, how will the seller, who may be another outside speculator like you, get together 38,000 pounds of pork bellies for delivery?

Only in extraordinary circumstances will either the buyer or the seller be forced to make good on a delivery. More than 95% of futures contracts are settled by an offsetting transaction. When the buyer wants to get out of the purchase, he or she sells an equal number of contracts for the same delivery period. To liquidate your July contract, you sell a July contract. If the price has gone up by more than the brokerage commission plus the interest lost by keeping the margin deposit with the broker, you have made a profit. If the price has risen by less or if the price has dropped, you lose.

But what about the seller? Any time up to the cessation of trading in July contracts the seller can "cover" his or her position by buying a July contract. That the customary sequence gets reversed by selling first and buying second makes no difference. If the seller can buy back a July contract for less then he or she sold one, he or she makes money. If the seller is forced to buy at a higher price, he or she loses.

Because trades are normally offset and must be wound up by a fixed expiration date, brokers base their commissions on a "round turn"—a buy and sell in either order.

Spreads and hedges. Straight speculative purchases and sales constitute only part of the activity on the exchanges. Alert traders need to know something about spreading, which people like yourself can do, and hedging, which is done by business people or farmers who deal with the actual commodity and who might be the seller when you buy or the buyer when you sell.

Spreads. In the usual spread you simultaneously buy a contract for delivery in one month and sell a contract for delivery of the same commodity in another month. They do not offset because they are not the same position. Why anyone should do that becomes clear with this illustration:

The May delivery of a commodity is selling for $2.50 a pound, the December for $2.95. Normally for this commodity, December is priced only 35 cents a pound over May instead of 45 cents, and you expect that relationship will be re-established.

You sell December at $2.95 and buy May at $2.50. Sure enough, the two positions close up to a 35-cent spread—the December declines to $2.82 and the May to $2.47. You then "unwind" your spread by selling a May contract and buying a December, offsetting both positions.

Now look at the results: You lost 3 cents a pound in the May contract, but you gained 13 cents on the short sale of the December delivery. That's a gross profit of 10 cents a pound.

Of course, that spread might have worked against you. If the May had held firm at $2.50 and the December had gone up to $3, you would have lost 5 cents a pound. Still, spreads in storable commodities are considered a relatively conservative operation and usually require less margin, because of the possibility that losses in one position will be offset to some extent by gains in the other.

Hedges.   Hedging is designed to protect commodity producers, dealers and users from price losses. The grain dealer who is storing wheat bought at $3.70 a bushel wants some insurance against a price decline. He protects his inventory by selling futures contracts at corresponding prices, taking into account storage and other costs. If prices decline, he can offset his position by buying back lower-priced contracts. That gain should compensate for some of the loss he suffers by having to sell the grain itself at a lower price.

The big attractions of futures markets are leverage and the promise of a fast turnaround. You can buy into a contract for about 5% to 10% of its dollar value, giving your profits—and losses—a boost that's hard to obtain anywhere else. As for speed, the overwhelming majority of futures contracts are liquidated within 60 days. Many last less than a week.

COMMODITY POOLS

Commodity pools, or funds, have some of the same potential advantages as mutual funds: professional management, the ability to diversify and, often, access to up-to-date information and high-quality research. The typical commodity fund is a partnership in which money put up by individuals is used by a professional trader to speculate in futures. The organizer, a company or individual, becomes the general partner and oversees operations and hires the trading adviser, or manager. The other investors are limited partners; their responsibility for losses is limited to the amount they invest. Partnership units usually cost $1,000, and investors as a rule must buy at least two to five units. They are bought and sold through brokers.

What you gain in professional management you lose in liquidity. There is virtually no secondary market for these investments; units usually can be redeemed only by selling them back to the general partner. Some funds execute redemption orders monthly, others quarterly. Usually, ten days' to two weeks' written notice is required to get out.

Some funds evaluate units for redemption purposes on specified dates, regardless of when you decide to sell. In addition, a fund may restrict you from selling units for a certain time after you buy them—three months, for example.

How do you make money? Some funds make cash distributions if substantial profits are realized. Others add the profits to the funds the managers use for trading. Still others do both. Because fund values can fluctuate sharply, when you get into a fund and when you get out can play the key role in whether or not you wind up a winner.

Prospectuses for public offerings must include the performance records of the pool sponsor and the trading adviser. The prospectus should also tell you the types of commodities that will be traded, whether cash distributions will be paid periodically if trading is profitable, how redemptions are handled, whether there are any conflicts of interest between the trading adviser and sponsor, whether the fund will be automatically dissolved after a certain period of time, and the circumstances under which the fund could be dissolved because of trading losses. Keep in mind that a pool may liquidate if half of its assets are lost, denying you the chance to recoup.

Fees and loads. Before investing in any commodity pool, find out how much of a load you would pay in sales commissions, start-up fees, and other charges collected by the general partner and sales organization. These charges must be in the prospectus, but it may take some hard scrutiny to figure it all out. The average initial load is about 10% of the amount invested, but some funds take 20% or more. Those charges may be added to the price of a unit, deducted from the amount you pay, or extracted—in part at least—from income produced by idle cash (only part of the money paid in by investors is used for trading at any one time; the rest is usually invested in Treasury bills). In addition to sales loads, annual management fees amounting to 20% or more of average annual equity are not uncommon.

The North American Securities Administrators Association, composed of state securities regulators, has said that organizing and offering expenses, including sales commissions, should not exceed 15% of the offering's gross proceeds and that management fees should not exceed 6% a year. Added to those charges are trading commissions, which are paid out of profits, if any, or out of the funds put up by investors. If profits are slim or nil, those commissions could eat heavily into a fund's assets and even force it into liquidation.

GOLD, SILVER AND OTHER HARD ASSETS

Once thought of chiefly as speculative havens for investors who feared economic calamity, precious metals and other so-called hard assets have found their way into the portfolios of less pessimistic investors. Whether such items belong in your investment plan depends on your willingness to familiarize yourself with the esoteric factors of supply and demand that influence their price movements.

Hard assets can offer profit potential to investors who take the time to be informed and have the ability to wait out the inevitable dips in price that affect all investment markets. In the meantime, gold, silver, gemstones and collectibles all share a significant drawback in comparison with stocks, bonds and other so-called financial assets: They pay no income while you hold them, you often must buy at retail prices and sell at wholesale, and you must pay to store and insure the assets while you're waiting for the price to rise. Beyond that, each major category of hard assets has its own potential rewards and pitfalls.

INVESTING IN GOLD

Despite its reputation, gold has not always been a reliable

long-term hedge against inflation. Its price movements have been erratic. On the other hand, gold has exceptional qualities in addition to its beauty, virtual indestructibility, and suitability for various industrial requirements. As an investment it generally performs well when stocks, bonds and other widely owned vehicles are doing poorly. It is one of the few mediums of exchange that has endured through the centuries: Governments and currencies have come and gone, but gold has survived wars, famine, pestilence and economic upheavals.

Because gold has traditionally thrived on adversity, its price has often been an anxiety index. When inflation, economic chaos, political violence or other troubles erupt or even threaten, many people turn to gold.

Conversely, when peace and prosperity prevail, gold may lose favor. This is the opposite of what usually happens to securities and other investments that benefit from human productivity. Additional factors affect the price of gold, including the output from mines, new discoveries, industrial demand, political stability in the countries where it is mined, and government monetary policies.

Should you invest? A number of professional financial advisers agree that diversified investment portfolios should include about 5% to 15% gold as insurance against runaway inflation. Many, but not all, independent analysts expect a generally upward trend in gold prices over the years. Much depends on investors' attitudes toward gold as opposed to financial assets such as stocks and bonds.

Ways to invest. There are several ways to invest in gold.

Bullion. It comes in everything from tiny wafers to 400-ounce bars and is sold by refiners, fabricators, currency dealers, so-called private mints, and some securities brokers and banks. The metal should be certified at least 99% pure and bear the stamp of a recognized refiner, such as Englehard, Johnson Matthey, Handy & Harman or Credit Suisse. The weight should be expressed in troy ounces.

Keeping gold around the house is foolhardy, and you'll normally need special insurance even in a safe-deposit box (few banks insure customers against losses from boxes). Some dealers provide storage facilities and insurance. You may have to have bullion assayed when sold to confirm its authenticity, at a cost of $50 to $100 or more.

Coins. Bullion coins, which contain a high percentage of gold, provide the safest, simplest and most convenient investment medium for most individuals. Before its importation into the U.S. was banned several years ago, the South African Kruger-rand was the most widely sold. More recently the one-ounce American Eagle has been the best seller in the U.S. Other popular coins include the Austrian 100 Corona, Mexican 50 Peso, Canadian Maple Leaf and the U.S. $10 and $20 Double Eagles. Gold coins are widely exchanged, easy to handle, and can be authenticated by gold dealers without an assay. Most sell at a premium of 5% to 8% above the value of their gold content. Most, but not all, contain exactly one troy ounce of the metal, which simplifies trading. Rarer gold coins, such as those that were once used as money, usually have numismatic value, which complicates matters for nonexperts. Their prices may move independently of the price of gold itself.

Stocks. By investing in U.S., Canadian or South African mining companies, you can play the gold market and collect dividends, too. Yields of some issues have sometimes topped 20%. The risk is that government policies, political disruptions and labor troubles can affect profits even if company management is good. Several mutual funds invest all or part of their assets in precious-metal securities. (See Chapter 17.)

Depository certificates. You can buy an interest in bullion stored in a vault and receive a non-negotiable certificate as proof of ownership. A major provider of these is the Deak-Perera Group, an international dealer in currencies and precious metals. Dreyfus Gold Deposits has a similar plan, as does the Rhode Island Hospital Trust of Providence. The gold is kept in a vault in the U.S. or abroad, as you direct, and is insured. For depository certificates, you usually pay a small fraction of the asset value annually for storage and insurance, plus a sales charge of about 1% to 5%, depending on size of the order. There is also a charge for sale, transfer or delivery of your holdings.

Gold jewelry. It's an investment you can wear while hoping for a price rise. Selectivity is all-important, however. Quality varies over a wide spectrum, and prices are, as a rule, substantially higher than the intrinsic value of the gold. Buy only from reputable, established dealers.

Before you invest. Add up the costs before you make a commitment: sales commissions, storage and insurance charges, taxes and assay fees. Figure how much the price would have to rise before you'd start making money. The more you buy, the lower the transaction costs are likely to be.

Never buy precious metals or metals-related contracts from strangers over the phone. Boiler-room operations, which are essentially banks of telephones staffed by high-pressure sales-people, are especially active in selling gold, diamonds and other hard assets. Report suspicious or objectionable calls to the Commodity Futures Trading Commission.

INVESTING IN SILVER

Investors who find gold attractive may also be drawn to silver. Like gold, its price often thrives on bad news. However, although gold and silver are often mentioned in the same breath, as investments they are quite different in several important respects. For one thing, the silver market is considerably smaller. It is so small, in fact, that the buying and selling of a relatively few very wealthy individuals can greatly influence the price—something that has happened in the past and could happen again.

Industrial usage plays a more important part in the market demand for silver than it does for gold. And when prices rise, industrial users, such as manufacturers of film, electronic parts, batteries and other products, have a strong incentive to find substitutes for silver or recycle what they use. Either action is eventually reflected in the market demand for the metal, which softens. Meanwhile, high prices also serve to spur faster production from the world's silver mines, thus adding to supplies. The combination of less demand and more supply is ultimately reflected in the price: It goes down.

Many silver investors base their hopes for profit on the belief that the world is running out of the metal. Although it is true that the demand for silver has sometimes exceeded supplies, forcing countries to dip into stockpiles to satisfy the market, supply and demand actually fluctuate quite a bit from year to year, with wide swings in surpluses or deficits due to differences in industrial usage, mine production and investor demand. In short, the world is not running out of silver—not for some time, at least—and the chief forces influencing its price are likely to remain fluctuations in industrial and investor demand.

Ways to invest. There are a number of ways to invest in silver. The most obvious is to buy bullion, which you can do through major dealers. Many also sell depository certificates that work the same way as gold certificates—the company holds the bullion for you; you get a certificate attesting to your ownership.

One popular method of buying silver is to purchase bags of pre-1965 U.S. silver coins. Dimes, quarters and half dollars were minted with 90% silver in those days, giving them a current value far above their original spending power. Bags usually contain $1,000 in face value and sell at prices determined by the market value of the silver in them at the time of transaction. Half bags are also available.

As you can imagine, coins with a face value of $1,000 take up space and weigh quite a bit. (A bag weighs about 55 pounds.) People holding bags of silver coins need a place to store them safely and should insure them against theft. Like gold, they produce no income until you sell.

There are other ways to invest in silver. Numismatic coins—those that increase in value because they are in demand by collectors, rather than strictly because of their silver content—tend to be more resistant to dips in silver prices, but they require an expert's eye or the advice of an expert for successful speculating.

If you'd rather not bother with actually holding onto silver or coins, you could still hook into silver's future by buying securities issued by mining companies, or mutual funds whose holdings include stock in such mines. Ask your broker for reports on these companies.

In addition, major brokerage firms have responded to the

demand for silver in recent years by setting up accumulation plans for their customers that allow them to make relatively small investments and relieve them of the problem of storage. A broker can supply details.

DIAMONDS AND OTHER GEMSTONES

Diamonds suitable for investments are not necessarily the kind you find in the average jewelry store. Diamonds vary greatly by color, clarity, cut and carat weight, referred to in the business as the four C's. Although there is no universal standard for what constitutes an investment-grade diamond, the most readily acceptable ones weigh at least a carat, rank very near the top of the scale in color and clarity, and have been expertly cut for maximum brilliance. A certificate from a recognized gemological laboratory attesting to a stone's four C's should be part of every investment diamond deal. The Gemological Institute of America is a recognized lab, as is the European Gemological Laboratory.

Most of the world's rough diamond sales are controlled by DeBeers Consolidated Mines through its Central Selling Organization. This cartel attempts to maintain an orderly market by controlling supplies. Confronting a market in which the price of diamonds is falling, DeBeers can cut back sharply on the amount of uncut stones it releases. This ability of DeBeers to control supplies and thus manipulate prices is what gives many investors their faith in diamonds. And indeed, DeBeers can be counted on to act in its best interest and, by extension, the interest of diamond investors.

All of this doesn't make diamond profits a sure thing. Despite DeBeers's efforts, prices of top-quality stones lost most of their value between early 1980 and early 1986 before recovering a bit the following year. Furthermore, most investors have no choice but to buy at retail prices and sell at wholesale. Since markups can range from 30% to even 100% or more, that builds in the necessity for considerable price appreciation just to break even. This makes diamond investing a long-term proposition. Furthermore, gems, like gold and silver, pay no current income. Instead, you pay to store and insure them.

When it comes time to sell, you must be willing to wait. Whether you sell the stones yourself, consign them to an auction house, or sell them to a local jeweler or through a broker, it takes time to find a buyer, time to ascertain certification, and time to get reliable appraisals. In all, arranging and carrying out a sale can easily take a month or two.

If you are interested in investing in diamonds, don't do it without investigating thoroughly. Know your dealer and insist on certifications from an impartial lab. Don't buy anything over the phone.

Colored gemstones. The special difficulties confronting diamond investors are multiplied for colored gems. Standards for grading aren't as well developed. The market isn't as organized. Records of historical price movements are harder to find. Investors don't always agree on what sorts of colored stones make good investments. In short, colored gemstones are a highly specialized investment best left to those who know the markets. Amateur investors should stay away.

INVESTING IN COLLECTIBLES

A painting by Vincent Van Gogh sells for $39.9 million. A few months later another Van Gogh, bought years ago for $9,000, goes for better than $20 million. A Philadelphia Chippendale-foot wingchair is auctioned for $2.75 million. This is the stuff that dreams are made of.

Collecting can combine the exhilaration of a treasure hunt with the joy of acquiring things you like. And the folklore of collecting is filled with tales of fabulous finds. Somebody discovers that the shade of an old lamp that had hung for years in a church rectory is a genuine Tiffany worth thousands of dollars. A baseball card picturing Honus Wagner, Hall-of-Fame shortstop for the Pittsburgh Pirates, turns out to be one of the most valuable of its kind. (Wagner forced a cigarette company to stop using his picture in its advertising, and only 19 of the cards are known to exist.)

Unfortunately, everyone doesn't come out a winner. Prices of collectibles can skid as well as climb. The market has always been heavily salted with fakes and flawed merchandise. When something becomes popular, forgers may grind out reproductions in massive quantities. There is also an abundance of schlock, such as certain commemorative medals and limited-edition offerings.

Collectibles pay no interest or dividends. They often entail costs for insurance and storage. They may be hard to sell. The most ready market, dealers, will give you a wholesale price for something you bought earlier at retail. And profits are often illusory. Say you pay $1,000 for a Victorian clock and sell it at an auction five years later for $1,500, less $300 for the auctioneer (commissions typically run between 10% and 25%). Your net gain is $200, about 4% a year.

Doing it right. None of the above should be cause for despair if collecting interests you. It can pay off, in enjoyment and satisfaction as well as in financial rewards, if you learn the ropes. What you collect should be something you like, perhaps period furniture, stamps, paintings, decorative objects or classic cars.

Whatever you choose, the best way to make money collecting is to know more about your collectible than others know. There is extensive literature to guide you—books and book clubs, magazines, newsletters, price guides, show and flea-market directories and more. There are countless organizations of people with similar interests who meet, correspond, buy and sell, exchange information, and get together socially. The *Encyclopedia of Associations*, available in most libraries, lists more than 100 such groups, including the International Chinese Snuff Bottle Society and the Beer Can Collectors of America.

Taking courses, attending auctions, shopping at shows and flea markets, visiting museums and talking with other devotees will increase your knowledge. Try to find and cultivate a reputable dealer. Buying from a dealer can have advantages over other methods of building a collection. A dealer can offer you a better selection of pieces and will generally stand behind their authenticity.

When you start collecting, buy the best you can afford. The higher the quality the less risk you take, assuming the price is fair. Articles you can use in your home—lamps, furniture, rugs, paintings, chandeliers, musical instruments and such conversation pieces as windup phonographs—are usually good bets.

Be sure to get signed receipts, plus any other papers that attest to the value, and record such information as the price, auction lot number, and description of the object. A provenance, or fact sheet on prior ownership, comes with more expensive pieces.

Auctions are probably the best places to find bargains. In most other places you can probably beat the asking price by haggling, which nearly everyone tries. Prices of comparable items vary widely and tend to be lower in small towns.

Obtain an expert's appraisal before making a major outlay. Experienced personal-property appraisers are scarce—only a few hundred are tested and certified by the American Society of Appraisers (P.O. Box 17265, Dulles International Airport, Washington, D.C. 20041), but some others are doubtlessly qualified. The ASA roster includes specialists in antiques, gems, coins and stamps.

Part Five

NEW WAYS
TO CUT TAXES

GET ALL THE TAX BREAKS
YOU'VE GOT COMING

Funny thing about taxes: Most people approach them backwards. They sit down between January 1 and April 15 and start sifting through the records of things they've already done, looking for ways to save.

The problem is, by then it's too late to take advantage of many of the opportunities that do exist. A smarter way to approach the task would be to look ahead, not behind. You can chart a tax strategy that will take you through the year in a manner calculated to yield the lowest possible tax bill come the following April 15. Sitting down and filling out your return is only the last step in such a strategy.

The Tax Reform Act of 1986 made mincemeat of a lot of traditional tax-saving techniques. But smart planning can still pay off in handsome rewards. Run through this list of five tax-saving ideas to make sure you're taking advantage of the opportunities that remain.

CHECKLIST OF TAX-SAVING IDEAS
THAT STILL WORK

1. Seek tax-free income. No federal tax at all is due on interest from municipal bonds issued by states, cities and towns, although your state might tax it. This federal subsidy of state and local borrowing is especially attractive to people in higher tax brackets, as discussed in Chapter 22.

2. Defer taxes. Certain kinds of investments allow you to postpone paying taxes from the year in which income is earned to a later year, when perhaps you'll be in a lower tax bracket. A sure advantage of tax deferral is that money that otherwise would go to the government continues earning for you. Series EE U.S. savings bonds (Chapter 16) offer this feature, as do deferred annuity contracts (Chapter 24) and whole life insurance policies (Chapter 10). Interest on savings bonds isn't taxed until the bonds are cashed. With an annuity you postpone taxes on the interest until the income is actually paid out. Taxes are also delayed on income that builds up in individual retirement accounts and Keogh plans (Chapter 24). In some cases you can even deduct from taxable income the amount you contribute to your plan each year.

3. Watch the small stuff. If you own a vacation home, you have a chance for some tax-free income. If you rent out the house for 14 or fewer days during the year, you don't have to report to IRS any of the income you receive. Go beyond that 14-day limit, though, and all rental income is taxable.

There are only a few other ways that you can receive money without the IRS stretching out its hand. Life insurance proceeds and gifts you receive aren't subject to income taxes. If you drive for a car pool, you can pocket the money from riders without paying tax on it.

4. Use gifts and trusts. Income from property you own—stock dividends or rent, for example—has to be reported by you and is taxed in your top bracket. If the assets were owned by another family member in a lower tax bracket, however, the income might be treated more gently by the IRS. By using gifts or trusts, you may be able to shift the tax burden to a lower bracket. Assume, for example, that to save for your daughter's college education, you deposit in a special account the dividends from a group of securities. Say the dividends in a given year come to $800, on which you have to pay tax. In the 33% bracket, that costs you $264, so you have only $536 to put aside for the future college costs. Had your daughter owned the securities, the entire $800 might have been saved, depending on her age and other earnings (Chapter 5).

Under the federal gift-tax law, you can give any number of people up to $10,000 each year without incurring any gift-tax liability. If you are married and your spouse participates in the gift, the tax-free limit is $20,000. Bigger gifts may be subject to the gift tax, but your unified estate and gift tax credit would probably cover it. See Chapter 25.

5. Keep good records. As you're pulling together information to do your tax return, flaws in the year's record keeping will become apparent. Haphazard record keeping can cost you money in the form of lost deductions and credits.

Don't let that happen. Get your files in order and commit yourself to keeping them up-to-date. Here are some of the categories in which good records can yield tax savings.

Your car. For those who don't bother with receipts, the IRS lends a hand with the standard mileage rate. For unreimbursed business use of your car you can deduct 21 cents a mile for the first 15,000 miles, 11 cents a mile thereafter. (If you use your car exclusively for business you can deduct the entire allowance; if you are an employee, you get the deduction only to the extent that your unreimbursed business expenses exceed 2% of your adjusted gross income.) For auto use connected with charitable purposes you get 12 cents a mile. In addition to the standard rate, you can also deduct the cost of tolls and parking. You need records of such expenses.

But running your car might be costing you far more than the standard allowances. If you want to try to beat the standard business rate, you need to keep track of what you spend for gas, oil, repairs, maintenance, insurance, licenses and garage rent, and how much depreciation costs you each year. However, the IRS says that when you're figuring your actual per-mile cost for charitable driving, you can count only out-of-pocket costs, such as oil and gas.

Medical expenses. Into this file go receipts and canceled checks for health insurance premiums and for doctor and hospital bills. Remember, too, to keep track of what it costs to get to and from physicians and dentists, what you pay for medicine and drugs (right down to the aspirin and cold remedies) and expenses for such items as eyeglasses, hearing aids, false teeth and crutches. Save records of any expense connected with, as the IRS says, "the diagnosis, cure, relief, treatment, or prevention of disease." Since you can generally deduct only the share of medical costs and insurance that exceeds 7.5% of your adjusted gross income, it's important to keep track of all expenses that move you toward that threshold.

You can count medical expenses you pay for yourself, your spouse, and anyone who qualifies as your dependent. You can also count medical bills you pay for someone who receives more than $1,950 in taxable income ($2,000 in 1989) or filed a joint return but would otherwise qualify as your dependent.

Suppose that you and your brother support your elderly mother, but neither of you can claim her as a dependent because her independent income exceeds the threshold. You could arrange for whichever of you is in the higher tax bracket to pay your mother's medical bills while the other directs his support to nondeductible items. That way Uncle Sam will pick up the biggest possible share of the medical expenses.

Charity.   Set up a file for records of charitable contributions to your church or synagogue, the United Way campaign, your college and so forth. When you don't get a receipt, write a note showing the date, amount and recipient. Your contribution doesn't have to be money to earn a tax deduction. Old clothes, a car or furniture given to a charitable organization generates a deduction based on the item's fair market value, which you must be able to document. If you drive in connection with church or synagogue work, to get to the Red Cross to donate blood, or for other charitable purposes, you can deduct the actual cost or 12 cents per mile plus the cost of tolls and parking.

Your house.   If you want to cut your tax bill, buy a house. The major tax advantages of homeownership are described in Chapter 6. Everyone knows that deductions for mortgage interest and property taxes can significantly cut taxes in the year they're paid. Other tax advantages of homeownership take longer to earn, and you'll need good records to claim them.

What you spend to maintain the place isn't deductible, but improvements will affect your tax bill sooner or later. The cost of a fence or a new driveway where none existed before, for example, increases your cost basis for the house—that's the figure you subtract from the sales price to determine the taxable profit when you sell. Whenever a household bill might qualify as an addition to the cost basis, keep the receipt.

Expenses of working. Whenever you spend money for a job-related expense, ask yourself: "Is this deductible?" When the following expenses exceed 2% of your adjusted gross income, they become deductible: job-hunting costs, union dues, the costs of special work uniforms, subscriptions to professional journals, and certain unreimbursed business travel expenses, including food and lodging if you're away from home overnight.

In some cases the cost of education can be deducted as a business-related expense. The key test is whether the course of study prepares you for a better job or is necessary to keep your performance up to snuff in your present job. Expenses in the first category aren't deductible; expenses in the second are deductible, subject to the 2% threshold described above.

If you have to hire someone to care for your children or other dependent while you work or look for work, you may be able to take advantage of the child-care credit. It permits a direct deduction from taxes of up to 30% of actual expenditures. The top credit allowed is $720 for the care of one child or disabled dependent and $1,440 for the care of two or more. When income exceeds $10,000, the credit is reduced in stages, down to 20% of qualifying expenses if your adjusted gross income is above $28,000.

YEAR-END TAX TACTICS

If you keep suggestions like the above in mind throughout the year, you should see results the following April. But remember that December 31, not April 15, is the deadline for most tax-saving moves. That makes the last couple of months of the year an important time for reviewing where you stand and taking steps to protect your position.

Shifting income. Sometimes there are good reasons for packing as much income as possible into either the current year or the next one. Suppose you expect a big infusion of income next year from the sale of property, perhaps, or from moving to a much higher-paying job. In such cases it may make sense to concentrate as much of your income as possible into the current year, to protect it from the possibility that next year's tax bracket will be higher.

On the other hand, suppose you expect to retire next year or take some other action that will cut your income considerably. Then you might want to shift as much income as possible into next year, when your tax rates may be lower.

Unfortunately, we don't often have a great deal of control over the timing of our income. Salaries and wages are usually paid on a fixed schedule and there's not much you can do to change it. But if your employer pays an unexpected year-end bonus, for example, you may be able to arrange to receive it in the more advantageous tax year. If you're self-employed and a cash-basis taxpayer, you could speed up or slow down sending bills to customers near the end of the year, in hopes of having the desired effect on income flow.

Timing capital gains and losses. Although the tax law no longer bestows favorable treatment on long-term capital gains, it still differentiates them from short-term gains.

A long-term gain or loss is one that results from the sale of property or securities held for more than six months. A short-term gain or loss results from a sale of property or securities held for six months or less. Both types of gains are fully taxable, and both types of losses are fully deductible up to a $3,000 annual limit for capital-loss deductions. Excess losses may be deducted in future years.

The timing of sales can be critical because a dollar of capital loss—whether long- or short-term—neatly offsets a dollar of ordinary income. Because there is no longer any advantage in holding property long enough to qualify for the special treatment long-term gains used to get, your decision about when to sell can lean more heavily on the need to shift income or losses from one year to the next.

Guarding dependents' exemptions. These are worth $1,950

apiece in 1988 and $2,000 each in 1989. It's important to remember that they are by no means guaranteed from one year to the next. Five dependency tests must be met each time: Generally, you must provide more than half your dependents' support; their gross income must be under $1,950 each for the year ($2,000 in 1989), unless they are your children under age 19 or full-time students for at least five months of the year; in most cases they must live with you, unless they are your children, parents, close relatives or in-laws; they generally must be U.S. citizens or residents of the U.S., Canada or Mexico; and they must not file a joint return with someone else. Unusual circumstances can sometimes imperil dependency exemptions.

If it appears that a potential dependent may end the year supplying more than half of his or her own support, consider whether to step up your payments between now and the end of the year. Would it save you money in the long run? To a couple filing a joint return with $40,000 of taxable income, a $2,000 dependency exemption is worth about $560 in the pocket. You can also suggest that the dependent put a larger portion of his or her own earnings in savings rather than spending it for self-support.

If you share the cost of supporting a dependent with others but none of you contributes enough alone to claim the exemption, any one of the contributors paying more than 10% of the cost of support can claim the dependent, assuming all the other dependency tests are met. The other contributors who gave more than 10% must declare to the IRS in writing that they won't claim the exemption that year. You accomplish this with form 2120, called the Multiple Support Declaration, available from IRS.

Assessing medical expenses. Unless your medical expenses amount to more than 7.5% of your adjusted gross income, they are worthless to you as tax reducers. Late in the year you can look back on expenses you've paid so far and anticipate the nonemergency care that lies ahead. If it is apparent that the bills won't amount to more than 7.5% of income this year, consider delaying optional treatment and putting off payment of some bills until the following year. Your medical expenses may be higher then, and maybe the government will absorb some of the cost.

Timing other transactions. As the end of the year draws closer, your timing of transactions with tax consequences becomes crucial. Look for deductions you can shift from one year to the next by speeding up or slowing down payment. In addition to payments for medical care, good candidates are charitable contributions, subscriptions to professional or job-related publications, union or professional association dues, rent on a safe-deposit box (if the box is used to store papers related to taxable income-producing property or securities), and certain state and local taxes.

GETTING HELP WITH YOUR TAX RETURN

Every year about half of all Americans hire someone else to do their tax returns. Counting those who get someone to do their taxes for them free, the proportion of taxpayers needing help filing returns rises to about three-fourths. Fortunately, there is plenty of assistance available.

The IRS. With offices scattered throughout the nation and toll-free telephone lines, the Internal Revenue Service itself is the busiest of the taxpayer helpers, providing instructions and forms and answering your questions. The phone number of the nearest IRS office is in your local phone book and in your annual tax package.

To some people, going to the IRS for tax help may seem like asking for trouble. It's true that many tax rules are open to different interpretations and the IRS may take a stingier view of your tax liability than other authorities may allow. Looking beyond IRS for assistance usually means having to pay for it, but remember that the cost is deductible on your tax return, to the extent that your miscellaneous deductions top 2% of your adjusted gross income.

Commercial preparers. H&R Block, Inc., prepares more tax returns by far than any other firm in the country—about ten million or more a year. The convenience of Block's offices, many of which are open nights and weekends during the filing season, and the company's extensive advertising are part of the reason so many taxpayers are willing to pay an average of about $50 each to buy H&R Block's help in filing their federal and state returns. Short forms cost less.

How good is the help provided by Block and other national firms? Most preparers employed by national firms receive a substantial amount of training to learn the basics and keep up with changes in the tax law. And most returns are double-checked for accuracy. At Block offices, for example, another preparer goes over returns done by his or her colleagues.

There are no federal standards for commercial preparers. In fact, the IRS staunchly opposes any kind of testing or licensing program. But all taxpayers are covered by rules imposed by the Tax Reform Act of 1976 and the Tax Equity and Fiscal Responsibility Act of 1982. A preparer can be fined for deliberately or negligently understanding a taxpayers' liability, failing to give the taxpayer a copy of the completed return, or failing to sign the return personally. These regulations are aimed at rooting out unscrupulous and incompetent preparers.

By exercising care, you can eliminate much of the risk. Be wary of local tax-preparation operations that pop up in the spring and are likely to disappear just as quickly in mid April.

Here are some tips to help you choose a commercial preparer that will give you the most for you money.

Go early.   One criticism of commercial firms is that they rush taxpayers in and out to build a high-volume operation. If you're part of the last-minute crunch, you might be shortchanged.

Find out in advance how much you'll be charged.   The more complex your return, the higher the fee is likely to be. Ask whether the fee includes preparation of any necessary state and local forms.

Ask the preparer about his or her qualifications and experience.   Also ask how completed returns are checked for accuracy. Be suspicious of a preparer who doesn't ask you a lot of questions. The preparer's job is to probe into your financial affairs and apply what he or she learns to get you all the tax breaks you deserve.

Carefully check over your completed tax return.   Remember, you are the one who pays if your tax liability is overstated, and you are ultimately responsible for errors. Be certain all forms and schedules the preparer discussed with you are included. If, for example, you are eligible for a credit for child-care expenses and the preparer filled out the proper form, be sure it's attached to the return.

Professional help. The more complex your return, the wiser it might be to turn to a professional tax practitioner, such as an enrolled agent or an accountant. Many charge by the hour, for what they're selling is their knowledge of how to use the tax law to your advantage.

Public accountants' fees for preparing itemized 1040s vary with the complexity of the return. Some charge by the hour, some charge a flat rate. Enrolled agents and certified public accountants are usually more expensive. Fees vary widely, so the only way to find out what they are in your area is to ask. You need to know what it will cost to have your return prepared, whether the person doing the job will represent you in case of an audit and, if so, the estimated cost of that service.

Public accountants needn't be licensed in most states, and their competence and experience can vary a great deal. Before hiring an accountant, ask about his or her education and experience and find out whether he or she is a member of the state accounting society and the National Society of Public Accountants.

Enrolled agents are the only tax practitioners who have to meet IRS standards. Whether or not they're accountants, enrolled agents earn their status by having worked as IRS auditors for at least five years or by passing an IRS exam on technical tax matters and accounting. Enrolled agents can argue their clients' cases at IRS audits and appeals. (Though commercial preparers can attend an audit with a taxpayer, they appear as witnesses to explain how the return was prepared, not as representatives of the taxpayer.) Enrolled agents may be hard to locate, for there are only about 20,000 in the country. Check the Yellow Pages.

Certified public accountants must pass an examination and have a certain amount of experience to earn their title. If yours is a highly complicated financial situation, it might be wise to choose a CPA to help you with your tax return and also to offer tax-planning advice. You can expect to pay as much as $200 an hour for this caliber of help. Check with your banker or lawyer for recommendations. Some CPAs specialize in corporate accounting and have neither the time nor the inclination to do individual tax returns.

In some cases attorneys who specialize in tax law will help their clients with tax returns, although their primary activity is advising clients on knotty areas of the law. Lawyers and CPAs, like enrolled agents, can represent clients at IRS audits and appeals.

WHAT IF YOU'RE AUDITED?

The higher your income the more likely you are to be chosen for an audit. Statistics indicate that just 3% of returns showing income between $25,000 and $50,000 are likely to be examined. Less than 6% of those reporting $50,000 and up are audited. For all income groups combined, the odds against being audited are about 50 to 1. Still, it happens.

There are three types of audits. *Correspondence audits,* as their name suggests, are handled entirely through the mail and generally involve only minor matters requiring documentation. In a *field audit,* an IRS agent comes to your home or place of business to go over your records. Most common is the *office audit;* it means getting yourself and your papers to the local IRS office.

The audit notice will identify the items on your return that are being questioned—usually broad categories, such as employee business expenses or casualty losses—and outline the types of records you'll need to clear up the matter. Office audits are usually limited to two or three issues, so you won't be expected to haul in all your records and prove every entry on your return.

An exception is the Taxpayer Compliance Measurement Program audit. Each year, the IRS chooses about 50,000 returns at random and subjects them to excruciating scrutiny. The data from these audits are used in evaluating how well taxpayers comply with the law and to construct the portraits of typical taxpayers against which the computer judges returns when choosing candidates for audit.

Assuming your return will get the office-audit treatment, you'll probably have at least two weeks after being notified to get your evidence and your arguments together.

First, get a copy of the return that's being challenged. Before the IRS puts it through the wringer, do it yourself. Pore over the items being questioned and pull together the documents that support your entries. There are almost sure to be gaps—after all, it's likely that at least six months, and perhaps more than two years, will have passed since you prepared the return. Try to reconstruct missing records. Get copies of canceled checks from the bank, for example, duplicates of receipts, or written statements from individuals who can back up your claims. Where you can't come up with written evidence, prepare your oral explanation.

Your records don't have to be perfect. If you have a reasonable explanation for how you came up with a figure that's not fully corroborated by the evidence, the IRS may well accept it. The agency manual for auditors reminds agents that record keeping and accounting are not exact sciences and that the lack of an occasional receipt or other element shouldn't prevent the records from being adequate.

Do you need help? Do you need someone with you at the audit, perhaps an accountant or tax attorney? Although it might be nice to have someone accompany you, it's probably unnecessary during the first meeting with the auditor.

If someone else prepared your return, let him or her know about the audit and ask for help getting ready for it. Whether or not you want this person to go along may depend on how much it will cost you.

Although the IRS would like to wrap up the case with a single meeting, there can be follow-up meetings if you don't agree with the auditor. Unless you fear you might capitulate if you go in alone, it's probably okay to attend the office audit and settle as many issues as you can by yourself. If disagreements remain, and the dollar amounts justify it, you can take an adviser along to the next session. That way you'll have help when you need it but not pay for hand holding while you're clearing up routine matters.

Be on time for your appointment. Besides being simple courtesy, punctuality may work in your favor: The auditor will review your case just before the meeting and, if you are late, your return will spend extra time under the microscope. Be businesslike and cooperative, and restrict yourself to answering the questions asked. Being cooperative doesn't mean automatically giving in when the agent challenges something on your return. In fact, being too agreeable can raise suspicions. The IRS manual alerts agents that quick agreement to adjustments and undue concern about closing the case right away may be signs that a more thorough examination is needed.

You will be asked to present evidence that supports the items on your return that are being questioned. Rather than just dumping your receipts on the table, be as helpful as you can. If the auditor rejects a claim because of a gap in your records, ask what might be considered acceptable evidence. Perhaps you'll be able to mail it in later. The audit will probably be restricted to the items listed on your audit notice, but if it strays onto new issues, you'll get a chance to get your records together. You may be able to mail in the necessary documents or come back for a second meeting.

The audit could last from 20 minutes to more than two hours. You'll spend a lot of that time watching the agent work an adding machine. When it's over, the auditor will give you the decision, which in four out of five cases is that more tax is due. Each proposed change on your return and the reason for it should be explained.

If you agree, fine. But remember that the auditor doesn't have the final say. Sometimes auditors make mistakes that cost taxpayers money. If you disagree with the findings—say the auditor threw out a deduction or was less than reasonable about a lapse in your bookkeeping—tell the auditor so and restate your position. He or she may be willing to compromise to close the case promptly.

How to appeal the results. If you agree with the auditor's findings, you'll be asked to sign a form saying so and within a few weeks you'll get a bill for the extra tax, plus interest and any penalty that was imposed. Most audits end this way.

If you disagree, tell the auditor and go home. You will receive in the mail a report explaining the proposed adjustments to your return. At this point, you may want to seek professional advice. If, on reflection, you decide you might as well settle for the proposed amount, you can do so by signing an agreement form.

You have several choices if you want to keep fighting. You can ask for another meeting with the auditor to present new evidence, for example, or you can make an immediate informal appeal to the auditor's boss. If you're still unhappy, you can go to the IRS regional appeal level. At any point you can take your appeal to court.

You have to ask for a regional appeal within 30 days of the date of the audit report, but it will probably be at least a couple of months before the appeal is scheduled. Regional appeals are handled informally, and you don't have to take an accountant or lawyer with you.

If you can't get satisfaction at the regional appeal, you can take your case to court. Most tax disputes are settled in the U.S. Tax Court, although you can also take your case to the U.S. District Court for your area or the U.S. Court of Claims in Washington, D.C.

The Tax Court, which hears cases at sites around the country, has a special procedure for cases in which the disputed amount is $10,000 or less. With relatively informal procedures, you can represent yourself in a small tax case. Unlike regular Tax Court cases and those in the district courts and Court of Claims, however, the ruling in a small tax case can't be appealed.

How to improve your chances. As already mentioned, preparation for your battle should begin before the initial audit. The letter you receive from IRS will generally indicate the areas being questioned, but the auditor doesn't have to limit the examination to those items. You should review your entire return.

Remember, you don't have to decide whether you agree or disagree with the auditor at the meeting. If you're not sure of what you should do, wait for the auditor's report and study it in a more relaxed atmosphere at home. Then you can plan your approach.

At every step of the appeals process, you'll have to decide whether you want to continue to the next. Time and money will always be major considerations. If you stick with it and your case involves a question of law that a court must arbitrate, the dispute could stretch on for years. That helps explain why so many taxpayers decide to settle for a compromise somewhere along the way.

THE LAST GREAT TAX SHELTER

The Tax Reform Act of 1986 virtually eliminated most of the highly touted tax shelters of the past, and it did it without having to deal with them one by one. It did it with one bold stroke, by creating three separate categories of income and losses: active, passive and portfolio. Active income comes from work you do—wages and salaries are obvious examples. Passive income comes from activities in which the taxpayer does not "materially participate"—a limited partnership, for example. The third category is called portfolio income; it means dividends, interest and capital gains generated by traditional investments like stocks and bonds.

The clincher is this: The tax law says you generally cannot use losses in one category to shelter income from another. This hits hardest at passive losses. You can't use passive losses from, say, a limited partnership to escape taxes on active income—the salary from your job, for example—or to offset portfolio income from a mutual fund.

Bingo. Bye, bye, tax shelters.

Well, not quite. Rental real estate gets a partial exemption, as described in Chapter 18. And in fact, just about any use of your money that legally allows you to escape, reduce or defer taxes could be called a tax shelter. You already have one if you own your own home (see Chapter 6), have life insurance that builds cash values (Chapter 10), have an individual retirement account or Keogh account (Chapter 24), buy U.S. savings bonds (Chapter 16) or receive employee fringe benefits such as a pension plan or health insurance (Chapter 24). The tax-favored status of such activities puts money in your pocket.

This chapter is devoted to the one product that is expressly designed to be a tax shelter and survived the tax reform axe virtually intact: municipal bonds.

MUNICIPAL BONDS: STILL STRONG

The investment packagers of Wall Street have responded imaginatively to the public's demands for tax-free income from municipal bonds. Years ago they figured there was a market for a product that would help guide investors through the sprawling marketplace of municipal debt, where thousands of different governmental units compete for billions of dollars of investors' money. The result was the appearance in 1961 of the first municipal-bond unit trusts. They made available, for a small sales fee, portions of a fixed portfolio selected by the fund's professional underwriters. The minimum investment in most cases was $5,000.

Then in 1976, the mutual fund idea came to municipals. Minimum investment dropped to only $1,000 or less, for which you got a slice of a portfolio of bonds that the fund's managers would buy and sell to take advantage of market conditions.

There's a third way to acquire a portfolio of municipal bonds—the old-fashioned way, by buying your own instead of letting someone else choose them for you. If you are in the market for municipals, you'd do well to compare the different ways of acquiring them. You could discover that some prominent features of particular methods fade in importance while others you might have overlooked begin to loom large.

What is a municipal bond? It's a catchall name that describes the debt issues of cities and towns, states and territories, counties, local public housing authorities, water districts, school districts, and similar governmental or quasigovernmental units. Because interest paid is exempt from federal income taxes and, usually, income taxes of the state in which the bond is issued, municipals can pay less interest than corporate bonds of comparable quality and still deliver the same after-tax yield. The higher your tax bracket, the more valuable this tax-exempt feature becomes.

Municipal bonds come in two principal varieties.

• *Revenue bonds,* for which repayment is generally tied to particular sources of revenue, such as bridge or highway tolls, or to specific taxes, such as those on alcohol or cigarettes. Uses of revenue bonds include financing of construction projects such as waterworks, airports, rapid transit systems, and sports complexes. (*Industrial revenue bonds,* although issued by governmental units, are designed to raise construction capital for private corporations. They are backed by the credit standing of the corporation, not the issuing government, and their tax-free status is limited. See the discussion of taxable municipal bonds in Chapter 16.)

• *General obligation bonds* pledge the faith and credit of the government that issues them, meaning that the taxing authority of the issuer stands behind the bond to insure payment of interest and principal.

Just like corporate issues, municipals vary in quality according to the economic and financial soundness of the project or the credit worthiness of the issuer. To serve as quality guides for investors, Standard & Poor's Corporation and Moody's Investors Services, Inc., study available financial data and determine credit ratings for municipal bond issues. Bonds considered least risky get rated AAA by S&P and Aaa by Moody's. These triple-A's are considered prime or gilt-edge investments. Next in quality comes S&P's AA, the equivalent of Moody's Aa, followed by the A rating used by both services, then BBB (Baa by Moody's), BB (Ba) and so on down the line. Bonds rated below BBB or Baa are considered speculative issues that might make them risky investments over the long run.

It stands to reason that the higher a bond's rating—in other words, the safer an investment it appears to be—the lower the interest it needs to pay to attract investors, and vice versa. Thus, the riskiest bonds tend to yield the most.

Keep in mind that every revenue bond project is different and needs to be analyzed on its economic merits. There are also special legal and financial agreements that can be significant to investors. Whatever type of municipal bond you are considering, ask your broker to provide you with an official statement from the issuer. This should describe in detail the bond, the project, and the municipality. (If the bond is a new issue, your broker is required to give you one.) This document, unlike a corporate prospectus, has no standardized format. And unlike corporations, municipal bond issuers are not required to provide regular financial information to bondholders.

How costs affect yields. You should shop for the highest yield consistent with the risks you're willing to take. Let's assume for a moment that each of the three options mentioned earlier— unit trusts, mutual funds and individual bonds—offers precisely the same yield. Will your earnings be the same, whichever you buy?

The answer is no, and the reasons lie in the costs associated with the different forms of ownership. First comes the sales fee. If you buy the bonds directly from a broker, it is included in the cost. Brokerage houses normally sell bonds from their own accounts, and when they raise the price to add in their sales charge, they usually recalculate the yield to reflect the additional cost to the investor. This means that when you buy, for example, a bond issued to yield 8.25%, you might get a return on your investment of only 8%. Part of that missing 0.25% would be lost to the dealer's commission. From your point of view, what you are purchasing is a bond yielding 8%.

Unit trusts and mutual funds don't work that way. Trusts, and funds sold by brokers, carry fees that reduce your actual return. The front-end load, or sales charge, is deducted from your gross investment. If you buy $10,000 worth of a unit trust charging a 4.5% sales commission, what you get is $9,550 worth of bonds earning interest for you. The same thing happens with a mutual fund sold by a broker.

There are other costs involved as well. Mutual funds,

including the no-loads, require the services of investment advisers to manage portfolios. For this the managers generally take 0.5% or more of the fund's average net asset value as a fee. This reduces your return by the same amount. A mutual fund earning 8% on its portfolio and keeping 0.5% for management can pay out only 7.5% to its investors.

Because unit trusts normally don't trade in the market once the portfolio is set, they don't need managers. But they do require trustees and administrators, who must be paid. Their fees generally amount to about 0.1% of net asset value. Thus, a trust earning 8% on its portfolio will return 7.9% to its investors.

Insured bonds and market risks. All municipal bond investments entail some degree of risk. The bonds are rated on the same scales used for judging the quality of corporate bonds, but issuers aren't required to reveal as much about their financial affairs as corporations are. Municipal bonds have had an excellent safety record over the years, and defaults are rare. Nevertheless, there have been near-defaults by some large cities and at least one actual default of the Washington Public Power Supply System (WPPSS, or Whoops) Projects 4 and 5. These episodes have made insured municipal bonds attractive to many safety-conscious investors.

To insure its bonds, an issuer or underwriter pays an insurance premium of anywhere from 0.1% to 2% of total principal and interest. In return, the insurance company agrees to pay principal and interest to bondholders if the issuer defaults. Policies cannot be canceled and remain in effect over the life of the bond.

In the case of a unit trust, insurance is usually purchased for the entire portfolio rather than each individual bond. As long as a defaulted issue remains in the fund, shareholders have the same guarantee of principal and interest payments as owners of individually insured bonds. Bonds in the trust that have already been insured by the issuer don't carry portfolio insurance as well.

The first municipal bond was insured by the American Municipal Bond Assurance Corporation (AMBAC) in 1971. The

Municipal Bond Insurance Association (MBIA), the other major insurer of municipals, began operations in 1974.

Once a bond is insured, it is assigned an AAA rating by S&P, even if the bond has, say, a BBB rating based on its own creditworthiness. So it's important to remember that a broker selling an AAA-insured bond may actually be selling a BBB security with insurance.

Will having insurance affect your yield? Yes. Issuers of riskier bonds need to offer higher yields to attract investors. Because insured issues carry a relatively low risk, their yields will be about 20 to 40 basis points lower than a comparably rated uninsured issue. (A basis point is one-hundredth of 1%.) Lower interest costs, as well as increased marketability of insured bonds, are the reasons that issuers are willing to pay the one-time insurance premiums.

The main advantage of an insured municipal bond trust is that a defaulted issue in the portfolio will continue to pay interest and return principal at maturity. If you hold onto your shares until the defaulted issue matures, you'll feel no adverse effect. But if you decide to sell before then, having a defaulted bond even in an insured portfolio could affect the value of your shares on the secondary market.

Municipal bond insurance guarantees only that your principal and interest will be repaid in the event of a default; it does not guarantee the market value of a bond. An unexpected down-grading in the issuer's credit rating or a default by the issuer, as well as interest rate changes, could affect the market value of insured bonds.

Tax swapping. For the great majority of investors, a bigger risk than default is getting locked into a return that looks fine at the beginning but turns out to be inadequate in the face of rising interest rates. If you have to sell the bond under those circumstances, you'll suffer a capital loss.

You can ease the pain somewhat by performing what is known as a tax swap. Tax swapping is especially suited to municipal bonds and can be a valuable year-end tax-saving move. You merely sell your devalued bonds and reinvest the proceeds in bonds from a different issuer paying the higher, current rate. This gives you a capital loss for your tax return and, ignoring commissions, keeps your bond income at the same level.

Example: Say you are holding $5,000 in municipal bonds purchased in January and yielding 8%. That gives you an annual income of $400. By December, rates have climbed to 10%. You are still earning $400 from your bonds, but their market value is now down to $4,000. You sell the bonds, take a $1,000 loss and reinvest the proceeds in 10% bonds issued by another municipality. Since 10% of $4,000 is $400, you've maintained your level of income while achieving a capital loss that can be used to shelter taxable income from other sources.

But note: The IRS considers a transaction a "wash sale" if you sell a bond or other security and within 30 days acquire a substantially identical one. Losses from wash sales are not deductible. Relying on small differences between issues, such as maturity dates or interest rates, could put you on shaky ground, so be sure to check with your broker or tax adviser before undertaking a tax swap.

ZERO-COUPON MUNICIPALS

Zero-coupon municipal bonds are sold at a big discount from face value and pay no current interest. Their attraction lies in the combination of two things: the big payoff at maturity and the tax-free status of their earnings.

The description of zero-coupon bonds in Chapter 16 points out that one potential disadvantage of zeroes held outside an IRA or other tax-deferred account is that you must pay tax on the interest that accrues each year even though no interest is actually paid until the bond matures. Municipal zeroes eliminate that worry and constitute a nearly perfect long-term investment vehicle.

As with other bonds, risks lie in the possibility that interest rates will rise substantially while you own them, thus reducing their current market value. There is some risk of default, which you can minimize by paying attention to safety ratings, and there is risk of call with some bonds. If your zero is called prior to maturity, you lose one of the investment's biggest attrac-

368

tions: the certain knowledge of what it will be worth on a particular date in the future.

THE ADVANTAGES OF FUNDS AND TRUSTS

Mutual funds offer the opportunity to ride along with rising interest rates if their managers are alert enough to spot the signals in time to make the necessary portfolio changes. The risk with mutual funds lies in the possibility that the funds' managers will make the wrong decision or wait too long to make the right ones, thus depressing the fund's net asset value and leaving you with a loss if you have to sell your shares.

When interest rates are volatile, sticking to short maturities is a sensible way to hedge the risks of the market. That's the approach taken by a group of mutuals that have come to be known as the tax-free money-market funds. These funds put their money into short-term notes issued by state and local governments and their agencies. The notes are considered temporary financing that will be paid off with revenues from taxes, bond issues and other sources. You will find in fund portfolios such securities as these: bond anticipation notes (BANs), tax anticipation notes (TANs), revenue anticipation notes (RANs), grant anticipation notes (GANs), tax and revenue anticipation notes (TRANs), temporary loan notes (TLNs). There is a list of tax-free money-market funds on page 370.

In a unit trust or a mutual fund you get another measure of protection that is difficult to obtain on your own: diversity. Consider a unit trust consisting of 16 different issues. Because the great majority of individual bonds sell in $5,000 minimums, you'd need a portfolio worth at least $80,000 to buy that much diversity on your own. You can buy a piece of some trusts for as little as $1,000.

Tax treatment. Tax-free municipals pay interest that is exempt from federal income taxes, but you still owe state and local taxes in most cases unless the bond is issued by a unit of your state or local government. This can be an important distinction, depending on where you live.

You can control the taxability of bonds you purchase on your own by restricting your portfolio to state and local issues that carry the overall exemption. And there are unit trusts available that invest only in issues of a certain state. For example, underwriters have put together trusts that specialize in the issues of California, Indiana, Massachusetts, Michigan, Minnesota, New Jersey, New York, Ohio, Pennsylvania and Texas. You can calculate the effect of double tax-free income on your taxable-equivalent yield by consulting the table on page 371. With mutual funds and most unit trusts, though, you have no control over the proportion of out-of-state issues in the portfolio.

Liquidity. Mutual funds redeem their shares on demand, and unit trusts generally maintain a secondary market for units. There's also an active market for individually held bonds, but you usually have to pay a premium if you want to sell only one or two.

Convenience. To calculate what this is worth to you, consider what is involved in maintaining your own portfolio of municipals. You'll need a place to safeguard them, probably a safe-deposit box. You have to watch the papers and other sources if you own any callable bonds. Interest is nearly always paid semiannually, whereas most unit trusts and mutual funds let you choose monthly or quarterly distributions instead. In addition to professional selection and management, that's the sort of service they are selling you.

Unit trusts are put together by brokerage houses, and you have to purchase them there. The following are some examples of mutual funds that invest in municipal bonds. Before deciding to invest in any of them, call for their prospectuses and compare their portfolios, management staffs and shareholder services. No-load funds are indicated by an asterisk.

Dreyfus Tax Exempt Bond Fund
800-645-6561

Federated Tax-Free Income Fund
800-541-6133

*Fidelity Municipal Bond Fund**
800-544-6666

IDS Tax Exempt Bond Fund
800-328-8300

Kemper Municipal Bond Fund
800-621-1048
Oppenheimer Tax-Free Bond Fund
800-525-7048

*T. Rowe Price Tax-Free Income Fund**
800-638-5660

*Scudder Managed Municipal Bond Fund**
800-453-3305

The following funds stick to short-term municipal notes and permit shareholders to write checks on their accounts. All are no-load funds.

Fidelity Tax Exempt Money Market Trust
800-544-6666

Prudential-Bache Tax-Free Money Fund
800-872-7787

Scudder Tax Free Money Fund
800-225-2470

Vanguard Municipal Bond Fund Money Market Portfolio
800-662-7447

THE ALTERNATIVE MINIMUM TAX

The idea behind the alternative minimum tax is simple enough to understand and its goal is laudable: It's designed to make sure high-income individuals aren't so successful at sidestepping income taxes that they wind up paying little or no tax. So the rules governing the AMT say that if it looks like you're not paying your fair share, you must add certain deductions back

continued on page 372

HOW MUCH TAX-FREE INCOME IS WORTH

For a true picture of what you're earning, you must compare the interest available from tax-exempt bonds with the after-tax yield from taxable issues. This table provides multipliers that take into account both federal and state income taxes. To find the taxable equivalent yield for a municipal bond issued by the state in which you live, find your state, then multiply the bond's yield by the figure appearing in the column under your tax bracket. Example: If you're in the 33% federal tax bracket, live in California and can get a California-issued municipal bond paying 8%, multiply the yield by 1.646 to find its taxable equivalent—13.17%. Kidder Peabody, the brokerage firm that calculated the multipliers, took into account federal and state tax rates as well as peculiarities of some state laws. The figures assume that a municipal bond is not taxed by the state in which it is issued.

	28% FEDERAL TAX RATE	33% FEDERAL TAX RATE
Alabama	1.463	1.572
Alaska	1.389	1.493
Arizona	1.513	1.626
Arkansas	1.493	1.605
California	1.531	1.646
Colorado	1.458	1.567
Connecticut	1.578	1.696
Delaware	1.505	1.617
D.C.	1.535	1.649
Florida	1.389	1.493
Georgia	1.472	1.582
Hawaii	1.526	1.642
Idaho	1.513	1.626

continued

	28% FEDERAL TAX RATE	33% FEDERAL TAX RATE
Illinois	1.425	1.531
Indiana	1.438	1.545
Iowa	1.548	1.664
Kansas	1.530	1.645
Kentucky	1.479	1.590
Louisiana	1.479	1.590
Maine	1.543	1.658
Maryland	1.502	1.614
Massachusetts	1.543	1.658
Michigan	1.511	1.624
Minnesota	1.510	1.631
Mississippi	1.462	1.571
Missouri	1.485	1.596
Montana	1.587	1.707
Nebraska	1.476	1.586
Nevada	1.389	1.493
New Hampshire	1.462	1.571
New Jersey	1.439	1.547
New Mexico	1.518	1.631
New York	1.550	1.665

continued

into your income and refigure the tax at a flat rate of 21%. If the AMT has you owing more than the regular way of calculating your tax bill, you pay the AMT.

What you must add back in are chiefly the kinds of items you'd expect: deductions taken for passive losses, depreciation on real estate and other property (placed in service after 1986), the portion of the value of charitable donations of appreciated

	28% FEDERAL TAX RATE	33% FEDERAL TAX RATE
North Carolina	1.493	1.605
North Dakota	1.443	1.561
Ohio	1.492	1.603
Oklahoma	1.478	1.588
Oregon	1.526	1.640
Pennsylvania	1.419	1.525
Rhode Island	1.480	1.607
South Carolina	1.493	1.605
South Dakota	1.389	1.493
Tennessee	1.478	1.588
Texas	1.389	1.493
Utah	1.506	1.618
Vermont	1.486	1.615
Virginia	1.474	1.584
Washington	1.389	1.493
West Virginia	1.485	1.596
Wisconsin	1.492	1.604
Wyoming	1.389	1.493

Source: *Kidder Peabody*

property that exceeds the cost basis of the property. You must also boost your income by some rather mundane deductions, such as state and local income taxes, real estate taxes and the tax-free interest received from certain municipal bonds judged to be floated for nonessential purposes but which were permitted to be issued tax-free nonetheless.

Taxpayers filing a joint return can protect $40,000 of income from the AMT; single filers get a $30,000 exemption. If your income is at or below those amounts, there's no way you'll incur the AMT no matter how many deductions you claim. But if your income is high—more than $150,000 for marrieds, $112,500 for singles—you begin to lose the exemption.

Could you possibly incur the alternative minimum tax? Probably not if your income is modest and your deductions are reasonable. But if it looks close, there's only one way to find out: Figure your tax both ways, and pay the higher amount.

Part Six

YOUR JOB, YOUR RETIREMENT, YOUR ESTATE

MAKING THE MOST OF YOUR JOB

ARE YOU KEEPING UP?

In many ways your job is your most important asset of all, because it demands so much of your time and energy. You should know whether the pay you're getting is keeping up with inflation, whether your fringe benefits compare favorably with other people in the same line of work, and whether there are opportunities for growth and advancement ahead. If your job is seriously deficient on any of those points, it's probably time to do something about it.

First consider your salary increases over the past several years. Despite being tamed quite a bit, inflation has still damaged our purchasing power, but most groups of workers have managed to come close to matching the year-by-year increases in the cost of living.

It would be fairly easy to compare the increases in your pay with the inflation rate for any given period and arrive at a quick conclusion about whether or not you've been keeping up. It would also be misleading, because your salary is only part of your compensation. If you wanted to make an accurate assessment of where you stand, you'd also have to calculate the value of your fringe benefits and conduct an assessment of how much taxes have taken from your pay. You'll find help with taxes in Chapters 21 and 22. This chapter will help you size up your job.

THE VALUE OF FRINGE BENEFITS

Your fringe benefits include some items that are worth a big chunk of money. And an especially appealing aspect of fringe benefits is that normally they don't increase your tax bill the way cash income does. The total dollar value of your combined benefits can be considerable, depending on how generous, enlightened and prosperous your employer is. If you receive an average amount, your fringes are worth more than a third of your annual salary.

The fact that some fringes cost your employer money is obvious—health insurance and pension contributions, for instance. Others aren't so obvious. Your employer considers as fringe benefits everything it pays out for you in addition to your salary. Fringes include your vacation time and sick leave, lunch and coffee breaks, and what the company pays for you into government-required social security, unemployment and workers' compensation funds.

You would be perfectly justified in noting that these kinds of fringe benefits don't help put food on the table now. But there are other fringes that do. If you are a heavy user of medical services—for example, if you have children of the age at which trips to the doctor's office are frequent—and your company-paid or subsidized health insurance covers most of the bills, that fringe benefit has shielded you from one of life's fastest-rising expenses. As medical costs continue to increase, the insurance will become all the more valuable.

Some fringes help in another way, too, by easing the need for cash in certain categories of spending, thus making more money available for use in other categories. Fringes that clearly free up cash include low-priced meals (in a company cafeteria, for instance), free parking, use of a company car, van-pool rides, free job training or funds for extracurricular education, payment of your dues in clubs and associations, and free legal services.

You can use the fringe-benefits checklist on page 380 to evaluate the elements of your benefits package. Put down only what your employer pays for your fringes, not any share you contribute. You may have to ask your personnel office for some information—for instance, how much your employer pays for your medical and hospitalization insurance coverage, how much the company puts into your pension fund each year, and so on—but you can figure out the value of many benefits yourself. If you have a free parking spot, value it at the going rate for commercial space in the same neighborhood. If you eat lunch in the company cafeteria, its value to you is the difference between the cost of meals there and what you'd pay for comparable ones in a restaurant. If you've called in sick, multiply the number of days by your daily pay.

When you consider the dollar value of your total compensation from the job—cash income plus fringes—you may conclude that even though your salary increases have barely kept even with rising prices, you are better off than you thought, because fringe benefits are cushioning you against certain kinds of price increases.

HOW TO IMPROVE YOUR SITUATION

If your analysis shows you've done all right so far, congratulations. But if you conclude that corrective action is in order, here are your options.

Ask for a raise. If you're convinced you're falling behind—and you believe that your job performance entitles you to more pay—ask for a raise. Your chances of success are best if you can make your case in terms of your own demonstrably increased productivity.

Earn a promotion. Don't expect a promotion just because you want and need the increased income. Build a solid case by demonstrating your value to your employer on the basis of efficiency, productivity, initiative, dedication and ability to deal effectively with others—all the attributes that go into making a person promotable.

A critical factor, of course, will be your relationship with your boss, who will probably have the biggest, if not the sole, say on

HOW DO YOUR BENEFITS COMPARE?

FRINGE BENEFIT	% OF COMPANIES THAT PROVIDE IT	AVERAGE ANNUAL AMOUNT EMPLOYER PAYS
Legally required payments*	99%	$2,333
Pension or profit sharing plans Defined benefit pension plan	58	851
Defined contribution plans	43	398
Life insurance and death benefits	93	127
Hospital, surgical, medical and major medical premiums	98	1,604
Retiree payments	34	157
Short-term disability, sickness or accident insurance	41	139
Long-term disability insurance	61	50
Dental insurance	56	148
Paid rest periods	76	879
Vacations	86	1,357
Holidays	83	820
Sick leave	76	354
Parental leave	61	48
Company discounts	18	63
Employee meals	25	26
Employee education	76	41
Child care	61	159
Other	35	86

*Employer's share of FICA, unemployment compensation and workers' compensation.
Figures are from a survey of 833 companies by the U.S. Chamber of Commerce.

your promotion. The decision could turn on any number of considerations, ranging from how consistently you've brought work in on time to how conscientiously you've studied the corporate culture, to how much support you've provided in compiling a record that makes the boss promotable.

Get a transfer. Say your work is excellent. You deserve a promotion. Your boss says so. Unfortunately, there just aren't any openings on the next rung of the ladder.

If that's the case, maybe you'd be wise to get into another part of the company where there is more chance of moving up. In many companies the career path in various divisions is different and so is the pace of promotion.

For example, a department like purchasing may offer limited opportunities for advancement, particularly if the people in jobs to which you aspire are solidly entrenched and sitting tight. But over in sales or systems analysis things may move at a breakneck pace. Business growth has an immediate impact there, and as the number of jobs expands, more supervisors are needed. Employees who are on the ball can move to higher-paying positions with regularity. In short, the situation is made to order for fast promotions.

Getting the transfer may not be difficult if you have a good work record and the company wants to hold onto you. Many companies encourage internal transfers by routinely posting openings in every department and offering any training needed for a new spot to qualified employees who want to make a switch.

Improve your fringe benefits. Some employers now offer fringe benefits on the cafeteria plan. Each employee is given a benefits allowance, and within it can select from a variety of fringes the combination that is most valuable. For instance, young employees with no dependents might pass up some life insurance for more time off and as much job training and education as they can get at company expense. Senior employees might prefer to increase their medical coverage.

In a typical cafeteria plan there are a few basic, or "core," benefits to which you can add to suit your current needs, with the option of altering the package as your circumstances change. And you might earn additional benefit credits as you gain seniority with the company.

If your employer offers such a plan:

• Take advantage of early announcements to learn the value of the benefits you have and compare them with what's being offered. Many employees don't know much about their benefits. Those who do will make better choices.

• Study the range of choices as you would when purchasing automobile insurance, comparing deductibles and amounts of coverage in light of your personal needs and finances. By all means, discuss the pros and cons of various options with coworkers, but when you have a question about plan details, take it to the benefits staff.

• Pay attention to the tax angles. The way you choose your flexible benefits can affect the amount of income tax you have to pay. Company brochures generally describe the tax considerations.

If you conclude that a flexible program doesn't offer you any real advantage, don't forget that you can often choose to stick with what you already have.

If your employer doesn't take the cafeteria approach to benefits or doesn't provide some fringes that most employers do, maybe you can start the company thinking about making improvements that will help keep good employees. In some circumstances a company might be more agreeable to boosting benefits than raising salaries.

Add another income. If the lid is firmly on at work, you may have to use your off-duty time to produce the extra income you need. You could take on a moonlight job or start a sideline business. A word of caution about this approach: Extra jobs bring extra costs in dollars and personal energy. Analyze your situation and goals carefully before taking such a step. You don't want to jeopardize your primary source of income or any savings you've socked away in your effort to boost your earnings on the side.

Get a better job. It's the obvious last resort and a valid choice. A job change of your own choosing should bring a pay increase as well as career advancement, but don't be too quick to jump.

Better be sure you won't land in the same sort of trap you are in now, even if you would be starting out at a higher salary.

JOBS WITH A FUTURE

For thousands of workers, the last several years have been devastating. Many who lost jobs in the auto, steel, rubber and other basic industries will never return to their factories. Hopes for the economic rejuvenation of their companies are riding on new technologies—from robot devices to banks of computers—that will allow the companies to operate more efficiently with far fewer workers.

The decline of jobs in the "smokestack," or core, industries wasn't unexpected. Government and industry had been reporting for years that white collar jobs were muscling out blue collar jobs. But in the longer run there should be ample jobs, and good ones, for those with the right training.

What is the right training? In some cases it will prepare workers to cope with new ways of doing their old jobs. In other cases the training will have to be designed to prepare workers to perform jobs that didn't exist a few years ago. But not all of tomorrow's good jobs will be in new occupations. The revamped smokestack industries will still employ a sizable segment of the work force.

The notion that workers who have lost jobs in the core industries can simply move over to the emerging high-tech industries is simplistic. Although growing fast, the high-tech industries are not as labor intensive as the older industries. The number of high-tech jobs created in the next several years will be fewer than the number lost in basic manufacturing industries.

At the same time, the basic industries will continue to be a source of good jobs. In their rejuvenated form some may well be considered high-tech themselves. The Department of Commerce includes a broad array of industries in its category of high-tech fields: machine tools, much of the chemical industry, the bulk of electrical- and medical-equipment manufacturing, and all electronics-related manufacturing, for instance.

There's no doubt that it will take specialized training to land a specialized job. But you'll be better prepared to launch or change careers in the future if you also possess a broadly based education gained at college or on your own. Employers will be looking for this combination in their future executives:

• Imagination and creativity—the knack for finding ways to perform any task better.

• The ability to motivate other people to achieve peak productivity.

• A solid grounding in the humanities and social sciences, especially communications skills (both oral and written), economics and history.

• Comfort and familiarity with—but not necessarily virtuosity on—business computers.

• Dual-degree college education, especially undergraduate study of science or engineering coupled with graduate work in business or law.

In drawing up a list of promising jobs of the future, it would be tempting to lean on the new and the exciting: housing rehabilitation technician, holographic inspector, battery technician, lunar miner. But reality, fortunately, is more down to earth. Most of the jobs already exist: accountants, engineers, actuaries, computer-systems analysts, nurses, lawyers, legal assistants, public relations specialists, financial service sales workers.

That list of occupations is really only a cross section of the fields offering bright career prospects as we move toward the 21st century. The tables on the opposite page and page 386 list what are expected to be the top 25 job fields over the next decade or so and the metropolitan areas in which they are likely to be found. Here's a closer look at some of the jobs.

Health services.   Demand will be especially strong for primary care workers such as nurse practitioners, nutrition counselors and gerontological social workers.

Hotel management and recreation.   This category includes restaurants, resorts and travel, as well as opportunities in conference planning.

Food service.   Managers and chefs will be in demand for all those restaurants and hotel kitchens, as well as for food-processing labs and plants.

THE FASTEST-GROWING JOBS

OCCUPATION	GROWTH 1985–1995
Legal Assistants	98%
Computer Programmers	72
Computer Systems Analysts	69
Medical Assistants	62
Computer Service Technicians	56
Electrical and Electronics Engineers	53
Actuaries	51
Electrical and Electronics Technicians	50
Computer Operators	46
Health Services Managers	44
Travel Agents	44
Physical Therapists	42
Physicians' Assistants	40
Podiatrists	39
Financial Services Sales	39
Engineers	36
Lawyers	36
Accountants and Auditors	35
Corrections Officers	35
Mechanical Engineers	34
Registered Nurses	33
Public Relations	32
Computerized-Tool Programmers	32
Occupational Therapists	31
Medical Record Technicians	31

Source: *Bureau of Labor Statistics*

THE FASTEST-GROWING JOB MARKETS

METRO AREA	ANNUAL JOB GROWTH 1985–2010
Naples, Florida	2.81%
Fort Myers, Florida	2.75
Fort Pierce, Florida	2.61
Orlando, Florida	2.42
Atlantic City, New Jersey	2.40
Anaheim–Santa Ana, California	2.37
Las Vegas, Nevada	2.36
West Palm Beach–Boca Raton–Delray Beach, Florida	2.33
Fort Lauderdale–Hollywood–Pompano Beach, Florida	2.31
Bradenton, Florida	2.25
Reno, Nevada	2.22
Ocala, Florida	2.13
Phoenix, Arizona	2.11
Sarasota, Florida	2.09
Gainesville, Florida	2.08
Bryan–College Station, Texas	2.07
Tucson, Arizona	2.07
Boulder–Longmont, Colorado	2.06
Portsmouth–Dover–Rochester, New Hampshire	2.04
Santa Rosa–Petaluma, California	2.02
Santa Fe, New Mexico	2.01
Monmouth–Ocean, New Jersey	2.01
Oxnard–Ventura, California	2.01
Tallahassee, Florida	2.00
Boise City, Idaho	1.99
U.S. Average	1.22%

Source: *National Planning Association*

Engineering.   Specialties in demand will be as diverse as robotics, aviation and aerospace, and waste management.

Basic science.   Molecular biology, chemistry and optics.

Computers.   Opportunities will continue to be strong in design, engineering, programming and maintenance.

Business services.   Accounting, statistical analysis and payroll management.

Human resources or personnel.   Call it whichever you want, this field includes job evaluation, hiring and firing, benefit planning and job training.

Teaching.   Demand is growing in primary and elementary grades to serve the children of the baby-boom generation, especially in certain specialties: math, science, engineering, computer operations and foreign languages such as Russian and Japanese.

Maintenance and repair.   Somebody's got to take care of all the equipment that will keep tomorrow's world running.

That list contains plenty of encouragement for those who are technically inclined, as well as for those who aren't. If you know exactly what you want to do, then the best thing to do is get specialized training. But over the long run, too much specialization doesn't pay off. Although companies like to hire specialists for entry-level jobs, they tend to seek out generalists for middle- and upper-level management positions. It pays to keep your options open.

MONEY ENOUGH TO RETIRE ON

What you hope will be your golden years can lose their glitter fast if you don't take steps to polish them up before you get there. Most people don't spend much time worrying about retirement in their early adult years, but even if you're in your 30s or early 40s, it isn't too soon to start planning. If you wait until retirement is near to take stock of what awaits you, it could be too late to do anything about it.

The hope for a comfortable retirement is probably behind a lot of the decisions you make about saving, investing, tax planning and other financial matters. Still, there are a number of considerations that have to do directly with retirement.

HOW MUCH INCOME WILL YOU NEED?

Fortunately, retirees can usually get along on a lower income than people working full time. You tend to spend less on clothing, transportation, food and other daily expenses, and you generally pay out less in taxes, due to your lower income and the special tax breaks available to people 65 and over.

Actuarial experts estimate that a retired couple ordinarily needs anywhere from 60% to 75% of preretirement income to maintain the same standard of living. But it's difficult to state a rule because there are so many variables—where you live, whether you rent or buy a place, the level of income you had prior to retirement. It stands to reason that the lower your preretirement income, the greater the proportion of it you will need after retirement.

Where will you get the money you need? The kinds of investments that can help produce it are described in earlier chapters of this book. But chances are you will be relying heavily on the traditional sources of retirement income—social security and pension plans, whether the plans be those of your employer or ones that you devise yourself.

SIZING UP YOUR PENSION PLAN

Working for a company with a pension program does not necessarily mean you are a member, that you will actually receive a pension, or that the pension will be adequate.

Ideally, you should check a company's pension plan before you take a job; it could influence your decision. A one-time examination even after you're hired isn't enough. The company may amend the plan's provisions from time to time, and your benefits will change with your salary and years of service. You have to keep track of pension rights just as you do your other fringe benefits.

Most of the required information should be clearly presented in the annual statements to members and in the plan description, which the company must provide employees under terms of the 1974 Employee Retirement Income Security Act, known as ERISA. Although it doesn't require employers to offer any pension benefits at all, ERISA sets minimum disclosure, funding and administrative standards for those that do.

If the summary of the plan leaves unanswered questions, you may be able to get some clarification from the company's pension officer or your union. The ultimate authority is the plan's formal agreement, a document that, unfortunately, is probably weighted down with dense legal wordage. To penetrate those complexities, concentrate on ten crucial questions.
1. **What kind of plan is it?** Essentially, there are two types.

Defined-contribution plan. In this arrangement the company contributes a specified amount each year to a fund that's invested in securities or some sort of insurance contract. When you retire, the money credited to your account is given to you in a lump sum or used to purchase an annuity. You get only as much annuity income as your fund will buy, and the amount is not guaranteed. Defined-contribution plans include deferred profit-sharing and stock-bonus programs. You may hear those and similar plans referred to as money purchase plans.

Notice that with a defined-contribution plan you take two risks: First, that the cost of annuities will rise while you are employed, thereby reducing the monthly income that the amount in your fund will buy; second, that the fund will earn a subpar return or take a loss, thus reducing the amount available to purchase an annuity or make a lump-sum payment to you. With a defined-benefit plan, the employer bears those risks.

Defined-benefit plan. This kind of plan uses a formula for determining your pension, and it's up to the employer to contribute enough into the pension fund to buy an annuity that will provide the income prescribed by the formula when you retire. The pension is usually tied to years of service and salary. All other factors being equal, you stand to come out best when the plan bases the pension on a few top-earning years or your salary in the final few years of service, when you're likely to be earning most. Least favorable is a plan that gears the pension to your average earnings for all years of service.

Both types of plans may require or allow contributions by employees.

2. When do you become a member? Ordinarily, you can't join the plan until you've met certain age and service requirements. The Retirement Equity Act of 1984 mandates that you must become a member—and thus begin the all-important process of vesting (explained later)—no later than age 21 with one year of employment. Educational institutions get special treatment if they require no more than one year of service and grant full vesting upon membership. In that case, the minimum age for membership is 26. Those limits constitute the maximum restrictions. An employer can make you a member sooner.

There is one special ERISA provision you should be aware of, particularly if you're in your fifties and considering a job change. The law permits a defined-benefit plan to exclude from membership a person who begins work within five years of the plan's normal retirement age.

3. How fast do you accrue benefits? Once you become a member, you start building up pension benefits year by year. In a defined-contribution plan your accrued benefit at any point equals the amount credited to your account. If the plan puts the money into a cash-value life insurance policy, the amount for which the policy could be surrendered represents your accrued benefit.

The accrual process works differently for defined-benefit plans because your pension isn't a special sum set aside for you in the pension fund but a fixed monthly income that will be paid on retirement. One accrual formula employs a ratio of actual service to the time you could spend in the plan. As an example, say you join the plan at age 35 and, therefore, could work another 30 years until normal retirement at 65. If you leave the company after 20 years of covered service, you will have participated for two-thirds of the potential period and be entitled to two-thirds of the estimated pension you would have qualified for at age 65.

Other arrangements for defined-benefit plans schedule accruals at a fixed percentage each year.

4. How fast will you be vested? The fact that you've accrued part of your ultimate pension does not necessarily mean that if you left the company, you would be entitled to benefits when you reach retirement age.

You own any money you may have contributed to the plan, but you don't completely own the accrued benefit created by the employer's contributions until you're 100% vested. If you are only 20% vested, then you own 20% of the accrued benefit. If you have not been vested at all when you go, you have no rights to that pension. If you change jobs frequently, it's possible to work a lifetime for companies with plans and not earn a pension.

ERISA permitted a variety of vesting systems, which are in effect through 1988. The most generous immediately vests all benefits 100%. One of the least favorable and most common arrangements, called cliff vesting, defers all vesting until after ten years and then vests 100%. The "rule of 45" vests 50% when your age and service add up to 45 and you have a minimum of five years of service. You get an additional 10% each year thereafter. Graduated plans vest on a schedule of up to 15 years. Profit-sharing and similar plans that vest each year's contribution into the pension fund separately are covered by another set of rules.

Beginning in 1989, companies must speed up their vesting to one of two schedules: cliff vesting of 100% after five years of service, or gradual vesting that starts at 20% after three years of service and adds 20% for each of the next four years so that vesting is complete after seven years of employment with the company.

Vesting schedules may actually progress somewhat faster than is apparent because a plan must (with some exceptions) credit years of service you completed before you became a pension plan member. By contrast, accrual schedules ordinarily credit you only for those years in which you participate in the plan.

5. What do you lose for interrupted employment? Each plan lays down rules defining your pension status when you have interrupted employment or fail to work what the plan considers a full year. Minimum standards reduce the chances that you will lose all rights because of a layoff or other break in service. These standards protect nonvested employees but do allow employers some leeway. For example, the plan need not use a calendar year in measuring the break. It can base service on hours completed during any 12 consecutive months, provided it applies the same limits in all cases. Such a provision might help or hurt you, depending on when you happen to lose time. Look for the sections in your pension plan that define plan year, hours of service, years of service and break in service.

6. What will your plan pay if you retire early? You will be entitled to a smaller monthly income than at the usual retirement age of 65, but the question is, how much smaller? A number of things will affect it. The accrual period will be shorter. Your salary may be lower than if you waited. And normally the pension is reduced by an actuarial formula that takes into account the likelihood that you will receive the pension for more years. The effect of these adjustments will vary with the provisions of the plan, but they can be substantial. The table on the opposite page, prepared by Hewitt Associates, a consulting firm, demonstrates how early retirement might reduce the pension of a worker under a more or less typical pension plan.

7. Will you earn benefits for work after 65? Companies can't force employees to retire because of age. Most plans, though, have designed benefits for normal retirement at 65. The legal bars against age discrimination don't require a company to increase pensions for post-65 service. Your plan might nevertheless recognize that service in some way by increasing the normal pension by an annual interest increment or by including the additional years of service or post-65 earnings in the pension computation.

8. How much will you receive if you are disabled? The company may have a long-term disability program that pays a monthly income until you become eligible for retirement. An alternative is to put employees on a retirement pension if they become disabled after they work for the company a prescribed number of years. The plan will specify any disability benefit to which you're entitled.

9. What are the death benefits? When you retire, you can choose one of the various types of annuities that will pay an income or lump sum to your spouse or other heirs on your death. Under the Retirement Equity Act, an annuity must be provided for the surviving spouse of a vested plan member who dies before collecting benefits. The joint-and- survivor-annuity form (defined later) will automatically be used then and at retirement if you make no choice before then. That is one of the law's most important safeguards for spouses, but keep in mind that the joint and survivor annuity reduces your pension in order to offset the potential increase in cost to the plan of paying survivor benefits.

In a plan paid for entirely by your employer, you can elect not

THE COST OF EARLY RETIREMENT

CURRENT AGE	AVERAGE PAY, LAST FIVE YEARS	YEARS OF SERVICE	PENSION BENEFIT		
			STARTING AT AGE 65	STARTING AT AGE IN LEFT-HAND COLUMN	
50	$40,000	20	$12,000	$ 7,200	
56	42,000	21	13,230	8,467	
57	44,100	22	14,553	9,896	
58	46,305	23	15,975	11,502	
59	48,620	24	17,503	13,302	
60	51,051	25	19,144	15,315	
61	53,604	26	20,906	17,561	
62	56,284	27	22,795	20,060	
63	59,098	28	24,821	22,835	
64	62,053	29	26,993	25,913	
65	65,156	30	29,320	29,320	

Assumptions:

1. Pay increases at 5% for each year you continue working.
2. Pension formula is 1.5% of final five-year average pay times years of service.
3. Pension is reduced 4% per year for retirees below age 65.

Source: *Hewitt Associates*

to receive the joint and survivor annuity, provided you do so in writing and your spouse agrees to the waiver in writing.

10. Do you have any inflation protection? You're lucky if your plan adjusts pensions after retirement to compensate for cost-of-living increases. The few private plans that do usually limit the annual rise to a relatively small amount, say 3%. Some companies, though, have made voluntary increases for retirees.

PROFIT-SHARING PLANS

It's more difficult in some ways to evaluate a profit-sharing plan than a straight pension program. Employers' contributions to such plans are linked to company profits, which vary from year to year, so you can't depend on a fixed minimum amount. Also, according to the Profit Sharing Council of America, smaller companies tend to reserve the right to contribute as much or as little as they like, instead of using fixed percentages. And the amount you eventually receive depends to a large extent on how successfully the money is invested.

If the contributed profits, or part of them, are paid out to employees each year, it's up to each person to invest the cash. Most plans, though, defer payouts until you leave. Meanwhile, that money is usually invested by professional investment counselors under the supervision of the trustees of the plan or an investment committee. A small percentage of profit-sharing plans give employees a voice in the selection of investments.

Some plans invest part of their funds in the company's own stock. That can prove an advantage or disadvantage for the employee, depending on the company's dividend payment policy (the stock held by the plan earns dividends), and on whether the stock appreciates or declines in value.

Although they lack the guarantees of regular pension plans, profit-sharing programs make it possible to accumulate sizable retirement funds when you work for a successful company. The ideal arrangement would probably be a pension program that provided an adequate defined benefit along with deferred profit sharing.

INDIVIDUAL RETIREMENT ACCOUNTS

Anyone with earned income to report on a tax return is

eligible to set up a tax-sheltered individual retirement account. You can put aside up to $2,000 of your earnings each year and deduct all or part of it from your taxable income if you or your spouse are not covered by a pension plan at work or you meet certain income tests. See the table on page 398 to determine your eligibility to deduct your IRA contribution. Whether or not you qualify for the deduction, you owe no taxes on the earnings in the IRA until you withdraw the money.

Money withdrawn from an IRA before the owner reaches age 59½ is subject to a 10% penalty tax. You must begin withdrawing the money shortly after your 70th birthday—specifically, no later than April 1 in the year following the year you reach age 70½. Thus, if you reach age 70½ in 1990, you must begin withdrawing your IRA money by April 1, 1991. When you do withdraw the money, it will be taxed as ordinary income if you took the deduction when you put it in; only the earnings will be taxed when you make qualified withdrawals from a nondeductible IRA. IRAs do not qualify for the special five- or ten-year forward averaging rule available to lump-sum Keogh and qualified pension plan distributions, as described later in this chapter.

As long as the money is in your retirement account, earnings accumulate tax-free, giving the power of compound interest added strength. A series of $2,000 nondeductible IRA contributions earning 10% per year compounded annually over a 20-year period will grow to nearly $102,000. If the earnings on that account were taxed annually in the 28% bracket, the earnings would accumulate to only about $90,000.

Contribution schedules. Each year's contribution can be made in one lump sum or in installments. Since dividends and other earnings that accumulate in IRA accounts do not have to be declared immediately for tax purposes, it is normally to your advantage to make contributions early in the year.

IRAs can be opened any time before the April 15 deadline for filing your federal tax return. For ongoing plans, this gives you time to make sure that contributions do not exceed the legal limits. There's a 6% penalty for overages, and the excess is included in taxable income when withdrawn. You can absorb

CAN YOU TAKE AN IRA DEDUCTION?

This chart sums up whether you can take a full deduction, a partial deduction, or no deduction.

IF YOUR ADJUSTED GROSS INCOME IS		IF YOU ARE COVERED BY A RETIREMENT PLAN AT WORK AND YOUR FILING STATUS IS				IF YOU ARE NOT COVERED BY A RETIREMENT PLAN AT WORK AND YOUR FILING STATUS IS		
At Least	But Less Than	Single, or Head of Household	Married Filing Jointly (even if your spouse is not covered by a plan at work) Qualifying Widow(er)	Married Filing Separately	Married Filing Jointly (and your spouse is covered by a plan at work)	Single or Head of Household	Married Filing Jointly or Separately (and your spouse is not covered by a plan at work) Qualifying Widow(er)	Married Filing Separately (even if your spouse is covered by a plan at work)
		YOU CAN TAKE	YOU CAN TAKE	YOU CAN TAKE	YOU CAN TAKE	YOU CAN TAKE	YOU CAN TAKE	YOU CAN TAKE
$-0-	$10,000	Full deduction	Full deduction	Partial deduction	Full deduction			
$10,000	$25,000	Full deduction	Full deduction	No deduction	Full deduction			
$25,001	$35,000	Partial deduction	Full deduction	No deduction	Full deduction	Full Deduction	Full Deduction	Full Deduction
$35,000	$40,001	No deduction	Full deduction	No deduction	Full detection			
$40,000	$50,000	No deduction	Partial deduction	No deduction	Partial deduction			
$50,000 or over		No deduction	No deduction	No deduction	No deduction			

Maximum deduction. You can deduct IRA contributions up to the amount of the deduction (full or partial) you can take, or 100% of your taxable compensation which-ever is less.

$200 floor. The partial deduction has a $200 floor. For example, if your deductionwould have been reduced to less than $200 (but not zero), you can deduct IRA contri-butions up to $200 or 100% of your taxable compensation, whichever is less. If the deduction is completely phased out (reduced to zero), no deduction is allowed.

Source: IRS

398

excess contributions by contributing less in a subsequent year.

Custodial or trustee arrangements. IRA investments must be made through a custodian or trustee—in practice, a company that supervises the account and reports to you and the government each year. Banks, savings and loan associations, mutual funds, and others who provide IRA plans have standard custodial or trustee arrangements that you join by completing a simple form. You are permitted to maintain more than one IRA account with the same or different companies.

Moving your money around. Despite the law's penalty for premature withdrawals, you are not required to keep your money in the same IRA from the time you open the account until you reach age 59½. The rules offer great flexibility for shifting the money around. There are two ways to do it: direct transfers and rollovers.

In a direct transfer, as the name implies, funds are transferred directly from one custodian or trustee to another—from a bank IRA, for example, to one sponsored by a mutual fund, or from one mutual fund to another. The key is that you never gain possession of the money. You can move your IRA money around and open and close accounts at will using this method. However, charges imposed by plan sponsors, such as fees to set up an IRA or early-withdrawal penalties if you cash a bank CD before it matures, may make frequent shifts costly.

If you take possession of the funds during a transfer—you close an account with a stock mutual fund, for example, and then put the money in an insurance company's IRA—the law considers the transaction a rollover. You can use this method only once each year. Once you withdraw funds from an IRA, you have only 60 days to complete the rollover. Any money that isn't contributed to a new account within that time is considered a premature distribution, which would be fully taxed as ordinary income and trigger the 10% penalty.

Where to invest? Once you decide to open an IRA, you still face the choice of where to put the money. The opportunities are almost unlimited. You can find approved sponsors—banks, s&l's, credit unions, mutual funds, insurance companies— offering almost every imaginable investment. But you can't invest directly in gems, precious metals, or collectibles, which the law prohibits from being used for IRAs. The only exceptions are the American Eagle gold and silver bullion coins, which the U.S. Treasury began minting in 1986.

Although there's no law against using them, tax-exempt bonds have no place in an IRA for three reasons. First, their earnings are already tax-free; second, higher yields are available from other issues; and third, when you begin to withdraw money from your IRA, it will be taxed and you will have killed the advantage of municipal bonds.

If you want to put together your own portfolio rather than rely on mutual fund managers, you can do it with a self-directed IRA. These accounts, usually set up through brokers, let you choose what you want to invest in and give you IRA opportunities you can't get anywhere else—such as zero-coupon bonds, real estate limited partnerships, or oil and gas deals.

You decide what and when to buy and sell, but if you wheel and deal too much, trading commissions can eat up a lot of your nest egg. The fees attached to this type of account demand close attention, especially in the early years of your IRA, when it holds a relatively modest amount.

Company-sponsored plans. You have an added option if your company is among those that have a qualified voluntary employee contribution plan. Through these plans, employees can make their IRA contribution to a special account in the company's retirement plan.

If you have the chance to piggyback your IRA on the company plan, judge the opportunity just as you would any other IRA offer. What's the track record of the investments? What would be involved if you decided to transfer your funds to a different IRA sponsor?

Taking the money out. Not only will the government penalize you if you dip into your retirement fund early, there's also a stiff penalty if you don't withdraw the money fast enough later on. Between the time you reach age 59½ and the year you turn 70½ you can withdraw without penalty as much or as little as you want from your IRA. Once you reach approximately age 70½, there is a minimum withdrawal schedule. It's based on your life expectancy—or on that of you and your spouse—and is designed to make sure you make a serious effort to deplete the account (so the IRS can finally tax the money) before you die. If you don't withdraw as much as you should each year, you'll be socked with a 50% penalty tax. Assume, for example, that a single man, age 70½, owns an account that has grown to $975,000. Under the IRS schedule he'd have to withdraw about $80,000 the first year. If he took out only $60,000, the 50% penalty would apply to the $20,000 underwithdrawal and cost him $10,000.

KEOGH PLANS FOR THE SELF-EMPLOYED

Keogh plans are for people who are self-employed, either full or part time. Favored by doctors, dentists, architects, attorneys and other professionals, as well as moonlighting consultants and free-lance writers, a Keogh plan can be used even if you're already participating in a company pension program and have an IRA. Keogh rules can be somewhat complex, but these are the essentials:

Qualified annual contributions to the plan are deductible from taxable income in the year in which they're made. The contribution limit for a defined-contribution Keogh plan is generally 25% of earned income, to a maximum of $30,000. (The definition of earned income for Keogh contributions, however, takes into account deductions for those contributions, thus lowering the effective limit to 20%.)

You can contribute more in some cases with a "defined-benefit" Keogh, a plan designed to produce a preset amount of retirement income. With a defined-benefit plan you decide, within broader limits, how much you would like to receive in annual retirement income, and then an actuary designs a savings program to attain that defined benefit. You pay the actuarial fee, but the expense is tax-deductible.

You can also set up a profit-sharing Keogh, which has smaller annual limitations on contributions but is more flexible and favored by part-timers whose self-employment income isn't very reliable. The maximum deductible contribution is 15% of earnings per year, which is reduced to an effective rate of only about 13% for the same reason the effective limit on defined-contribution Keoghs works out to 20%.

Dividends, interest and other gains made by your Keogh investments accumulate tax-free. Neither the contributions nor earnings are subject to tax until the money is withdrawn at your retirement.

You can't start dipping into your Keogh funds without incurring a 10% penalty until you're 59½ and retired, unless you become disabled. But you don't have to start drawing from the fund until you reach 70½.

Keogh funds may be paid out in a lump sum, installments, or annuity payments, and they are taxed accordingly. The pay-outs, though, can't be scheduled to exceed your life expectancy or the life expectancies of you and your spouse. Again, the intent is to restrict the Keogh plan to its retirement objective.

The law does not require you to purchase an annuity in order to arrange for annuity-type payments. The proper installments can be calculated from IRS tables prepared for that purpose. A special method known as five-year forward averaging permits you to pay tax on a lump-sum Keogh's distribution as if it were paid out in equal annual installments spanning those years, thus greatly reducing the tax in the year in which you take out the money. (Special rules permit Keogh participants who were age 50 or older on January 1, 1986, to choose between five-year averaging and a ten-year schedule, which may be even more advantageous.)

Any full-time employees must be included in your Keogh plan no later than the third year of employment. That could prove a burden, but it also presents the opportunity to bring in family members and give them tax-deferred pensions. You may include part-timers, provided you include all the eligible ones.

Brokerage firms, banks, mutual funds and other types of financial companies offer standardized Keogh accounts. For a plan tailored to your particular needs, consult an attorney or actuary who specializes in this field.

DEFERRED-PAY PLANS

Known generically as 401(k) plans, after the section of the

Internal Revenue Code that authorizes them, deferred-pay plans give employees of a company sponsoring them the option to divert a portion of their salary to a tax-sheltered savings account set up by the employer. The IRS agrees to postpone taxing the portion of the pay you agree to postpone receiving. Earnings accumulate tax-free. The tax bill doesn't come due until you ultimately put your hands on the cash.

As tax-favored savings vehicles, 401(k) plans have a lot in common with individual retirement accounts. You can have both, in fact, because joining a deferred-pay plan doesn't affect your right to contribute to an IRA. There are differences between the two tax shelters, however, and most of them tip the scales toward the 401(k).

First, you can put more into a deferred-pay account, meaning bigger immediate tax savings and more money set aside to grow without annual pruning by the IRS. The law caps IRA contributions at $2,000 a year. You can put as much as $7,313 into a 401(k) in 1988 (the limit is indexed for inflation) and your employer can contribute more, as long as your combined contribution doesn't exceed $30,000 or 25% of your pay, whichever is less. Most companies set lower limits, however.

Although the company plan determines the maximum contribution, workers choose how much, if any, to shave their paychecks. The plans are flexible, letting employees adjust the percentage being deferred. If financial demands increase, you could suspend contributions and have 100% of your pay show up in your paycheck.

Unlike IRA contributions, which may or may not be deductible on your tax return, funds channeled into a 401(k) plan escape the IRS by not showing up on your wage statement in the first place. (The amount deferred is subject to social security tax, however.)

The company match. A special attraction of 401(k) plans is that most firms offering them sweeten the pot by matching part of the employee's contributions, commonly kicking in 50 cents for each $1 of employee contributions. Some plans match dollar for dollar, others a quarter or less. Usually, the company's generosity applies only to a portion of the salary a worker elects for the 401(k).

Unlike the wide-open field of investment opportunities available for IRA contributions, you have limited options under a salary-reduction plan. Your choices are restricted to those offered by the company. They may include company stock, a stock, bond or money-market mutual fund, or a guaranteed-interest contract. You'll get to decide where your periodic contributions go and have the opportunity to move your funds around among the investment alternatives.

Getting the money out. Like IRAs, the aim of 401(k) plans is to encourage saving for retirement. That's why, along with the tax breaks, there are restrictions on getting at the money. Basically, salary funneled into a 401(k) account is locked up until you reach age 59½ or leave the company. A major exception to that rule, though, lets employees tap the money they've contributed to their accounts in the event of financial hardship. Just what qualifies as a hardship is not always clear, but the rules have gotten tougher in recent years.

You don't necessarily have to pay any tax on the 401(k) distribution when you receive it. You can roll over all or part of it to an IRA, a technique that lets you continue to defer taxes until you tap the IRA. Rolling over into an IRA means forfeiting the right to use forward averaging, though.

SIMPLIFIED EMPLOYEE PENSIONS

A simplified employee pension plan, or SEP, permits small business owners to contribute up to 15% of employee compensation to employees' IRAs, and 13.04% of profits to their own IRAs, to a maximum of $30,000 per year. If employees are taking voluntary salary reductions, the limit they can take is $7,313 in 1988, same as under a 401(k). Because of the IRA connection, they are sometimes called SEP IRAs or Super IRAs. Employees' contributions are simply excluded from their pay, much like a 401(k).

The advantage of a SEP over a Keogh for an employer is that it is simpler to administer; the paperwork burden isn't quite so onerous. Like a profit-sharing Keogh, SEPs let the employer vary the contribution from year to year or skip it entirely if the profits aren't there. On the other hand, the vesting rules are more inclusive than those of a Keogh, and even part-time and seasonal workers must be included. Furthermore, SEPs aren't protected from the claims of creditors, as are Keoghs and other types of qualified pension plans.

THRIFT PLANS

Employees can typically contribute between 2% and 6% of their after-tax pay to a thrift plan, and companies often offer a 50% matching contribution. Withdrawals are often permitted before you retire or leave the company. You can take out your contributions without paying tax at the time because they've come from after-tax dollars. Thrift plan contributions are not deductible, unlike those made to IRAs. Earnings on your money, as well as employer contributions and the earnings on those amounts, accumulate tax-free but are subject to taxes when you take them out. Some employers require you to work a specified time—generally about five years—to qualify for the maximum matching contributions.

BUYING PART OF YOUR COMPANY

In an employee stock ownership plan (ESOP), employees buy stock in their company through payroll withholding or some other way, or the corporation contributes shares of its stock to funds that allocate the shares to employees based on their annual compensation. The advantage to employees is that they acquire stock of the company they work for at no or reduced cost. In a no-cost plan, the stock can't be distributed to participants until 84 months after it is allocated to them, unless they die (in which case their heirs would receive the shares), become disabled, or leave the company. Employees must pay taxes on the value of the stock when it is distributed to them. In the meantime, the stock can appreciate tax-free. When it is received, employees can continue the tax-favored treatment by rolling it over into an IRA or taking advantage of five-year averaging.

As retirement programs, though, ESOPs have some potential drawbacks. Because all or most of your stake is invested in one company, you lose the protection of a diversified investment portfolio. And you can never be sure how much the stock will be worth when you pull out of the plan.

WHAT'S SOCIAL SECURITY GOT FOR YOU?

Social security benefits have a couple of distinct advantages over most other forms of retirement income. First of all, for the majority of retirees, benefits are tax-free. You may owe tax on up to half the benefits, but only to the extent that your adjusted gross income, plus nontaxable interest plus one-half of your social security benefits, exceeds $25,000 if you're single, $32,000 if you're married.

For example, assume that you and your spouse get $10,000 in social security benefits. If half that amount plus your adjusted gross income and tax-exempt interest total less than $32,000, none of the benefits would be taxed. If the combination totals $33,000, however, $500 worth of your benefits (one-half of the amount over the threshold) would be subject to tax. The one-half-of-the-excess rule would operate until your income plus half your benefits totaled $42,000. From that point on, half of your benefits—$5,000—would be considered taxable income.

The other advantage of social security benefits is that they increase automatically along with inflation.

How can you find out whether the program has something for you? Or how much you can expect to receive? Or how to apply?

First write to, call or visit one of the approximately 1,300 social security offices scattered around the country. They are listed in telephone directories under U.S. Government, Social Security Administration.

If you're unable to travel to a social security office because of ill health, call the nearest office and request that someone visit you. The administration regularly sends out representatives to assist people in their homes.

It's especially important to contact a social security office if someone in your family dies, if you're unable to work because of an illness or injury that's expected to incapacitate you for a year or longer, or if you're 62 or older and plan to retire soon.

If you're nearing retirement and wonder how large your payments will be, you can make a rough estimate with the help of a pamphlet, Estimating Your Social Security Retirement Check, available from all social security offices. Or if you make a request on Form 7004, the office will calculate an estimate for you.

Even if you intend to keep working after 65, you should check in with the social security people three months before your 65th birthday to enroll in medicare, which will become available to you at 65 whether or not you retire.

Whatever your situation, be sure to obtain a set of explanatory pamphlets that the Social Security Administration gives free to anyone who requests them. They're concise, informative and easy to read. The basic publication is *Your Social Security*. Another publication, *Your Right to Question the Decision Made on Your Claim*, tells how to go about applying for reconsideration of an adverse decision.

Actually, social security is far more than just a retirement program. There are several kinds of help available if you're covered.

Retirement checks.   You'll get them if you have worked a certain length of time under social security. (You are generally considered fully insured if you have worked in a covered job for at least one quarter out of each calendar year after your 21st birthday, but you needn't be fully insured to qualify for benefits. Check with your social security office.) Benefits automatically increase in step with the consumer price index following any year in which the index rises by 3% or more. (If the assets of the plan fall below a certain level, the increase will be limited to the lesser of the increase in prices or the increase in wages during the measurement period.)

You can retire at 62, but your payments will be reduced. If you retire at 65, your spouse, if 65, will receive an amount equal to half of your benefits or a reduced amount as early as age 62. And a spouse entitled to benefits from his or her own work record receives whichever is larger, his or her entitlement or an amount equal to half of the spouse's.

Beginning in the year 2000, the age at which you can qualify for full retirement benefits will be raised gradually from 65 to 67. Eligibility for reduced benefits at age 62 won't change, nor will the age of eligibility for medicare.

Disability income. People who are blind or disabled in ways that prevent them from working may receive assistance based on their average earnings under social security.

Disability is defined as an inability to work because of a physical or mental impairment that has lasted or is expected to last at least 12 months or to result in death. Blindness means either central visual acuity of 20/200 or less in the better eye with the use of corrective lenses, or visual field reduction to 20 degrees or less (tunnel vision). A person who was disabled before age 22 may qualify for benefits when a parent, or sometimes a grandparent, begins receiving retirement or disability payments or dies, even if the claimant has never worked.

Supplemental security income. SSI is a separate program that provides a basic cash income for people in financial need who are 65 or older and for the needy of any age who are blind or disabled. Financial need is defined as receiving an income of less than about $500 a month for a couple, about $330 for an individual.

It's possible to receive SSI even though you have other financial assets. Single people are allowed to own a home and, in addition, other personal assets worth up to $1,700. For married couples, the personal asset limitation is $2,550.

Survivors' benefits. The spouse, children, parents and, in some cases, grandchildren of a deceased eligible worker may be entitled to cash benefits. Specifically eligible are:

1. A widow or widower 60 or older, 50 if disabled.

2. A widow, widower or surviving divorced mother if caring for the worker's child who is under 16 (or disabled) and who is receiving benefits based on the deceased worker's earnings.

3. Unmarried children under 18, or under 19 if full-time students at a secondary school.

4. Unmarried children who were severely disabled before 22 and who remain disabled.

5. Dependent parents 62 or older.

In addition, if the marriage lasted ten years or more, checks can go to a surviving divorced wife of 60 or a disabled surviving divorced wife of 50.

In general, a marriage must have lasted one year or more for dependents of retired or disabled workers to be eligible for social security payments, and survivors can receive checks if the marriage lasted at least nine months.

Medicare. Medicare provides hospital and medical insurance to social security recipients. If you're eligible, coverage takes effect automatically at age 65 and extends to people under 65 who have been entitled to social security disability payments for 24 consecutive months or more, and to people receiving kidney-disease benefits.

Beginning in 1989, medicare hospital patients are eligible for 100% coverage of most hospital bills, after paying an annual deductible of about $565. But there is a 190–day lifetime limit on psychiatric hospital services.

Starting in 1991, medicare will pay 100% of approved doctors' charges (if they meet the "reasonable" standard imposed by regulations), after the patient pays about $1,400.

In addition to hospital and doctors' bills, medicare provides limited coverage for prescription drugs, certain preventive medical procedures (including mammograms every other year), professional home health care services and care in a skilled nursing facility. There is no coverage for so-called custodial nursing home care.

As a medicare recipient, you pay for the coverage you get via monthly premiums deducted from your social security checks. In addition, if your income is above about $7,000 as an individual (about $11,500 for a couple), you may have to pay an "income-related premium"—a tax surcharge—for your medicare protection.

Widowers' benefits.   A father can receive monthly payments if his wife died while insured under social security, he has not remarried, and he cares for an unmarried child under 18 (or older if disabled before 22) who is entitled to benefits.

Earnings limitations while retired. You can do some paid work after retirement and still collect social security, and from age 70 on you can earn any amount and still receive your full benefits. If you're between 65 and 70, you can earn up to $8,400 in 1988 and no benefits will be withheld. If you make more than that, $1 in benefits will be withheld for every $2 you earn above that amount. Retired beneficiaries under age 65 can earn up to $6,120 in 1988 without losing benefits. The amount is indexed for wage inflation and rises a bit each year.

A rule that allows retirees to collect full benefits for the months in which their earnings are below one-twelfth of the annual rate applies only in the year in which they retire.

Social security benefits, which rise each year on a scale tied to wage and price increases, should provide some protection against inflation for those who retire over the next decade. The table on the opposite page shows the monthly payments you could expect to receive in the first year of retirement at age 65 if you always earned the maximum covered wage and thus qualify for the maximum benefit, or if you earned an average amount in your last year before retirement. Calculations were done by the Social Security Administration.

WHAT TO DO WITH A HUNK OF MONEY

How can you turn lump sums of money into a guaranteed lifetime income without incurring any more tax than absolutely necessary? It's a problem faced by many people when they retire.

One thing you could do with the money, if it is a lump-sum distribution from a retirement plan, is roll it over into one or more IRAs or annuities within 60 days of receiving it. In most cases that would let you postpone any tax until you started taking the money out. A couple of things you must take into account are your life expectancy (see table, page 413) and how much of the money you can afford to take out each year (see table, page 414).

In any case, you should also consider carefully the potential tax advantages of taking the money as a lump sum and using the ten- or five-year forward averaging rule discussed earlier. If you don't need all or part of the income from the money right away, an IRA could shield it from taxes until you are ready to take it out. However, distributions would be taxed as ordinary income

WHAT TO EXPECT FROM SOCIAL SECURITY

YEAR OF RETIREMENT AT AGE 65	WAGES IN YEAR PRIOR TO RETIREMENT FOR MAXIMUM BENEFIT	ESTIMATED MAXIMUM MONTHLY BENEFIT	AVERAGE EARNINGS IN YEAR PRIOR TO RETIREMENT	ESTIMATED AVERAGE MONTHLY BENEFIT
1988	$43,800	$838	$18,036	$626
1989	45,000	903	18,924	670
1990	46,800	975	19,974	720
1991	49,200	1,014	20,990	745
1992	51,600	1,058	22,202	774
1993	54,600	1,112	23,429	810
1994	57,900	1,166	24,663	846
1995	61,200	1,239	25,992	891
1996	64,500	1,320	27,374	943
1997	68,100	1,403	28,867	994
1998	71,700	1,489	30,455	1,047
1999	75,600	1,581	32,130	1,103

Assumes 5.5% wage inflation and 4% price inflation
Source: *Social Security Administration*

then, and even a partial rollover into an IRA forfeits the opportunity to use forward averaging on the entire sum.

Annuities. Under an annuity contract you pay money to an insurance company and receive in return a guaranteed income, starting right away or later on, or a lump-sum settlement at some later date. There are basically two types of annuity contracts: immediate and deferred.

With an immediate annuity the payout begins as soon as you put up your money; with a deferred annuity it begins some time later. Deferred annuities can be paid for with a single payment or with installment payments in fixed or flexible amounts.

Deferred-annuity contracts may guarantee a minimum yield, or rate of interest, on premium payments during the accumulation period and a minimum income when payouts begin. A variable annuity may give you a choice of investments and the chance at higher returns, but a lower guaranteed rate in the meantime.

By contracting for a deferred annuity, you can assure yourself of a specified income for life (or a shorter period if you so choose) at annuity prices in effect at the time of the purchase.

You can usually choose from several ways to receive the annuity—as a lump sum you can reinvest, for example, or as a guaranteed income for ten years, or as a guaranteed income for as long as you live or for as long as you and your spouse live. Naturally, the size of the payments will vary accordingly.

Annuity contracts have a tax advantage—no federal or state income taxes are owed on the interest or other investment earnings until the money is withdrawn.

There are other benefits, too. Should you die, the contract value would pass directly to your designated heirs without probate. Annuity contracts can, with certain exceptions, be used to fund individual retirement accounts and Keogh plans.

But there are drawbacks. There is a 10% penalty tax on amounts you withdraw or borrow from an annuity before age 59½. Most variable annuities have stiff charges for surrendering (cashing in) the contract within the first several years of its purchase. When both you and your designated survivor have

WHAT'S YOUR LIFE EXPECTANCY?
(AVERAGE LIFE EXPECTANCY, AGE 45–65)

Age	Male	Female	Age	Male	Female
45	35.6 yrs.	40.2 yrs.	55	26.8 yrs.	30.8 yrs.
46	34.7	39.3	56	25.9	29.9
47	33.8	38.3	57	25.1	29.0
48	32.9	37.4	58	24.3	28.1
49	32.0	36.4	59	23.4	27.2
50	31.1	35.5	60	22.6	26.3
51	30.2	34.5	61	21.8	25.4
52	29.3	33.6	62	21.0	24.6
53	28.5	32.7	63	20.2	23.7
54	27.6	31.8	64	19.4	22.8
			65	18.6	22.0

Source: *Life Insurance Fact Book; American Council of Life Insurance*

died, the purchase money usually stays with the company. Also, income can be relatively low in proportion to the amount invested. Some contracts pay less than insured, long-term savings certificates. And if price inflation continues, which is all but certain, any kind of fixed income will buy less and less as years go by. Here's a look at four popular types of annuity payout plans.

Life annuity. It guarantees a stipulated monthly income for life. There are no death benefits or surrender values.

Life with ten years certain. This type provides a lifetime income as well and also guarantees that should you die during the first ten years, the payments would continue through the tenth year, going to your designated beneficiary.

Installment refund annuity. It guarantees you a lifetime income and provides that should you die before the total of the payouts equals the purchase price, payments would be made to your beneficiary until the payout equaled the purchase price.

HOW LONG WILL YOUR MONEY LAST?

The table, prepared by the U.S. League of Savings Associations, shows how long it would take to deplete an account at various interest rates and withdrawal amounts. It is assumed that withdrawals are made at the end of each month, that there are not premature withdrawals or penalties (such as there could be in the case of certificates of deposit), and that interest is compounded continuously under a formula called 365/360. In the case of daily compounding, funds would be exhausted slightly faster.

PERCENT OF ORIGINAL PRINCIPAL WITHDRAWN EACH YEAR

Interest Rate Paid	5%	6%		7%		8%		9%		10%		11%		12%		13%		14%		15%	
		ys*	ms*	ys	ms	ys	ms	ys	ms	ys	ms	ys	ms	ys	ms	ys	ms	ys	ms	ys	ms
5%	—	37	0	25	6	19	11	16	5	14	0	12	3	10	10	9	9	8	11	8	2
6%	—	—		33	8	23	7	18	7	15	6	13	3	11	8	10	5	9	5	8	7
7%				—		31	1	22	1	17	6	14	8	12	8	11	2	10	0	9	1
8%						—		28	11	20	9	16	7	14	0	12	2	10	9	9	8
9%								—		27	2	19	7	15	9	13	4	11	8	10	4
10%										—		25	7	18	7	15	1	12	10	11	2
11%												—		24	4	17	9	14	5	12	4
12%														—		23	2	17	0	13	11
13%																—		22	3	16	4
14%																		—		21	4
15%																				—	

— = infinity   *ys = years   ms = months

Joint and survivor annuity. This guarantees payments over your lifetime and a reduced level of payments for the life of your surviving spouse.

Some annuity buying tips. When comparing contracts, watch closely for disclaimers, qualifiers and ambiguities. Be sure the net income you would receive after payment of any commissions or service charges is clearly stated in the contract. Special taxes could lower your net income, too: Some states collect premium taxes on annuity purchases.

When you buy an immediate annuity, you're betting that you'll live long enough to come out ahead, or at least break even. Suppose that kind of gamble doesn't appeal to you. Well, you could set up a retirement fund yourself by putting the money into income-producing investments such as those described in Chapter 16. You wouldn't get the same kind of ironclad guarantees, but neither would you surrender your capital. And the assets would not be lost at your death—they could be willed to members of your family or anyone else. Of course, you'll be liable for taxes on whatever your investments earn.

Another thing: Part of the principal could be used in an emergency, an option you don't get with an annuity. In fact, you could provide yourself with a bigger income by drawing out small parts of the principal along with the interest in accordance with a schedule that would preserve the nest egg for as long as you expect to live. The table on the previous page shows how long your money would hold out.

To illustrate how to use the table, let's say you're a 65-year-old woman with $50,000 to invest. If your life span is average, you'll be around for another 22 years or so.

Now assume you invest the money in a way that yields 9% for the foreseeable future. Reading along the 9% line, you'll see that the money would last 27 years and two months if you withdrew 10% of the original principal each year. That would give you a monthly income of $416.67 and a five-year margin of safety.

Whatever type of plan you choose, be sure to factor in the tax consequences in calculating the monthly return. If you invest

continued on page 418

NUMBERS YOU'LL NEED TO PLAN YOUR RETIREMENT

The first table shows how large a fund you'd need to yield $100 a month over a number of years when invested at various rates. For example, if you needed the money over 20 years during which you can earn 9%, you'd need a starting fund of $11,114 (the point at which the 20-year and 9% columns meet). Thus, to generate $500 a month, you'd need a fund that was five times larger, or $55,570.

You can also use the first table to find out how much you'd get each month if you already have a hunk of cash that you want to draw down over your retirement. Suppose your retirement fund totaled $250,000, on which you figured you could earn 9% over 20 years. Tracing the 20-year and 9% columns gives you $11,114—the amount that will yield $100 per month. Because your fund is 22.5 times greater, you can expect a monthly payout that's also 22.5 times greater than $100, or $2,250.

The second table shows how much you'd have to save monthly at various interest rates over a number of years to accumulate $1,000. For example, if you wanted to build your kitty over 20 years by investing in a 9% account, you'd need to put away $1.49 a month. If you wanted to accumulate $55,000, you'd need to save 55 times $1.49, or $81.95.

HOW MUCH CAPITAL YOU'LL NEED TO YIELD $100 A MONTH FOR THE PERIOD INDICATED AT INTEREST RATE INDICATED

	5½%	7%	8%	9%	10%	11%	12%
5 years	$ 5,235	$ 5,050	$ 4,932	$ 4,817	$ 4,706	$ 4,599	$4,496
10 years	9,214	8,613	8,242	7,894	7,567	7,260	6,970
15 years	12,238	11,125	10,464	9,860	9,306	8,798	8,332
20 years	14,537	12,898	11,955	11,114	10,362	9,688	9,082
25 years	16,284	14,149	12,956	11,916	11,005	10,203	9,495
30 years	17,612	15,030	13,628	12,428	11,395	10,501	9,722

MONTHLY INVESTMENT NEEDED TO ACCUMULATE $1,000 OVER THE PERIOD INDICATED AT INTEREST RATE INDICATED

	5½%	7%	8%	9%	10%	11%	12%
5 years	$14.45	$13.89	$13.52	$13.16	$12.81	$12.46	$12.12
10 years	6.24	5.76	5.43	5.13	4.84	4.57	4.30
15 years	3.57	3.14	2.87	2.62	2.40	2.18	1.98
20 years	2.29	1.91	1.69	1.49	1.31	1.14	1.00
25 years	1.55	1.23	1.04	0.89	0.75	0.63	0.53
30 years	1.09	0.81	0.67	0.54	0.44	0.35	0.28

INFLATION'S EFFECT ON YOUR FIGURES

To use this table, start with your estimated expenses for your first year of retirement. To see how they would grow after five years of 5% inflation, for example, find where the five-year and 5% columns intersect and multiply your original expense figure by the number shown there.

	3%	4%	5%	6%	7%	8%	9%	10%
5 years	1.16	1.22	1.28	1.34	1.40	1.47	1.54	1.61
10 years	1.34	1.48	1.63	1.79	1.97	2.16	2.37	2.59
15 years	1.56	1.80	2.08	2.40	2.76	3.17	3.64	4.18
20 years	1.81	2.19	2.65	3.21	3.87	4.66	5.60	6.73
25 years	2.09	2.67	3.39	4.29	5.43	6.85	8.62	10.82
30 years	2.43	3.24	4.32	5.74	7.61	10.06	13.27	17.45

the money and withdraw interest only, leaving the principal intact, all of the income may be subject to federal income taxes. By contrast, part of the proceeds from annuities and self-liquidating funds is excluded from tax, since it is a return of your own money. Whether this would make a significant difference depends on your tax situation, but it definitely should be taken into account in making income comparisons.

To determine how the proceeds from annuity contracts would be taxed, ask any Internal Revenue Service office for a free copy of Publication 575, *Pension and Annuity Income.* Publication 590, *Individual Retirement Arrangements (IRAs),* tells about the tax treatment of employee-benefit rollovers.

LIVING OFF YOUR HOME EQUITY

Many retired people face a common problem after a lifetime of making mortgage payments: Their paid-off home is a substantial asset, but they can't get any income out of it when they need it the most. That's the problem that equity conversions were created to solve. Equity conversions take several forms. The most appealing is the reverse mortgage.

A reverse mortgage turns the lender-buyer relationship on its ear. A bank or other institution accepts your house as collateral for a loan, but instead of giving you all the money at once, it doles it out on a monthly basis. One way to look at it is to say the bank is making mortgage payments to you. Meanwhile, you stay in your house and don't have to pay anything back until the term of the loan is up—typically ten to 15 years later. Presumably you pay back the loan by selling your house.

The lender's monthly disbursements are based on the amount of equity you have in the house. Reverse mortgages are available in only a handful of states, typically through government agencies and nonprofit groups that work with the aging. But other kinds of home equity conversion plans are more widely available, including sale-leasebacks, special-purpose loans and home-equity lines of credit.

Sale-leasebacks.   In this sort of arrangement, you sell your house and rent it back from the buyer. Typically the buyer is a son or daughter who leases the place back to you for life.

Assuming you are 55 or older, you can take advantage of the once-in-a-lifetime exclusion of $125,000 in profit on the sale. Because your son or daughter is in effect your landlord, he or she gets all the tax advantages that go with owning rental real estate. Most sale-leasebacks are financed by the seller, who gets an infusion of cash from the down payment and regular income from the mortgage.

Special-purpose loans.   These are usually made by government agencies or private nonprofit organizations and must be used for home repairs or improvements or for paying property taxes. They don't have to be paid back until you move, sell your home or die.

Home-equity loans.   The major disadvantage of using a home equity loan (described in more detail in Chapter 3) as a source of income is that repayment must start immediately. The loan's main advantage is that it is widely available and other forms of home-equity conversion can be hard to find.

You can get a free fact sheet containing names of lenders who make equity-conversion loans from the National Center for Home Equity Conversion, 110 E. Main St., Room 605, Madison, Wis. 53703. Send a stamped, self-addressed, business-size envelope with your request.

The American Association of Retired Persons, 1909 K St., N.W., Washington, D.C. 20049, also has free equity-conversion guides available. Address your request to AARP Home Equity Information Center in the Consumer Affairs Section.

MAKE A WILL, PLAN AN ESTATE

THE IMPORTANCE OF A WILL

Making a will is a sobering act that's easy to put off, which is probably why so many people don't have one. But it's also sobering to realize what could happen if you don't leave a valid document describing how your property should be distributed.

If you die without a valid will, the state will supply a ready-made one devised by its legislature. Like a ready-made suit, it may fit and it may not. Abraham Lincoln, a president with great experience in the practice of law, died without a will, and his estate was divided, as it still would be in some states, into a third for his widow and a third for each of their sons. One son was grown and the other was 12 years old, so the arrangement may not have been considered ideal by Mary Lincoln.

The possibilities of inequities when there is no will are nearly endless. A hostile relative might be able to acquire a share of your estate, for example, or a relative who is already well-fixed might be able to take legal precedence over needier kin.

So you should have a will, a carefully drawn, written will.

Oral, or nuncupative, wills are not legal in a number of states and valid only in narrow circumstances in states where they are legal. Handwritten, or holographic, wills are legal in some states but can create complicated and expensive problems for the survivors.

That's why it makes sense to pay a competent lawyer a reasonable fee to write a document that lays out your wishes and will stand up later to scrutiny in probate court. Trying to save a few dollars, or even a few hundred if you have a complex estate, can cost far more in the long run.

Before you see a lawyer. A lawyer's time is money, so have some basics straight before you go to see one. Start by drawing up a list of your assets—real estate, bank accounts, stocks, bonds, cars, boats, life insurance, profit-sharing and pension funds, business holdings, money owed to you, and the like. Note for the lawyer's benefit any trusts and jointly held property so he or she can determine whether those assets can pass to your heirs via a will. You usually needn't list every piece of jewelry or every stick of furniture. Making specific bequests of long lists of items like that in a will can needlessly complicate matters and lead to extra costs and delays. The executor of your estate can carry out your separate instructions simply and directly. Ask your lawyer's advice on this.

Choose your executor carefully. Naturally, he or she should be someone you trust—a relative, a friend, your lawyer, anyone you feel is able to take on the responsible task of disposing of your estate. The person should be willing to do the job, so check before you name someone who might later refuse, thus forcing the court to appoint someone you might not have chosen.

A husband and wife need to decide together whether to name each other or a mutually agreed upon person as executor in their wills. You'll also have to choose someone who will serve as executor if for some reason your first choice can't do it.

If you have minor children, you'll have to decide who you want to take care of them if you and your spouse both die. This involves setting up a guardianship, a task that has two principal functions. The first is to provide for the proper care of the children until they reach the age of majority. The second entails managing prudently the money and property you leave to the children and distributing it to them as you would wish.

You might pick one person for both tasks if you know someone who could handle them. Or you might name a warm-hearted relative to raise the children and a business-minded relative (perhaps the executor) to handle the financial end. Naturally you should try to pick people who get along well together.

Next you'll have to decide how you want your estate distributed. This is obvious and straightforward in many instances, such as leaving everything to your spouse or to your children if both of you die.

But your intentions could be more complicated. Say you want an aged aunt to live in your house for the rest of her days and then you'd like the house to go to your children in equal shares. Your lawyer can show you how to arrange that.

Choosing a lawyer. For simple wills a competent generalist should be able to do the job at a reasonable price. If your estate is substantial, it may be a good idea to consult an attorney who specializes in estate planning so you can minimize the effects of federal and state taxes. Don't conclude hastily that your estate is too small for you to worry about taxes. Insurance policies, company benefits, investments, and rising real estate prices could make your estate larger than you expect.

When you first talk to a lawyer, get a clear understanding of the fee. Depending on the lawyer, the size of the city or town, and the complexities of the document you need, the fee can range from as little as $150 or so for a simple will to $100 an hour or more for the time involved in planning a complex estate. There is no such thing as an average price.

Using the lawyer. When you sit down with your lawyer, state clearly and completely what you want to do. The lawyer will likely explain several ways of accomplishing your objective. If you specifically want to leave someone out of your will, especially a child, be sure to say so. Your lawyer will probably advise you to mention the person by name so that he or she can't later contest the will, claiming that you merely forgot.

The lawyer should recommend wording broad enough to cover a rise or drop in your fortunes and provisions for a common disaster that takes the lives of you, your spouse and your children.

If your situation changes in the future, you can always amend the will. But don't do it yourself. You could invalidate the entire document in the eyes of the court, thus undoing the good you've done so far. Go to the expense of having the lawyer make the changes.

Don't keep the will in a safe-deposit box because it may be sealed after your death, making the document unavailable for a period of time. Perhaps you can keep it in the lawyer's vault or with your other important papers. You may also want to give a copy to the executor or the principal beneficiary. Subject to your lawyer's advice, consider including a letter of last instructions that will help your executor gather your affairs together and carry out your wishes.

PLANNING YOUR ESTATE

Everything you own and property over which you exercise decisive control, such as certain kinds of trusts, are considered part of your estate when you die. In understanding the importance of planning for the distribution of your estate, consider all the things that can affect it.

Probate. This is the procedure by which state courts validate a will's authenticity, thereby clearing the way for the executor to collect and pay debts, pay taxes, sell property, distribute funds, and carry out other necessary tasks involved with settling an estate.

The process can be slow and expensive. Probate fees average around 6% to 10% of assets, but can run to much more.

How probate is handled usually depends on the nature and size of the estate and, in some cases, the wishes of the heirs. About three-fourths of the states have a streamlined procedure for certain small estates. The maximum size is often between $5,000 and $10,000. In most jurisdictions no probate is required if the estate is much smaller than that. About half the states have informal procedures requiring little court supervision.

Sometimes all that's necessary is for the appropriate person to file an affidavit with the court and have relevant records, such as title to property, changed. In most states formal probate, where major steps along the way are supervised by the court, is commonly used for larger estates.

Not all of your estate has to go through probate. Among the items exempted from probate—but not necessarily from taxes—are life insurance payable to a named beneficiary, property left in certain kinds of trusts, and such assets as homes and bank accounts held in joint tenancy with right of survivorship.

Trusts. Essentially, a trust is an arrangement whereby you give assets to a legal entity (the trust) created in a separate agreement to be administered by an individual or institutional trustee for a beneficiary, who may be yourself or some other person.

An inter vivos, or living, trust operates while you are alive. A testamentary trust goes into effect after your death. A revocable trust's provisions can be changed; an irrevocable trust can't be materially modified.

Flexibility is the main attraction of a revocable trust. You can transfer legal ownership of assets without giving up control of them. In most states, you can name yourself both trustee and beneficiary. And you can revoke the trust at any time and take back ownership of the assets. You can also change the agreement if you want, or transfer assets in and out of the trust as you desire.

Having a trust doesn't relieve you of the need to have a will. But you'll probably need only a simple will, directing that any assets not in the trust be "poured over" into it upon your death. Any so-called poured-over assets have to go through probate, but their ultimate distribution is controlled by the provisions of the trust.

Trusts can reduce taxes by transferring the ownership of property from a high-tax situation to a lower-tax situation. They also help in such situations as the following.

• James is the sole support of his elderly father. If James dies before his father, there is no assurance that the father will be able to care for himself. Therefore, instead of willing his money directly to his father, James set up a testamentary trust with a bank as trustee. If James dies while his father is still living, the bank will invest the money and use the proceeds for the father's support. When the father dies, the remaining funds will be distributed to another beneficiary designated in the trust.

• Henry and Sally intend to leave a substantial sum to their son but are concerned about his ability to handle that much money. Rather than give him the entire amount at once, they set up a trust that will pay him the income annually, then half the capital when he reaches 25 and the remaining half when he turns 30.

Banks and professionals such as attorneys charge fees for administering trusts. The cost might rule them out for small trusts. In any case, you might prefer to appoint a friend or relative who knows the trust's beneficiary and who might be willing to serve for a small fee or expenses only. Husbands and wives can sometimes act as trustees for each other's trusts. You may also want to appoint two or more trustees to guard against the possibility that one will be incapacitated, and to name a successor who will take over if a trustee dies.

Joint tenancy. Property that is jointly owned with a right of survivorship—the form commonly used by married couples—automatically passes to the other owner when one owner dies. The pluses and minuses of joint ownership are discussed in detail later on in the chapter. For now, suffice it to say that it is an important estate-planning tool.

Estate and gift taxes. Unless you are reasonably well-off, your estate will have to pay little or no federal estate tax. An estate has to amount to more than $600,000 before it begins to incur any federal tax at all. And with proper planning, married couples will be able to defer tax on the entire estate of the first spouse to die. (Actually, the tax-free allowance is accomplished by what's called the unified estate and gift tax credit. The credit stands at $192,000, which is enough to protect $600,000 in assets.)

You should also be aware that the federal government is not the only official authority wanting a piece of your estate when you die. Most state governments levy some form of death taxes that cut into much smaller estates than the federal tax. The most commonly imposed state levy is an inheritance tax. An inheritance tax is paid by each of the heirs out of his or her inheritance unless the will directs that the estate cover it. (An estate tax comes out of the estate before its proceeds can be divided up among the heirs.) There is also something in most states called a pickup tax, which doesn't actually increase the tax but claims for the state the amount of the credit allowed on the federal estate-tax return for death taxes paid to a state. It applies only to estates owing a federal tax. See the listing of state death taxes on page 428 and 429.

There is also the federal gift tax to take into consideration. The law permits an individual to give away up to $10,000 a year to as many recipients as he or she desires without incurring a gift tax. For married couples the limit is $20,000. (To be strictly accurate, people rarely pay any gift tax. Rather, the tax, if incurred, serves to reduce the estate tax credit available at death.)

If a tax on gifts seems unfair, think of the loophole its absence would create. People of means could give away much of their wealth to prospective heirs and thus escape the estate tax entirely. The gift and estate tax schedules are the same and range from 18% to 55% of the taxable amount, reaching the top bracket for taxable gifts or estates of $2.5 million or more.

Gifts and estates may be further protected from taxes by exemptions for gifts made by one spouse to another and for estates inherited by one spouse from another. There is no limit on gifts between spouses and there is no limit on the marital deduction. This means that, with proper estate planning, the marital deduction and the estate-tax exclusion can be used to pass estates of any size from one spouse to the other without incurring any federal estate tax. To make sure that you take full advantage of this opportunity and to minimize estate taxes upon the death of the second spouse, consult with an experienced estate attorney familiar with the laws of your state.

INS AND OUTS OF JOINT OWNERSHIP

Joint ownership is a traditionally popular way for husbands
continued on page 430

DEATH TAXES, STATE BY STATE

An estate tax is levied on the value of the entire estate, normally at one tax rate in a manner similar to the federal estate tax. An inheritance tax is levied on the share of each heir at rates that vary with the heir's relationship to the deceased person. A pickup tax for estates with a federal tax liability allows the state to collect a tax equal to the full amount of the credit permitted on the federal estate tax return. In some states the names used for estate and inheritance types of taxes do not clearly describe them; the pickup tax is also called a credit estate tax.

	ESTATE TAX	INHERITANCE TAX	PICKUP TAX
Alabama			•
Alaska			•
Arizona			•
Arkansas			•
California			•
Colorado			•
Connecticut		•	•
Delaware		•	•
District of Columbia			•
Florida			•
Georgia			•
Hawaii			•
Idaho		•	•
Illinois			•
Indiana		•	•
Iowa		•	•
Kansas		•	•
Kentucky		•	•
Louisiana		•	•
Maine			•
Maryland		•	•
Massachusetts	•		•
Michigan		•	•

Minnesota			●
Mississippi	●		
Missouri			●
Montana		●	●
Nebraska		●	●
Nevada			●
New Hampshire		●	●
New Jersey		●	●
New Mexico			●
New York	●		●
North Carolina		●	●
North Dakota			●
Ohio	●		●
Oklahoma	●		●
Oregon			●
Pennsylvania		●	●
Rhode Island*	●		●
South Carolina**	●		●
South Dakota		●	●
Tennessee		●	●
Texas			●
Utah			●
Vermont			●
Virginia			●
Washington			●
West Virginia			●
Wisconsin***		●	●
Wyoming			●

*Rhode Island's estate tax will be phased out by January 1, 1991.
**South Carolina's estate tax will be phased out by July 1, 1991.
***Wisconsin's inheritance tax will be phased out by January 1, 1992.

and wives to hold property. It's a nice symbol of economic togetherness. Joint ownership is used here as shorthand for two ways of owning property: joint tenancy with the right of survivorship and tenancy by the entirety. Although they differ in some respects and about half the states don't recognize the entirety variety, both forms of joint ownership provide a survivorship feature that's especially attractive to married couples. When one partner dies, the other joint owner automatically becomes sole owner of the property. Beyond the security offered by this assured continuity, joint ownership permits property to bypass probate, avoiding delays and usually trimming the costs of that final accounting process. In some states it can also ease the inheritance tax bite, and such property may be exempt from seizure by creditors of the deceased.

Possible problems with joint ownership. Those advantages, buttressed by some imagined benefits that don't actually exist, help explain the appeal of joint ownership. Offsetting the advantages are several potential problems.

For one thing, control of jointly held property is sometimes muddled. Depending on what's involved, one spouse may be able to dispose of it without the other's knowledge (as is generally the case with the entire balance of a joint checking or savings account). Or each may be hamstrung, unable to sell the property without the other's consent (a situation that can apply to a home or to stocks and bonds).

Another potential problem of joint ownership lies in a common misconception: It is often seen as a substitute for a will. Sometimes it is even called the poor man's will or mini-estate plan, because it guarantees that the surviving owner will get the property when his or her joint owner dies.

Although joint ownership may appear better than nothing because it gives you some control, it is not a substitute for a will. For one thing, if the surviving owner later dies without a will, the property will be divvied up according to the state's scheme of who should get what.

Also, joint property can dilute the power of a will to parcel out assets as you wish because it can't be controlled by a will. Say, for example, that you and your sister buy a mountain cottage. If you take title as joint owners and you die first, your share disappears and your sister automatically becomes sole owner. That may be what you want, or it could mean unintentionally disinheriting someone else.

It is essential that you recognize this implication of taking joint title. Your interest in the property can't be left to one or more heirs by your will, nor can it go to a trust for expert management. Taking joint title makes the decision: Your fellow owner gets the property if you die first.

(Two or more people can co-own property without being joint owners. If you take title as tenants in common, which has no right of survivorship, your will controls what happens to your share of the property.)

Many people make the mistake of assuming that jointly owned property escapes estate taxes just as it avoids probate. In the past the full value of jointly owned property was generally included in the estate of the first owner to die, except to the extent the survivor could prove he or she paid for the property. That's still how it works for unmarried joint owners, so the full value of the property might be taxed in the estate of the first to die and taxed again when the surviving owner dies. For husbands and wives, though, only 50% of the value of jointly held property goes into the estate of the first to die. The marital deduction will shield it from the estate tax, but the 50% rule can have adverse income tax consequences later on.

In the past, when the full value of the property went into the first estate, the entire property also received a stepped-up basis. That is, the basis—which is the value from which gain or loss on sale of the property is judged—became the value at the date of death of the owner. Effectively, the income tax on any profit that built up during his or her lifetime was forgiven. Now that only half of the property goes into the estate, only half gets a tax-saving, stepped-up basis.

Who should own what? Choosing the right kind of ownership can be tricky. It's clear that the more property you own, the more attention should be paid to the consequences of how you own it. Today's ownership decisions should be made with an eye to the future. There can be clear advantages to joint ownership, and in many circumstances they easily outweigh the potential drawbacks. A lawyer well versed in federal estate and local property laws can help you make the right choice. You may decide that the best course for you and your spouse is a careful mix of joint and individual ownership, depending on the property involved.

Your house. Joint ownership's survivorship feature may be especially appealing here. Talk with your lawyer about other options, though.

Savings and checking accounts. Joint accounts are convenient, but with some types of accounts in some states part or all of the balance may be frozen at the death of either owner. Since that could strap the survivor at a difficult time, you may want to have individual accounts, too. Ask your banker about local rules.

Life insurance. If you own a policy on your own life, the proceeds will be included in your estate regardless of who receives them. It might be advisable for each mate to own the policies on the other's life. This keeps the proceeds out of the estate of the insured. It also means that the insured must give up all "incidents of ownership," including the right to change the beneficiary and borrow against the cash value. Depending on your circumstances, creating a life insurance trust to own the policies may be beneficial. Check with your attorney or insurance agent for details.

Stocks and bonds. Joint ownership could restrict flexibility in managing investments because both signatures are needed to buy or sell.

Your car. There's not much advantage to joint ownership and one drawback: The assets of both owners could be vulnerable to a suit for damages.

Safe-deposit box. Pitfalls exist here, too. Check local law. A jointly owned box may be sealed upon the death of either owner until authorities take inventory.

Community property states. Community property states add a special twist to the ownership puzzle. They are Arizona, California, Idaho, Louisiana, Nevada, New Mexico, Texas,

HOW LARGE IS YOUR ESTATE?

Although you don't have to worry about federal estate taxes until
your taxable estate exceeds $600,000, you might be surprised by all
the things the government counts in getting there.

In the worksheet below, the "ownership" column is included
because how you own property is pivotal to how much of its value
will be included in your estate when you die. In the "value" column,
include the following:

- the full value of property of which you are the sole owner;
- half the value of property you own jointly with your spouse with
right of survivorship;
- your share of property owned with others;
- half the value of community property if you live in a community
property state (see list on page 432).

Also include the value of the proceeds of an insurance policy on
your life if you own the policy, your vested interest in pension and
profit-sharing plans, and the value of property in revocable trusts.

ASSETS	OWNERSHIP	VALUE
Cash in checking, savings, money-market accounts		
Stocks		
Bonds		
Mutual funds		
Other investments		
Real estate		
Personal property, including furniture, cars, clothing, etc.		
Art, antiques, collectibles		
Proceeds of life insurance policies you own on your life		
Pension and profit-sharing benefits, IRAs, etc.		
Business interests: sole proprietorship, partnerships, closely held corporations		
Money owed to you, such as mortgages, rents, professional fees due		
Other		
Total assets		

continued

LIABILITIES	OWNERSHIP	VALUE
Mortgages		
Loans and notes		
Taxes		
Consumer debt		
Other		
Total liabilities		
Net estate (total assets minus total liabilities)		

Washington and Wisconsin. (The rest are called common-law states.)

In those nine states, salaries and assets acquired during marriage are generally considered community property, which means they are owned 50/50 by each spouse. Community property doesn't carry the right of survivorship, so when one spouse dies, the other does not automatically assume full ownership. The deceased partner's half is disposed of by will or the state's intestate rules and only that part is included in the estate for tax purposes.

Community property laws in these states usually permit couples to set up other types of ownership, either separate or joint. For details, check on local laws that apply to your circumstances. If you move from a common-law state to one with community property rules, or vice versa, be sure to review your family's ownership arrangements and estate plans.

Index